THE SKY PEOPLE

A HISTORY OF PARACHUTING

THE SKY PEOPLE

A HISTORY OF PARACHUTING

Peter Hearn

Airlife
England

For
Paul and Danny

Also by Peter Hearn
Parachutist
Lonely On The Wing
From The High Skies
Sky High Irvin
When The 'Chute Went Up (with Dolly Shepherd)
The Yorkshire Birdman (with Harry Ward)

First published in the UK in 1990
by Airlife Publishing Ltd
This edition published 1997

British Library Cataloguing in Publication Data
A catalogue record for this book
is available from the British Library

ISBN 1 85310 869 3

Printed in Hong Kong.

Airlife Publishing Ltd

101 Longden Road, Shrewsbury SY3 9EB, England.

Contents

Foreword

When I started free fall parachuting in the early '60s, Peter Hearn was one of my heroes, for it was he who, with other like-minded, individualistic, instructors at No. 1 Parachute Training School, Royal Air Force, had pioneered, on a self-help basis, early military free fall training and had then founded the RAF's first free fall parachute display team, the forerunners of the modern day 'Falcons'. Their achievements were regarded with awe by those of us who aspired to fly in free fall ourselves, for sport parachuting (or skydiving) was in those days somewhat in its infancy, with all the equipment being military surplus and modified (sometimes to hair-raisingly individual designs) for free fall use. As a young subaltern serving in the Parachute Regiment, my weekend skydiving activities were regarded with raised eyebrows by many of my colleagues — particularly when military parachute pay was an extra 7/6 a day and we were spending two or three times that amount per jump at the local civilian parachute club. A quarter of a century later the sport of parachuting has gained respectability, with the British Parachute Association receiving vital grant aid from the Sports Council, both to promote this challenging sporting aviation activity and to assist in sending British Teams to compete in World Parachuting Championships.

Peter Hearn was constructively very much involved in these early development years and thus his qualifications to assemble this comprehensive history and entertaining collection of parachuting memorabilia are impeccable. He was a member of the British Parachute Team at the 5th World Parachuting Championships in Bulgaria in 1960 and, the following year, Peter and fellow RAF Instructor, John Thirtle, became the first pair of parachutists in the United Kingdom to maneouvre close enough together in free fall to pass a baton from one to the other. He later commanded No. 1 PTS, the RAF organization responsible for the training of military parachutists and where both the Prince of Wales and the Duke of York completed parachute courses; the former gained his military parachute wings and is now Colonel in Chief of the Parachute Regiment. Apart from that, Peter Hearn has previously written two other excellent works on parachuting — *Parachutist*, a delightful personal reminiscence, and *Sky High Irvin*, a well researched biography of the parachuting pioneer and founder of the Irvin Air Chute Company.

I must admit to having thought that I had read just about everything that had been written on the history of parachuting, until I opened the pages of this exhaustively researched and entertainingly written book. His idea of presenting this history in five different categories of parachutist is both simple and logical, and his selection of illustrative stories, whilst inevitably being somewhat personal, provides appropriate examples which do much to paint fascinating portraits of the successive generations and types of 'Sky People'. I was delighted to see included Jackie (Smith) Young's delightfully recalled and typically modest account of her winning the World Championship Gold Medal in 1978, when she became the first person, male or female, to score ten consecutive 'dead centres' in the accuracy event at the World Championships, particularly as 'Smiff' is unquestionably this nation's most accomplished competitive parachutist.

Sport parachutists are still asked at monotonously regular intervals: 'Why jump out of a perfectly serviceable aeroplane?' Apart from their replying that if the aeroplane wasn't serviceable they wouldn't be able to jump out of it, this splendid book will undoubtedly provide the definitive answer and I have no hesitation in commending it unreservedly.

Charles Shea-Simonds
Vice President
Royal Aero Club of the United Kingdom

Preface

Charles Shea-Simonds, who is amongst the foremost of our Sky People and who has kindly provided the foreword to this book, once said of parachuting: 'If you haven't been there, you can never quite understand, and if you have been there, you can never quite explain.'

Well Charlie — I've tried!

I have tried, in tracing the history of the parachutist, to convey to those who haven't 'been there' the fears, delights, wonderment, exhilaration, and the physical sensations known to those who have. If in this I have succeeded in any measure, it is because, wherever possible, I have used the words of the parachutists themselves — for theirs is the true voice of the skies. For those who *have* 'been there', the book may serve to remind them of their own experiences, and of their parachuting heritage.

Parachuting takes several forms, and those who have indulged in it fall into recognisable categories. There are those who paved the way: the Pioneers. There are those who have jumped primarily for display and profit: the Show-Jumpers. There are those who have jumped from a crippled aeroplane through necessity rather than choice, and in the same category those whose test-jumping has made it possible for them to do so: the 'Caterpillars'. There are those who use the parachute as a means of transport to war: the Paratroopers. Finally, there are those who jump for the sheer joy of it: the Skydivers. Many jumpers belong in more than one category, but the sequence is broadly chronological and only slightly over-lapping in time and form, and it is therefore within these five categories that I present the history of the parachutist.

In one volume, such a work must be selective rather than fully comprehensive. I have tried to record the most significant events and trends, and to illustrate them with the most appropriate stories, but I am aware that many worthy jumpers are excluded; many an anecdote and adventure untold; many a technical advance not acknowledged; many an airborne operation dismissed too briefly or not mentioned at all. As the story approaches the present, it becomes even more selective, for I have concentrated more on the roots of parachuting than on its recent growth, which has not yet been assessed by time. In the Bibliography I recommend books that have concentrated on individual 'categories', and which may serve to expand on my more general survey.

Sources of quotations are indicated in the text, or acknowledged in the Reference section. I am grateful to those publishers and authors who have allowed me to quote from their works.

The early literature of parachuting, particularly that written during the 1920s and '30s, contained much that was inaccurate. Accounts were rarely written from practical experience, and the parachutists from whom those early stories were taken were usually show-jumpers, for whom an element of exaggeration was part of the trade! To separate fact from much of the consequent folk-lore I have drawn heavily on long conversations with the late Dave Gold who was advisor on parachute history to the Smithsonian Institute; on the original manuscript of Lloyd Graham's 1933 book *Ripcord* that has a ring of truth about it; and on the proceedings of several legal battles over patent rights during which prominent Sky People of the 1920s and '30s were required to tell their stories under oath!

Much of the inspiration and information for this book has come from those Sky People that I have met, and with whom I have talked, and with whom I have sometimes jumped during thirty years as a parachutist. In writing the chapter on The Skydivers, I realised how long I have been out of the sport. Doug Peacock, Charlie Shea-Simonds, and John Meacock have been particularly helpful in bringing me up to date, and Dave Howerski provided a fascinating insight into the future of the sport.

I am most grateful to them and to the many others who have provided advice, material and information specifically for this book: Wing Commander F. T. K. Bullmore, Louise Dann, Leo and Mandy Dickinson, Donald East, Warrant Officer Joe France, the late Sidney Jackson, Mr Fred Lake of MOD Library, Wing Commander Roy McLuskey, Colonel Graham Owens, Sue (Burges) Phillips, Eileen Robinson on behalf of the Caterpillar Club, Carol Saunders, Molly Sedgwick, Flight Lieutenant Chris Simpson, Squadron Leader George Sizeland, Harry Ward, Dave Waterman, Frank Wootton, Sergeant Alistair Wright, Jackie (Smith) Young, my son Paul for the drawings, and the staffs of The RAF Museum, The Imperial War Museum, The Airborne Forces Museum, The Smithsonian National Air and Space Museum, and Martin-Baker Aircraft Company Limited.

1. Filling the Balloon.
2. Baldwin fixing the Parachute.
3. Baldwin's farewell to his wife before starting.
4. The moment before ascending.
5. The Ascent.
6. The Leap from the Balloon.
7. Parachute alighting in Coldfall Wood, Fortis-green.
8. Reception, going back to the Palace.
9. Portrait of Baldwin.

PROFESSOR BALDWIN AT THE ALEXANDRA PALACE.

"Professor" Thomas Baldwin's descents at London's Alexandra Palace in 1888 caused controversy and a resurgence of interest in show jumping. These sketches illustrate the sequence of ascent and descent using the revolutionary 'limp' parachute suspended from a gas balloon. (page 49)

CHAPTER ONE
The Pioneers

Every parachutist is a pioneer. That first jump . . . ! It is a jump into the unknown. It is a leap or a drop or a stumbling step — or even a push — into a new world. It is a world for which nature did not equip us, and for which no description nor simulation can prepare our senses. The first-time jumper is an explorer, not only of this strange new world that he now enters, but of himself. Leaping into space is against all human instinct. Bad dreams are made of it. So during the moments, or sometimes the hours, or sometimes the days, before that first jump, the parachutist tests himself against a level of fear that he has probably never encountered before, and when he overcomes that fear he knows a sense of achievement that again may exceed all previous experience. He may, in subsequent jumps, explore the joy and exhilaration that eventually replace that fear.

Yes, every first-time parachutist is a pioneer, and many jumpers continue to be pioneers. The trials-jumper, testing new equipment and techniques; the show-jumper seeking a yet more daring way to thrill those upturned faces; the paratrooper jumping at night onto an unknown and alien drop zone; the skydiver searching for perfect flight — they are still pioneering.

In tracing the story of the sky people, however, we shall use a more narrow definition of 'pioneer'. We shall confine it to those who paved the way, in theory and in practice, for modern parachuting. Modern parachuting? Let us say that it began with the first jump from an aeroplane in flight. That was on 1 March 1912. A lot happened before that . . .

Exactly when it began, we do not know. We know who made the first *recorded* parachute descent, but before then much happened in fantasy, theory, and perhaps even in fact.

The dream of flight is as old as man's first sight of a flying creature. We do not know when he first tried to change the dream into reality, but he almost certainly failed, and in failing he was likely to have become the world's first, but quite unintentional, free faller. Those early endeavours to emulate the birds by launching into

the air from high places sought to ascend into the skies, not to descend from them. Man wanted to fly, not to fall. The fact that inevitably and painfully he did fall and was perhaps supported to some small degree by the wreckage of his home-made wings, or by a billowing cloak with which he had endeavoured to float upon the air, does not qualify him as a parachutist. His intention was different. Icarus was not a skydiver: he was a failed aviator.

Nevertheless, the early 'birdmen' who hurled themselves with great ambition but little support from towers and cliffs and other high places, by their very mistakes and by their undoubted spirit of adventure, helped to point the way. One such was the monk Oliver of Malmesbury, who about the year 1020 . . .

> ' . . . Made and fitted Wings to his Hands and Feet; with these on the top of a Tower, spread out to gather air, he flew more than a Furlong; but the wind being too high, came fluttering down, to the maiming of all his Limbs; yet so conceited of his Art, that he contributed the cause of his fall to the want of a Tail, as Birds have, which he forgot to make to his hinder parts.'[1]

It is likely that the tower-jumpers of the Middle Ages had been preceded by others whose endeavours are now recorded only in folk-lore — particularly that of the Orient. The story is told of the Chinese Emperor Shun (*circa* 2200 BC) who as a youth was commissioned by his evil father to build a granary surmounted by a tall tower. When the work was completed and Shun was standing proudly on the tower, his father set fire to it, whereupon the ingenious lad escaped death by descending to the ground under the support of two large reed hats. It is quite conceivable that the Chinese were indeed the first to design and use some form of 'fall breaker'. They had the parasol and the kite by 200 BC. Why not a simple parachute? But there is no record of it outside legend, and we must look to fifteenth century Europe for the first known design of what we would now call a parachute.

In a notebook dated between 1470 and 1480, and believed to be that of an Italian engineer of Siena, there appears a drawing of a man suspended in flight beneath a conical 'fall breaker'. The device is well braced and has what appears to be a gore-construction. Sadly, the sketch is not annotated. The 'parachutist' has something in his mouth, held there by a band. The American aviation historian Lynn White believes it to be a sponge, gripped between the jaws to absorb the landing impact and held in place by the band so that 'if he cries out in terror he will not drop it.'[2.]

A little later than this (circa 1485) is Leonardo Da Vinci's rough sketch of a pyramidal shaped 'fall breaker' with the following design specification.

> 'If a man have a tent roof of caulked linen, twelve braccia broad and twelve braccia high he will be able to let himself fall from any great height without danger to himself.'[3.]

More than a century later, another Italian, Fausto Veranzio — influenced perhaps by the Siena notebooks but certainly not by Da Vinci, whose aeronautical sketches were not 'found' until the seventeenth century — depicted a 'Flying Man' in his book *Machinae Novae*. The engraving shows a man descending from a tower supported by a square sheet stretched within a wooden frame, and is annotated with some of the first glimmerings of parachute aerodynamics:

> 'With a square canvas spread between four equal poles, and having four cords attached to the four joints, a man could without danger throw himself from a tower or similar emminence. Even though there is no wind at the time, his weight will create the wind that inflates the canvas; he need have no fear of falling swiftly, for he will descend little by little. The man should proportion the spread of canvas to his own weight.'

These early scientists were pioneers of theory only, for there is nothing to suggest that they or anyone else constructed and used the devices which they depicted. Those who continued to leap from high places still put their trust in wings and optimism. The Marquis de Braqueville showed more discretion than most by launching himself from a roof that leaned conveniently over the River Seine, but his caution was ill rewarded, for he fell upon a washer-woman's barge and broke a leg.

Let us look again at the Far East, where Simon de la Loubère, French envoy to the King of Siam in 1688, tells the story of 'a tumbler exceedingly honoured by the King of Siam':

> 'There dyed one, some years since, who leap'd from the Hoop, supporting himself by two Umbrellas, the hands of which were firmly fix'd to his Girdle: the wind carry'd him accidentally sometimes to the Ground, sometimes on Trees or Houses, and sometimes into the River. He so exceedingly diverted the King of Siam that this Prince had made him a great Lord.'[4.]

Fact or folk-lore? Alas, we do not know. Perhaps a little of both. To find the first *recorded* parachute descent, we must return to Europe.

The appearance of a practicable, man-carrying, parachute required two things: it needed a vehicle to take the parachutist to altitude, and because it did not itself provide a solution to man's yearning to fly, it needed a purpose. The balloon was to provide the altitude. Showmanship was to provide the purpose.

Despite the energy and life expended on winged endeavour, man eventually floated rather than flapped his way into the air. In 1766, Cavendish discovered hydrogen and its 'lighter-than-air' quality. Shortly afterwards, two French papermakers, Joseph and Etienne Montgolfier, realized the lifting potential of hot air — which they believed to be some form of gas developed from burning substances. In June 1783, at Annonay, the Montgolfier brothers successfully launched an unmanned balloon made of paper-lined linen, fuelled by hot air from a fire of wool and straw. Two months later in Paris, Jacques Charles, aided by the brothers Robert, sent up the first hydrogen-filled balloon. It was also unmanned, which was just as well, for this strange creature that drifted from the skies some fifteen miles away was attacked and torn to pieces by the terrified villagers of Gonesse. The French Government issued a proclamation to assure the populace that these 'balloons or globes' need not cause alarm, and that they would 'some day prove serviceable to the wants of society'.

Interest was intense, and it was in the presence of Louis XVI and Marie Antoinette at Versailles that the Montgolfiers sent aloft the first aerial passengers — a sheep, a duck, and a cock. They served the same purpose as the dogs and monkeys who much later were to precede man into outer space, for in the eighteenth century, the air immediately above the earth was even more of a mystery, and was believed to hold untold perils. Thus, when the balloon landed in a forest two miles away and it was found that the cock appeared somewhat indisposed, this was attributed to the hazards of aerial travel until ten witnesses solemly testified that they had seen the sheep kick the cock before the balloon took off.

King Louis was still reluctant to send a man into the air, but agreed to commit two criminals to those unknown perils. A spirited young scientist named Pilatre de Rozier objected so strongly to *'la gloire de s'elever dans les airs'* going to common villains, that the King was persuaded to allow De Rozier and the equally bold Marquis D'Arlandes to become the first aeronauts.

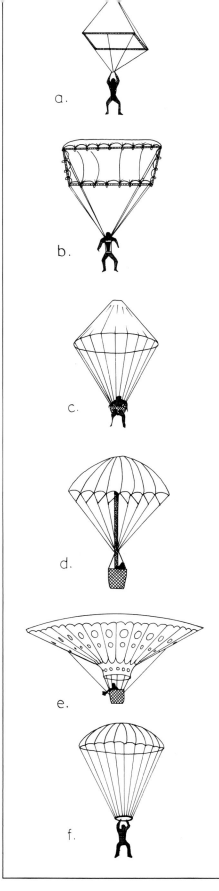

The development of the parachute in theory and practice. a. Leonardo Da Vinci's design, circa 1485; b. Fausto Veranzio's design, circa 1600; c. Sebastian Lenormand's design, 1783; d. André Garnerin's parachute, 1797; e. Robert Cocking's 'inverted cone' parachute, 1837; f. Thomas Baldwin's 'limp' parachute, 1887.

They did so on 21 November 1783, rising beneath their splendidly decorated balloon from the Bois de Boulogne, equipped with bundles of straw to feed the fire in its brazier, and a pail of water and a sponge apiece to dampen the ardour of any sparks that might settle on the balloon itself. They rose to some 3,000 feet, and landed unharmed five miles away.

It was a momentous occasion. Man had flown for the first time. Not exactly like a bird, but he had flown! Just over a week later, Jacques Charles made the first flight in a hydrogen balloon. Once the problems of producing hydrogen for the balloon had been lessened, the 'Charlière' would become a more reliable and more widely used vehicle than the 'Montgolfière'.

The balloon had arrived. Quite coincidentally, so had a parachute that in its basic design was the forerunner of the 'round' canopy that has subsequently carried generations of sky people to the ground.

Louis Sebastian Lenormand was a watch-maker and would-be physicist. After experimenting with braced parasols, he produced in 1783 a parachute that comprised a 'dome' of linen six feet deep and fourteen feet wide, beneath which a wickerwork seat was suspended by numerous cords. The porosity of the linen was reduced by glueing a layer of paper to it, and the canopy was strengthened by a cord running round its periphery. Successful tests were carried out from the tower of the Meterological Observatory at Montpelier, first using ballast, then several domestic animals. It has been suggested that Lenormand himself jumped with his parachute, but there is no evidence of this. Nevertheless, Lenormand made a major contribution to parachute design at a particularly appropriate time. He introduced the circular canopy and 'rigging line' concept; pointed to the need for peripheral strengthening; and showed an awareness that canopy porosity is an important factor — even though he went too far in making his material completely impermeable. What is more, he was the first to call his apparatus a 'parachute': we owe the word to the little watch-maker of Montpelier.

Several were influenced by Lenormand's design, and even took credit for it. Joseph Montgolfier made a copy of the parachute and used it to drop a sheep from the 100-foot tower of the Papal Palace at Avignon. The same sheep made the journey six times, but there is no truth in vague reports that Montgolfier entrusted himself to the device. Another who claimed Lenormand's ideas as his own without actually putting them into practice was the Abbé Bertholon.

So the balloon had taken to the air, and a basic design for a workable parachute was available. The first to combine the two in practice was another Frenchman, Jean Pierre Blanchard. He did so purely in the interests of showmanship. Although the first aeronauts had been motivated by a sense of adventure and occasion — as was Pilatre de Rozier — or by scientific enthusiasm in the case of Jacques Charles, it soon became obvious that there was money and fame to be made from ballooning. The impact on the public of those early flights was enormous. It was estimated that 400,000 flocked to the Tuileries Gardens to see the first ascent by Charles in his hydrogen balloon — half the population of Paris at the time. Not only would crowds gather, and perhaps pay, to watch the balloon take off, but there was handsome reward in prospect from wealthy backers and passengers. It was a role for which Jean Pierre was well suited. Although from a poor background, he had a natural aptitude for mechanics, which he combined with a flair for exhibitionism to become the most celebrated of the first generation of professional aeronauts, although not the most popular. 'A petulant little fellow, not many inches over five feet, and physically well suited for vapourish regions,' was the opinion of a contemporary.

Blanchard made his first balloon ascent in 1784, and soon became an efficient pilot, despite a misguided belief that he could influence the direction of his balloon by attaching wings, paddles and rudders. When Vincent Lunardi made the first balloon flight over London in September 1784, the initial scepticism of the British turned to effusive praise. 'You will observe, Madam, that the balloon engages all mankind,' wrote Doctor Johnson to Mrs. Thrale, for such was the effect in France and England of 'Balloonomania'. Seeing rich pickings across the Channel, Blanchard came to London, where he gathered about him a small group of wealthy enthusiasts and backers, and made his first flight in England a month after Lunardi. His most famous flight came the following year when he and his sponsor, Doctor John Jeffries, became the first to cross the English Channel by air — only just, for it was only by discarding every ounce of ballast including their coats and britches that they avoided ditching just short of the French coast.

Back in London, Blanchard invested some of the considerable earnings from that flight in the world's first flying school, in Stockwell Road, Vauxhall. He called it the Grand Aerostatic Academy. There he offered ascents and tutelage in tethered and free balloons, and a close-up view of the proceedings, and it was also there that, as an added attraction, he married the parachute to the balloon. He made a flexible parachute of silk, again based on Lenormand's principles, and with it he began to launch a succession of bemused cats and dogs into the sky above Vauxhall. The 'Academy' was unsuccessful and short lived. Attendance was lower than expected, and Blanchard was perhaps the first showman to realize that people are not going to pay to enter an arena when they can watch the aerial activity just as well from outside it. When an attempt to drop a sheep by parachute failed, the disgruntled audience demanded their money back. Two weeks later, when an Italian who had been billed to play a violin whilst making a parachute descent, jumped a mere ten feet to the ground with the instrument tucked under his chin, they wrecked the place. Blanchard returned to France. He toured Europe extensively and successfully, making numerous balloon flights and scattering more livestock about the countryside under his silk parachutes. The first parachute to be seen in the United States of America was one of his, used to drop a cat, a dog, and a squirrel under one canopy in 1793. No human ever used those parachutes, and Blanchard himself never jumped, despite vague claims that he did and that he broke a leg in the process. He suffered a heart attack during his sixtieth flight, and although it was not fatal, he never flew again. He had made a colourful contribution to the history of the balloon and the parachute.

Almost the first parachutist was an English seaman named George Appleby, who was assistant to the balloonist Stuart Arnold. On 31 August 1775 at St George's Fields near Rotherhithe, this intrepid seaman took his place on a flat basket attached beneath a silk parachute, that was in turn attached to a balloon about to be piloted skywards by Stuart Arnold, with his son as passenger. The balloon, however, was too heavily laden, and as it struggled to rise, the parachute was swung into railings and became detached. The 'car' of the balloon hit a wagon and also fell away, with Arnold senior inside. Relieved of so much weight, the balloon made a dash for it, carrying away Arnold junior clinging to the rigging and hoop. To the added dismay of the spectators, the balloon then burst spectacularly, but did so above Execution Dock, into which young Arnold plunged and whence he was quickly rescued. It is likely that he received some support from the balloon fabric being trapped inside the netting. No more was heard of George Appleby. He probably went back to sea, thinking that it would be safer off Cape Horn.

For the first man to make an intentional parachute descent with an apparatus designed for that purpose, we must look again to France.

André Jacques Garnerin is our man. He was born in 1770, made his first flight as a passenger in a balloon at the age of seventeen, and his first solo ascent at twenty. As 'Citoyen Garnerin' he fought with the French Revolutionary Army, was captured in battle, and imprisoned by the Austrians for three years in the fortress of Buda, in Hungary. It is said that whilst there he pondered the possibility of escape by some form of parachute. Quite likely. Others say that he was attracted to parachuting purely as a means of supplementing his income from balloon exhibitions. Equally probable. Whatever the motivation — and it was probably a combination of these two factors — in 1797 he constructed a parachute that drew on Lenormand's design but also incorporated enough originality to suggest that he had given the matter much serious thought. Garnerin did not record the exact measurements

A VIEW OF MONS.ᴿ GARNERIN'S BALLOON AND PARACHUTE,

By which he ascended from the Volunteers Ground, North Audley Street, Grosvenor Square, Sep.ᵗ 21 1802, to the haight of 8000 Feet.

And the Parachute he descended by in a Field near S.ᵗ Pancras Church, quite safe.

Published Oct.ᵗ 22 1802 by G. Thompson, N.° Long Lane West Smithfield London.

An artist's impression of the first parachute descent in England,
made in 1802 by André Jacques Garnerin, who landed close to where
Marylebone Station now stands.

of his 'chute, which has given parachute technicians and historians much scope for learned conjecture and argument ever since. The following specifications represent the majority view. The circular canopy was made of thirty-two 'gores' of cotton sailcloth and had a flat diameter of thirty-two feet, or perhaps larger. Garnerin followed Lenormand by lining the canopy with paper. At the apex was a circular piece of wood ten inches across, and about four-and-a-half feet below that, a wooden hoop eight feet in diameter was sewn inside the canopy. This was a novel and sensible idea, for when suspended beneath the balloon, the canopy would hang from the hoop like a cylindrical curtain and thus keep its mouth open to ensure that it took a good gulp of air when released. Whether Garnerin intended it or not, this would also prevent the lines from twisting as the balloon hauled the parachute into the air. A wicker basket two feet wide and four feet deep was suspended from the periphery of the canopy by thirty-six lines of braided cord, each thirty feet in length. From basket to apex ran a metal tube to provide a channel for the rope that would attach the whole contrivance to the underside of the balloon.

Garnerin committed himself to this parachute without first putting it through the usual 'live' trials. Perhaps he was an animal lover. More likely, he was in a hurry. In June 1797 a large crowd gathered in the Jardin de Byron in Paris to witness the first parachute descent by a man, a privilege for which they had payed handsomely. The 'chute was attached to a hydrogen balloon; Garnerin readied himself; excitement mounted; the ropes that held the balloon to the ground were released. Alas, too soon, for the balloon was insufficiently filled. It laid down, and refused to budge. Garnerin was abused by the crowd, ridiculed by the press, and accused of being an aerial charlatan.

On 22 October, at what is now the Parc Monceau, he tried again. Once more he had problems mounting the operation, and it was after five o'clock in the afternoon before all was ready. The scepticism of the Paris crowds turned to amazement as Garnerin, standing in his little basket beneath the fully extended parachute, was at last lifted into the sky beneath an unmanned hydrogen balloon. Some 2,000 feet above the expectant faces, André Jacques Garnerin cut the rope that attached him to the balloon . . . and became the world's first parachutist.

The crowd got their money's worth this time. As the parachute dropped away and the relieved balloon shot upwards, the separation speed gave an immediate but illusory impression that Garnerin was hurtling earthwards at a fatal rate. Then, as the canopy opened fully into its umbrella shape, it began to oscillate wildly, swinging the basket and the parachutist within it like an exuberant pendulum. When Garnerin came heavily but unharmed to earth he was mobbed by an enthusiastic throng, carried off shoulder high, and provided with a horse to carry him back in triumph to the launching site.

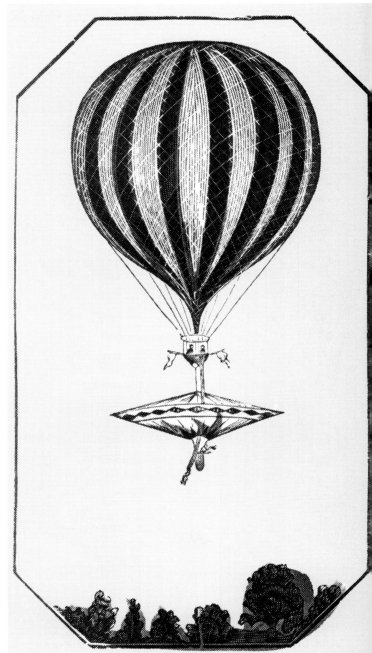

The Ascent of the Royal Nassau Balloon from Vauxhall, with the Parachute attached.

Published b

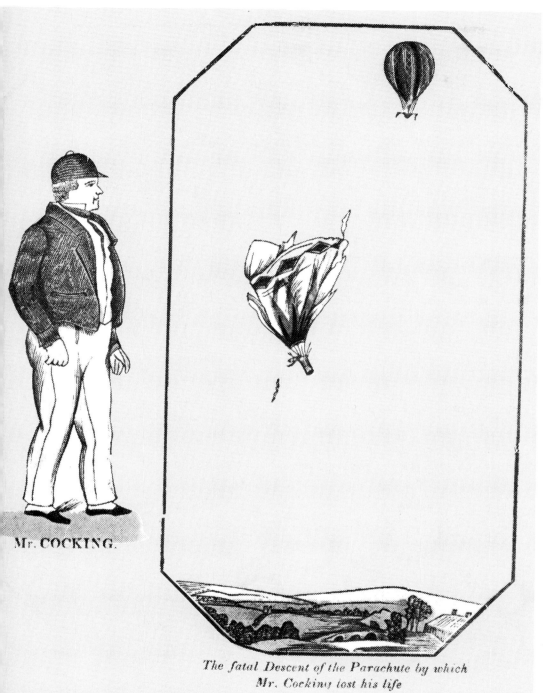

Mr. COCKING.

The fatal Descent of the Parachute by which
Mr. Cocking lost his life

MPSON, 41, Gloucester Street, Oakley Street, Lambeth.

Robert Cocking, the first Englishman to attempt a parachute descent, died in the wreckage of his 'inverted cone' parachute in 1837. (page 21)

ROYAL GARDENS, VAUXHALL.

GRAND DAY FÊTE,

On MONDAY, the 24th of JULY, 1837.

Extraordinary Novelty and Combined Attraction!

ASCENT IN THE ROYAL NASSAU BALLOON

BY MR. GREEN,

AND DESCENT IN A NEWLY-INVENTED

PARACHUTE,

BY MR. COCKING.

The Proprietors of Vauxhall have the satisfaction to announce that they are enabled to present to the Public another grand improvement connected with the Science of Aerostation; viz. a PARACHUTE of an entirely Novel Construction, by which a perfectly safe and easy descent may be made from any height in the Atmosphere attainable by a Balloon.

Mr. COCKING, a gentleman of great scientific acquirements, having, many years since, witnessed the descent of M. Garnerin, (the only one ever made in England,) was forcibly struck with the danger to which that gentleman was exposed on account of some error in the construction of his machine; and, after several years spent in numerous experiments, has succeeded in discovering the faults in M. Garnerin's instrument, and also in producing

AN ENTIRELY NEW PARACHUTE,

which is allowed by all who have seen it, to be constructed on unerring principles. The form is that of

An Inverted Cone 107 Feet in Circumference!

which, during the Descent, is quite free from oscillation; and as it will be in its proper form previous to the Ascent, it is not liable to the objection of falling several hundred feet without expanding, which was the case with the Parachute of the old form.

MR. COCKING WILL MAKE HIS FIRST DESCENT

ON MONDAY NEXT, JULY 24.

The great power of the Royal Nassau Balloon has afforded the means of making an experiment with the above-named Machine, which, from its great weight, would be impossible with any other Balloon hitherto constructed.

The plan adopted by M. Garnerin was to ascend alone and detach the Parachute from the Balloon, which having no person to conduct it fell in some very distant part, and was either lost or destroyed; but Mr. GREEN has undertaken to ascend in the Nassau Balloon, and to liberate the Parachute himself, a feat never before attempted by any Aeronaut.

THE PARACHUTE WILL BE EXHIBITED PREVIOUS TO ITS ASCENT.

In order to render this Fête more than usually attractive, the Proprietors intend giving a variety of Amusements during the Afternoon, the principal of which are—

A CONCERT in the Open Orchestra

A DRAMATIC PIECE in the Theatre, which will be lighted as at Night

The Extraordinary Performance of M. LATOUR, M. DE LA VIGNE, & their Sons

THE YEOMANRY AND QUADRILLE BANDS, &c. &c. &c.

AND A VARIETY OF OTHER ENTERTAINMENTS.

Doors will be opened at One; & the Ascent at Five.

The Descent will be made as nearly over the Gardens as possible.—ADMISSION, 2s. 6d.
VISITORS ARE REQUESTED TO COME EARLY.

The Admission to the Evening Entertainments will be as usual.——Parties can Dine in the Gardens.

[Balne, Printer, 38, Gracechurch Street.

'I believe that the interest shown was considerable. I have been told that all eyes were filled with tears and that women, equally adorable for their charms as for their sensitiveness, fell in a faint,' wrote Garnerin in a subsequent and modest letter to the *Journal De Paris*.

A great and widely-acclaimed success though it was, nobody rushed forward to become the second parachutist, and Garnerin himself was in no hurry to repeat the performance. He made only one descent each year in 1798, 1799, and 1800, all in Paris, and all well rewarded. In 1802 he came to London, and after completing several balloon flights, on 21 September he made the first parachute descent in England. The balloon was launched from the Volunteers Ground, near Grosvenor Square. Let this great pioneer tell his own story:

'The experiment of my thirty-first balloon ascent and of my new descent in a parachute, took place in London on a very fine day, and in the presence of an immense crowd of spectators, who filled the streets, windows and houses. The scaffolding erected round the place of my departure was, alas! the only spot not crowded with spectators!

'. . . I hastened the filling of the balloon, and at five pm I filled the pilot balloon which Mrs Sheridan did me the honour to launch. This pilot balloon ascended quickly and was soon out of sight, marking out my career towards the north east. Whilst the anxious crowd was following the path of my little pilot, I suspended my parachute to the balloon; this painful and difficult operation was executed with all possible address, by the assistance of the most distinguished personages. At length I hastened to ballast my cylindrical bark, and to place myself in it; a sight which the public contemplated with deep interest — it seemed at that moment as if every heart beat in unison; for though I have not the advantage of speaking English, everyone understands my signs. I ascertained the height of the barometer, which was at twenty-nine-and-a-half inches. I now pressed the moment of my departure, and the period of fulfilling my engagements with the British public.

'All the cords were cut; I rose amidst the most expressive silence, and, launching into infinite space, discovered from on high the countless multitude that sent up their sighs and prayers for my safety. I quickened my ascending impulse, and rose through light and thin vapours where the cold informed me that I was entering into the upper region. I followed attentively the route I was taking and perceived that I had reached the extremity of the city, and that immense fields and meadows offered themselves for my descent. I

Above: Thomas Baldwin headed the list of attractions at London's Alexandra Palace during the summer of 1888. (page 29)

Opposite: Robert Cocking's descent was well advertised, ostensibly in the interests of aeronautical science, in fact in the interests of the proprietors of Vauxhall Gardens. (page 21)

examined my barometer, which I found fallen to twenty-three inches. The sky was clear, the moment favourable, and I threw down my flag to endeavour to shew to the people that I was on the point of cutting the cord that suspended me between heaven and earth. I made every necessary disposition, prepared my ballast, and measured with my eye the vast space that separated me from the rest of the human race. I felt my courage confirmed by the certainty that my calculations were just. I then took out my knife and with a hand firm from a conscience void of reproach, and which had never been lifted against anyone but in the field of victory, I cut the cord.

'My balloon rose, and I felt myself precipitated with a velocity which was checked by the sudden unfolding of my parachute. I saw that all my calculations were just, and my mind remained calm and serene. I endeavoured to modulate my gravitation, and the oscillation which I experienced

increased in proportion as I approached the breeze that blows in the middle regions; nearly ten minutes had elapsed, and I felt that the more time I took in descending the safer I should reach the ground. At length I perceived thousands of people, some on horseback, others on foot, following me, all of whom encouraged me by their wishes, while they opened their arms to receive me. I came near the earth, and after one bound, I landed and quitted the parachute, without any shock or accident . . .

'A crowd soon surrounded me — laid hold of me, and carried me in triumph, till an indisposition, the consequence and effect of the oscillation I had

experienced, obliged the procession to stop. The interval of a moment, however, permitting me to get on horseback, a numerous cavalcade approached to keep off the crowd, whose enthusiasms and transports incommoded me not a little . . . At length, after several incidents, all produced by the universal interest with which I was honoured, I withdrew from the crowd without any other accident than that of having my right foot jammed between the horse I rode and a horseman who pressed too close to me . . .'[5.]

The use of ballast by Garnerin and other early parachutists indicates a continuing pre-occupation with the techniques of balloon flight, and it is interesting to

Above: The German show-jumper Katchen Paulus sits in her sling and shows how she would release herself and her two 'bundled' parachutes from beneath the balloon. (page 31)

Above left: Before taking off from Kinnoch Field for the first parachute descent from an aeroplane, pioneer jumper Albert Berry sits with pilot Anthony Jannus. The parachute is stowed beneath the jumper in the conical container, from which his falling weight will drag it. Date is 1st March, 1912. (page 34)

note that Garnerin carried a barometer to indicate altitude. For the spectators, the most noticeable feature of the descent was the violent oscillation of the 'chute as it came down into the fields where Marylebone Station now stands — violent enough to cause Garnerin to be sick all over his admirers. After his first descent in Paris and on the advice of the astronomer De Lalande, he had opened the apex of the canopy for his next drop, but this had not lessened the swinging, and he had closed the vent again. He had also removed the paper lining, but the cloth remained practically airtight, and we recognise now that the instability of the Garnerin parachute was caused mainly by the air spilling under the lip of the canopy because it had nowhere else to go. At the time, however, it drew much comment and argument. Not for the last time in the history of the sky people, theorists who would themselves never go near a parachute voiced strong opinions as to how such a device should be constructed and handled. They scoffed at Garnerin for being 'unscientific'. Also, despite the immediate adulation of the spectators, the event attracted criticism from the popular press:

'This is the first experiment of the kind in this Country, and we sincerely hope it will be the last,' said *The Sun*, a London evening newspaper. 'We mean not to detract from the skill and the courage displayed by M. Garnerin upon this occasion; indeed it would be impossible if we were so inclined; but the man who could feel any pleasure in seeing the life of his fellow creature exposed to such imminent danger, without any adequate cause, must possess either the most unjustifiable curiosity, or the most brutal apathy.'

It was an attitude that was to accompany parachuting through much of its history. In the early eighteenth century, many of the *The Sun*'s readers would have nodded in agreement. There lingered at that time — perhaps in the sub-conscious — the old belief that flying was devil's work, and it took little to persuade the populace that parachuting in particular bordered on the immoral; especially when performed by a Frenchman, and a Revolutionary to boot! Thirty-five years would pass before another parachutist would make his appearance in England.

Although there was less opposition to parachuting in France, none of his countrymen hurried to emulate Garnerin. The practical difficulties of making a parachute and of then hoisting it into the air were immense. There was also at that time a firm belief that anything approaching a rapid fall would itself cause suffocation and death. Few aeronauts, brave though they were, would be prepared to put that particular belief to the test. For more than a century, parachuting would remain an infrequent act, performed by an intrepid few.

Garnerin himself made only five descents. There is an unconfirmed report of a sixth, but there were certainly no more. He was primarily a balloonist, and one of the most accomplished of his day. He made flights throughout Europe and in Russia, and in Paris he became famous for night flights and for the aerial firework displays that he conducted above the City. He extended his showmanship and his parachuting into the theatre: at the Covent Garden pantomime in 1815 his adopted daughter Blanche, at the age of seven, was lowered from the Covent Garden ceiling beneath a fixed parachute.

Aeronautics was a Garnerin family business. Before she married André, Madame Garnerin became the first woman parachutist. As Mademoiselle Jeanne Labrosse she appeared at the Tivoli Gardens in Paris on 18 October 1799. A large crowd had gathered for the event, and she touched their hearts by the theatrical way she cried 'Adieu, tout le monde!' as she was lifted into the air, but she was back again within twenty minutes, having dropped successfully from some 3,000 feet. She only jumped the once, but with her husband became a proficient balloonist.

The most prolific and celebrated parachutist of the time was Elisa Garnerin, niece of André and daughter of his elder brother. Jean Baptiste Garnerin was a showman of sometimes devious method. For a start, one might consider it pretty devious for a man to let his daughter do all the jumping, but quite apart from any other considerations, Jean Baptiste knew that a pretty face — particularly when subjected to extreme hazard — would attract more attention and profit than his own. He would not be the last parent to put his daughter on the aerial stage while he collected the money.

Elisa made her first parachute descent at Tivoli Gardens on 20 September 1815, smiling prettily and waving flags to the spectators as she went up, and more surprisingly as she came down. She appears to have been quite fearless, and was to make a total of thirty-nine jumps in twenty-one years of parachuting. They were not without incident. The pioneer parachutists were almost entirely at the whim of the wind, and landings could be brutal. The Duke of Wellington was said to have been amongst her rescuers when she was smashed into railings during a show in Prussia. Nor were the hazards confined to the air. Elisa's father often fell foul of promoters, and sometimes of the public. He had a flair for advertisement that could raise the expectations of spectators beyond his capacity to fulfil them. It happened in Madrid in 1818 when, after a series of postponements and excuses, father and daughter were locked in prison to protect them from irate crowds, and then given an armed escort to the border. It was, apparently, not the only time that Jean Baptiste saw the inside of a gaol. His brother, André Jacques, would have nothing to do with him. In the air,

however, Elisa Garnerin was the star of the time. A crowd of 60,000 flocked to see her in Milan. In Paris, in 1817, her exhibition at the Jardin Ruggieri coincided with that of the aeronaut Margat at the Tivoli, where he was to ascend beneath a balloon whilst mounted astride a doe. Hardly anyone watched him. They were all at the Ruggieri watching Elisa. She was prettier.

It was purely for this reason — for the novelty that it added to the spectacle of a balloon ascent — that parachuting existed at all during the first half of the nineteenth century. It served no other purpose. Whereas the balloon was seen to have some relevance to scientific investigation, and even to offer some military potential, the parachute had no claim to usefulness. It was not even needed as a means of escape from a ruptured balloon, for in such events there was a tendency for the collapsed envelope to gather in the upper netting to provide a form of canopy of its own. This had been accidentally displayed in the case of young Arnold, and by others, and later it would be demonstrated purposely on a number of occasions by the American balloonist John Wise.

Whilst the Garnerins undoubtedly dominated the first forty years of parachuting, there were other aeronauts who included it in their exhibitions, and who introduced the parachute to new audiences. Michaud took it to Russia in 1803, and to Vienna in 1804; Bourget to Berlin, also in 1804; Gillaume Robert to Lisbon in 1818; and Louis-Charles Guillet to America in 1819.

When Elisa Garnerin finally hung up her pretty jump boots in 1836, nobody had parachuted in England since André Jacques had swung down from the skies over London in 1802. The next to do so would be a man who had stood in the crowd and wondered at that wild descent.

Robert Cocking was by profession an artist, specializing in delicate water colours. His interest in scientific matters was purely that of an enthusiastic amateur, and it found expression in the design of a parachute that he thought would overcome the main deficiency of Garnerin's 'chute: that fearsome oscillation. Following the Frenchman's own belief that stability was a factor of ballast, Cocking first considered a system of adjustable weights made to slide on a rod, but soon abandoned the idea in favour of Sir George Cayley's stated verdict on parachutes, to the effect that an 'inverted surface' would be far more stable than the Garnerin design. Cayley, whose ideas on dirigibles, gliders and powered flight would have a major influence on nineteenth century aviation, proposed the 'inverted cone' theory in a paper on Aerial Navigation in *Nicholson's Journal of Natural Philosophy* in 1810. It is a sound aerodynamic principle. Cocking applied it to the construction of model 'inverted cones' and must have been encouraged by the way his miniature parachutes performed when launched from the Monument at London Bridge and from small hydrogen balloons on Hampstead Heath. In 1814 he lectured to the City Philosophical Society and to the Society of Arts on the concept of the 'inverted cone' parachute, but he was not able to put his theory to practical test, for the parachute that he envisaged was of such size and weight that it was beyond the lifting capacity of any balloon of the time.

In 1832 the German scientist Lorenz Hengler also recommended the 'inverted cone' principle, and subsequently claimed to have made several descents with such a device, but this was certainly not known to Cocking.

In 1836, the managers of Vauxhall Gardens made a giant balloon to the specifications of the celebrated aeronaut Charles Green. With a capacity of 70,000 cubic feet and towering eighty feet into the air with its basket attached, it was by far the largest balloon yet built. It gained fame and a new name as the 'Nassau' balloon when Green and two companions made a record-breaking flight of 480 miles from London to Weilburg in the Duchy of Nassau in November 1836. It was quite capable of hauling Cocking and his parachute to altitude. When Cocking first made this proposal, the manager of Vauxhall Gardens, Frederick Gye, was not keen. Neither was Charles Green, who feared the effect on the balloon of the sudden release of so much weight at altitude. But Gye and Green were showmen, and such an event would surely draw a good crowd. They put their doubts to one side. An agreement was reached whereby Gye would fund the construction of the parachute and the launching, and Cocking would make the first descent for nothing; a second and third for twenty guineas each; and subsequent drops for thirty guineas. Robert Cocking wouldn't be the last parachutist to put his life on the line for peanuts. 'Trial' drops were apparently not considered, and although this is usually ascribed to supreme confidence on the part of Cocking, it probably had more to do with the economics of show business. Although Cocking himself was motivated primarily by the urge to prove a theory that he had carried with him for over thirty years, his parachute descent was not promoted in the interests of science: it was promoted in the interests of the Vauxhall Gardens.

The 'inverted cone' was constructed at Vauxhall under Cocking's direction. Like a shallow funnel, the great canopy tapered from a thirty-four foot diameter at the top to four foot at the base. One hundred and twenty-four square yards of Irish linen were stretched over a framework made of three hoops — the upper of tin and the two lower of copper — connected by ten wooden spars. A small wicker basket was suspended beneath the canopy, and was equipped with a 'liberating rope' which the parachutist would use to set himself free from the balloon, an act which Charles Green

Dolly Shepherd, the Edwardian 'Parachute Queen'. (page 31)

refused to perform from within the main basket. It has been suggested that there was also a device for tilting the cone-shaped canopy so that it might be 'steered' during the descent, but there is no proof of this. The total weight of the parachute was given as 223 lb, and some have claimed that it was even heavier. The canopy was elaborately decorated by E. W. Cocks, the Garden's resident artist.

It was a fine day on 24 July 1837. During the late afternoon, Charles Green and his colleague, Edward Spencer, took their places in the basket of the 'Nassau' and the parachute was attached beneath it. Inflated pigs' bladders were fixed to the underside of the parachutist's basket to absorb the impact of landing. It appears that Frederick Gye had last minute misgivings, but the sixty-one-year-old parachutist had no such doubts, and at half past seven on that fine summer evening he took his place in the tiny basket. The band of The Surrey Yeomanry struck up the National Anthem, the balloon was released, and brave Robert Cocking was lifted into the sky.

'As soon as we had attained the height of five thousand feet', said Charles Green, 'I told him that it would be impossible to get up as high as he desired in a sufficient time for him to descend by the light of day. Upon this Mr Cocking said, "Then I shall very soon leave you; but tell me whereabouts I am?" Mr Spencer, who had a moment before caught a glimpse of the earth, answered, "We appear to be on a level with Greenwich." I then asked him if he felt himself quite comfortable, and whether he found that the practical trial bore out the calculations he had made. Mr Cocking replied, "Yes; I never felt more comfortable or more delighted in my life." Shortly after, Mr Cocking said, "Well, now I think I shall leave you." I answered, "I wish you a very good night and a safe descent, if you are determined to make it, and not to use the tackle?" Mr Cocking to this question made no other reply than "Goodnight Spencer; goodnight Green." '[6]

Cocking pulled the liberating rope. Nothing happened. There was a pause, then he gave it a harder tug. The parachute fell away and the balloon was catapulted upwards by the sudden loss of weight. From the Greenwich Observatory the Astronomer Royal, Sir George Airy, had a telescope trained on the scene. He saw the parachute descend normally for a few seconds, then watched in horror as the inverted cone buckled inwards upon itself. Rotating wildly beneath a streaming tangle of broken spars and flapping linen, Robert Cocking hurtled to his death in a field near Lee Green.

Various reasons for the failure were suggested. Henry Coxwell, a contemporary aeronaut, claimed that the upper hoop had been broken before the ascent and there hadn't been time to repair it. There was also evidence that Cocking had twisted the liberating rope round his wrist for that second tug, and that this had slammed him up against the canopy as it was released, causing structural damage to himself and his parachute. Others have subsequently suggested that Cocking tried to use the supposed tilting device and had thus thrown undue pressure onto one side of the cone, but it is

unlikely that he would have endeavoured to steer the parachute so early in the descent. If all was well, he would have been too full of wonderment and exhilaration during those few seconds when he may have believed that his dream had come true: those few precious seconds of peaceful descent before the great canopy above him began to crumple. The fact, surely, is that poor Robert Cocking was, as scientist and aeronaut, no more than an enthusiastic amateur, whose calculations were sadly adrift, and whose 'inverted cone' was woefully lacking in strength. It was aerodynamically sound, but structurally fatal.

From where he crashed to the ground — apparently still alive but to die within minutes — Cocking was carried to the Tiger's Head inn, at Lee, where an enterprising landlord charged customers threepence a head to see the remains of the parachute, and sixpence to view the body. Poor Robert Cocking, painter of gentle water colours, and dabbler in the science of aeronautics — he never really aspired to showmanship. Yet it killed him, and pursued him even in death.

It was the tabloid extravaganza of the day. Newspapers not only featured the tragedy on their front pages, but also issued 'Parachute Disaster' supplements. All, with hindsight, condemned parachuting as an ill-advised search for sensationalism. Scientists and theorists again took the opportunity to wax eloquent and wise. Some sought to defend the principle of the 'inverted cone' whilst others condemned it. Certainly none of them tried it. The Garnerin-type parachute remained the vehicle for the parachutists of the time, and when another Englishman prepared himself to join their ranks, it was with an adaptation of the Garnerin model.

John Hampton was a professional aeronaut who, according to the American balloonist John Wise, '. . . determined to outstrip the competition by descending from his balloon by means of a newly constructed parachute.'[7] It was at a time when the appeal to the crowd of a straight-forward balloon ascent was wearing thin through repetition, and when showmen were seeking to brighten their acts. Hampton, entirely for financial gain, turned to the parachute. He made a 'chute in the form of a fifteen-foot wide canvas umbrella, with ribs of whalebone and 'stretchers' of bamboo. It had a central tube of copper similar to Garnerin's, and carried a basket for the parachutist. It differed from the French design by incorporating a block-and-tackle with which to open the canopy fully before release from the balloon. Hampton was taking no chances with slow openings, for there still existed in 1838 the firm belief that fast fall would kill.

There still existed, also, the belief that Hampton shouldn't be doing it at all. It was but little more than a year after the death of Cocking, and when it became

Opposite: Dolly, astride her sling and gripping the trapeze bar, waits to be hauled aloft for a descent at Wolverhampton in 1910. (pages 35–37)

known that Hampton was planning to make a parachute descent at Cheltenham, the local press condemned it vigorously, and efforts were made to dissuade the aeronaut. The manager of the gas-works where Hampton sought to fill his balloon agreed to supply the gas, but only if the aeronaut undertook to make a 'captive' ascent, which would allow the parachute to be displayed but not dropped. Hampton gave his solemn agreement. On 3 October at the Montpelier Gardens, when the 'captive' balloon had raised Hampton and his parachute some thirty feet, he cut the ropes that tethered him to the ground, and escaped into the sky. He used the block and tackle to open out his parachute, released it at 6,000 feet, and landed some thirteen minutes later at Badgerworth to become Britain's first successful parachutist, much applauded by all except the manager of the gas-works.

In 1839 he brought his parachute to London for the summer season. His first appearance was on 13 June, at the Cremorne Gardens in Chelsea: 'Admission 2s 6d; inner circle and reserved seats 5s; outward ground 1s; children half price.' It was a poor day for parachuting. Strong winds suggested that Hampton should postpone the drop; the crowd suggested that he should get on with it before they tore the place down. So away went the aeronaut, heading fast for the clouds. He released himself from the balloon before he entered them, which did not give him enough time under the parachute to throw out all of his ballast, so that his landing on the Fulham Road was rather heavy. His second drop that summer was mounted from the Flora Tea Gardens in Bayswater. He landed this time in a chestnut tree near Kensington Palace. Hampton, like many parachutists since, was discovering that the descent itself is fine; it is the arrival that is sometimes painful.

These exhibitions by Hampton were given a mixed reception. The immediate spectators loved it, of course, but subsequent press reports continued to lambast parachuting. *The Examiner* said of the Cremorne Gardens event:

> 'Now what is there in prize-fighting, or bull-baiting, more really savage than this, or betraying so much callous inhumanity in the spectators? Here was an immense throng of people whose pleasure consisted in seeing a fellow creature risking his life with every probability of losing it, in a way the most horrible to the imagination . . .'

The *Mechanics Magazine* wrote:

> 'Were these ascents and descents made by way of experiment with a view to testing any scientific fact, or for the investigation of any natural phenomenon, we of course could not properly object to them; but made as mere exhibitions to gratify the excited appetites of a mob of gazers, we must cordially agree in the just condemnation given to them.'

Hampton himself did nothing to lessen the impression that parachuting was the height of folly. He depended for his livelihood on that 'mob of gazers', and in fact encouraged them in their conviction that life was much at risk. He spoke in particular of the difficulties he experienced in breathing during a descent, thus strengthening the belief in the fatal consequences of rapid progress through the air, an opinion that would later be levelled against the motor car!

In their quest for novelty, most professional aeronauts of the time pandered to that 'mob of gazers'. The French couple, Monsieur and Madame Poitevin, specialized in making balloon ascents mounted astride suspended animals — even a bull — and in 1851 they found a balloon capable of lifting a carriage with two horses, a coachman and a groom. It was inevitable that they should add parachuting to the aerial extravaganzas which they staged regularly at the Champ de Mars in Paris, and it was perhaps equally inevitable that it was Madame Poitevin who did the jumping, not Monsieur. Surprisingly, it was John Hampton who loudly condemned this marital arrangement when Madame Poitevin made a successful descent at Cremorne Gardens in 1852, by which time the Englishman had himself given up parachuting after seven descents: a touch of professional pique, perhaps. Louise Poitevin proved to be a worthy successor to Elisa Garnerin. She travelled widely throughout Europe, and with her red silk parachute made some thirty-five descents, which included unintentional duckings in the Mediterranean off Gibraltar, Marseilles and Naples.

An even more prolific jumper of the 1850s and '60s was Eugène Godard, the star of the Hippodrome exhibitions staged in Paris by the impresario Arnauld to rival those at the Champ De Mars. He was said to have made at least fifty descents, also using a silk parachute based on Garnerin principles.

Accidents to the true professionals such as the Garnerins, Poitevins and Godards were rare. They confined themselves to a parachute of proven design, and suffered no more than the expected knocks of the trade. It was the dabbler in new ideas who was much at risk. Such a one was François Letur, who designed and made a 'governable parachute' comprising a braced canopy that could be 'warped' and supposedly steered by means of a foot-operated bar. With this apparatus he made two trial drops in France in 1853, and the following year sought to demonstrate it in England. After being lifted from Cremorne Gardens, Letur was unable to release himself from the balloon, and during the subsequent descent he was dragged through tree tops near Tottenham, and killed. Cremorne Gardens was the scene of another accident when in 1874 Vincent De Groof, a Belgian shoemaker, crashed to his death beneath a ridiculous 'winged parachute'.

Fanciful invention was not confined to the parachutists: aviation in general at this time combined

Dolly waves to the crowd at The Alexandra Palace as she ascends beneath her streamed parachute, suspended from a hot air balloon. (pages 35–37)

honest endeavour with much adventurous eccentricity. However, whereas the main thrust of aviation was moving slowly but surely towards the goal of heavier-than-air flight, parachuting seemed to have come to a stand-still. By the 1880s it still served no purpose other than exhibition, and the show jumpers were still using a design of parachute pioneered some eighty years before. Furthermore, exhibitions were confined to the larger cities where the considerable cost of mounting the show could be re-couped, and those city audiences were becoming blasé. With its value as a crowd-teaser in decline, and useful for nothing else, the parachute was in a poor state of health. In the 1880s, one man — with a little help from his friends — was to revive it.

Thomas Sacket Baldwin — he didn't like that middle name, and later changed it to Scott — was born in Quincy, Illinois, where at the age of twelve he saw his parents gunned down by Civil War raiders. Young Tom ran off to find jobs as newspaper boy, gas-lighter, railroad worker, and door-to-door book-salesman. In an Arkansas saw-mill he taught himself simple acrobatics, using a pile of saw-dust to lessen the pain, then at the age of fifteen he began a career as a travelling trapeze artist and tightrope walker. In San Francisco, he met a large man of Dutch extraction, called Park Van Tassell. Van Tassell too was a showman: an aerial showman. Whilst Tom Baldwin was walking a 700-foot wire above the sea between Cliff House and Seal Rocks every Sunday, Van Tassell was selling 'joy rides' in a tethered balloon, winching it up to 1,000 feet to give astonished passengers a birds' eye view of the harbour. He was not the first aeronaut to decide to brighten his act with a little dare-devilry, and he chose to do so with a parachute descent. He said that he got the idea when he was browsing through an encyclopaedia, and came across a picture of a parachute. He decided to make one.

Van Tassell's home-made parachute was crudely constructed but, probably because his mind was not encumbered by scientific theory, it was devastatingly simple. Gone were all the struts and stiffeners of whalebone and wood. Gone were the central 'tube' and liberating rope. Gone were the basket and the ballast. In their place was a plain, round canopy made of canvas, to which a square trapeze was attached by suspension lines of manilla rope. The only concession to prior art was a hoop at the very top of the canopy which would cause it to hang with its mouth partially open when suspended. Van Tassell wasn't too bothered about the actual dimension of the hoop: he used the rim from an old sulky-wheel. The whole assembly weighed some eighty-five pounds. The method of operation would be as simple as the parachute itself. It would be suspended from the netting of the balloon at its 'equator' by a break-cord. The parachutist would ascend within the balloon basket and when at the required height, would hop over the side, hanging onto the trapeze. His falling weight would snap the break-cord, thus releasing the parachute to go about its own business. If it opened . . .

It was to ascertain this that Van Tassell gladly accepted the partnership of the wire-walker, Tom Baldwin. They obtained the use of the Mechanics' Pavilion which had a domed ceiling from which they suspended the 'chute, tied sandbags to its trapeze bar, and let it go. It seemed to work. So Tom Baldwin tried it. He came down fast, but safely. The drop was only some eighty feet, so the opening characteristics of the canvas canopy must have been impressive. He made a second descent, then Van Tassell entrusted his greater bulk to his invention, and that too was successful. They were in business.

They approached the street-car company who operated the Golden Gate Park, and offered to make a parachute descent from any height between 350 and 1,000 feet, at a dollar a foot. The company agreed to buy a thousand feet. Baldwin would do the jumping, Van Tassell would operate the balloon. Some 30,000 people gathered at the Park on 30 January 1887, and watched the stuntman leap from the balloon basket, dragging the extended 'chute behind him until it banged open and brought him swinging down to enthusiastic acclaim.

There appears to have been an instant difference of opinion over the division of the 1,000 dollars, and the partnership broke up. They would never have got on, anyway. Van Tassell was a dour man, always impeccably dressed, and not given to the usual extravagances of show business. Tom Baldwin, on the other hand, was an engaging extrovert: a scruffy opportunist. The opportunism showed, for when they parted company, it was Baldwin who took the 'chute.

He took it to his home town of Quincy, where on 4 July 1887, aided by his brother Sam, he made his second jump, for which he received much local acclaim, a gold medal set with diamonds, and $250 in cash. During the remainder of that summer he toured the eastern states, making a series of descents at Rockaway Beach in New York, and others at Syracuse, Kansas City, and Minneapolis. Most of his jumps were from a tethered gas balloon called 'The City of Quincy' and rarely did he jump from above 1,000 feet, which meant that he remained within sight of the paying crowd — not always the case with his predecessors who, with their free balloons and more complicated systems were sometimes out of view before they gave their 'show'. Baldwin heightened the dramatic effect of his performance by replacing the balloon basket with a simple sling-seat, and for the occasions when he had to use a free balloon he evolved a 'ripping cord' method of releasing gas as he dropped away, so that the unmanned balloon would follow him down at a safe distance.

Veteran show-jumper William Morton, dressed in lavender-coloured tights, looks decidedly unhappy about making one of the earliest jumps from an aircraft, at Venice Beach, California, in 1912. (page 34)

The response to his shows was, as usual, mixed. The crowds applauded: authority frowned. 'The manoeuvre shows a want of aeronautic common sense' wrote balloonist Henry Coxwell of Baldwin's Rockaway performance.[8.] Chicago city authorities cancelled his planned appearance because they thought it all far too hazardous. One who was impressed, however, was 'Buffalo Bill' Cody, who saw Baldwin jump in Minneapolis and strongly advised him to take the show to England. So in 1888, leaving brother Sam to look after the exhibition jumps in America, Tom Baldwin came to London.

The parachute that he brought with him had been progressively improved during his 1887 performances. It was now made of silk, and the sulky-wheel had long been replaced by an eighteen-inch rope ring, which left an adequate vent-hole but dispensed with any attempt to hold the canopy even partially open. It was the first truly 'limp' parachute. Just as Garnerin had provided the basic design for the first ninety years of parachuting, so Baldwin, with his improved version of Van Tassell's 'chute, now produced the basic model for the next ninety years. Through practical trial rather than through scientific deduction these two pioneers had discovered the simple fact that a plain circular canopy, when correctly presented to the airflow, will open without the aid of mechanical contrivance. It was a discovery that practising parachutists would quickly accept, but that would somehow elude more scientific minds for many years to come. Baldwin became a very proficient parachutist, and must have been one of the first to steer a parachute with a basic technique still used today with plain round canopies:

> 'The parachute I can pull down on any side according to the direction I wish to go. I can tilt up the ring at one side and pull it down on the other, or I can seize the rope on one side of the parachute and pull the silk down, so as to give it more or less resistance.'[9.]

The parachute was registered as British patent number 10.937 on 28 July 1888 in the names of Thomas Baldwin and Guillermo Antonio Farrini. This Farrini was no parachutist: he was an impresario, who knew a good act when he saw one. Earlier that summer he had undertaken, for half a share of the improvement in revenue, to bring back the crowds to the Alexandra Palace, which as London's largest pleasure ground was having a lean time. 'Professor' Baldwin was to be the means of doing so. Farrini's advertisement of the forthcoming series of parachuting exhibitions was more effective than the enterprising Italian could ever have imagined. There were those who remembered Robert Cocking. The press stoked the public imagination with frequent reference to 'suicide jumps', and the alarm and controversy spread to the House of Lords, where the Earl of Milltown asked the Government

> ' . . . whether the attention of the Home Office has been directed to an announcement in the papers that Professor Baldwin would at the Alexandra Palace on Saturday next, jump out of a balloon, a thousand feet above the ground; whether it was believed the announcement was genuine, and if so, whether measures would be taken to prevent so dangerous and demoralizing an exhibition'.

Replying for the Government, Earl Brownlow assured the Lords that

> ' . . . the attention of the Home Secretary had been directed to the subject, but no definite information was forthcoming of the exact nature of the advertised performance. The police had been instructed to attend and warn the intended performer.'

The jumps from Tower Bridge, left and above, by Major Orde Lees and the Hon. Lieutenant Bowen in 1917 provided a dramatic demonstration of the low-level opening characteristics on Calthrop's 'Guardian Angel' parachute. Later, Orde Lees made frequent jumps from aircraft. (page 40)

The outcome of all this free publicity was a crowd of over 40,000, gathered at Alexandra Palace on 28 July 1888. They weren't disappointed. The show that Farrini and Baldwin put on was staged with outstanding professionalism. It began with the inflation of the balloon in a roped enclosure ringed with the great throng of spectators. It was a symbolic act, tension and excitement rising with the swelling of the great bag. When the balloon was tugging at the ropes that tethered it to the ring of sandbags, the dapper figure of Farrini came forward to tie the apex of the parachute to the netting. Then Baldwin himself appeared. Farrini had insisted that the American dress as became an aerial 'professor' and less like a cowboy, and Tom was an impressive figure in collar-and-tie, jacket, waistcoat, trousers and polished black shoes. He addressed the spectators in a loud, calm voice, telling them that he intended to jump from 1,000 feet but would release himself from as low as 500 if he was being carried too far away. He asked for absolute silence during the final preparations, then, after bidding a fond and visible farewell to his wife, he removed his jacket and took his place in the sling as the tethering ropes were slowly paid out. Holding on with one hand, in the other he took the trapeze of the parachute that was hanging in a fully extended loop from the side of the balloon. All this in utter silence, broken suddenly by Baldwin's loud command, 'Let go!'

The balloon was released, and the parachutist, sitting in his flimsy sling, was whisked from the ground. There was none of the solemn majesty normally associated with balloon ascents — this was a rapid and dramatic dash for the sky, for the impact of Baldwin's show depended on him getting up there quickly and dropping whilst still within easy viewing distance. Forty thousand heads tilted backwards; 40,000 pairs of eyes watched the dwindling figure; 40,000 voices cried out in alarm as the man above fell suddenly from the sling and hurtled earthwards at what appeared to be terrifying speed before the streaming canopy blossomed into life. The cries became cheers as the parachutist swung jauntily from his trapeze, and the cheers followed him all the way as he came swaying down out of the sky to land alongside the 'Ally Pally' racecourse. It was an outstanding display.

The subsequent response was the usual mixture of condemnation and admiration. The *Court Circular*:

'We cannot but think that it would be as well if the Home Secretary were to direct the police to put a stop to 'Professor' Baldwin's descent from a balloon in a parachute. It is true that last Saturday he accomplished the feat successfully, but on the next occasion he may not be so fortunate, and may be dashed to pieces in the presence of thousands of people. It is well known that many of the spectators who visited Alexandra Palace on Saturday went there with the full impression that they were going to witness a tragical occurrence. The descent by means of the parachute serves no scientific purpose. It can only appeal to the morbid interests of the mob, and should certainly be at once stopped.'

The Times:

'The performance was a marvellous one, and, whether it deserves to be regarded as one of any scientific value or not, it was certainly one of the most extraordinary and successful sensational feats of modern times.'

During the next three weeks, whilst controversy raged and Members of Parliament made further attempts to have the performances banned, Tom Baldwin made ten more successful jumps at the 'Ally Pally'; a piece of music called 'The Cloudland Waltz' was written and dedicated to him; the British Balloon Society awarded him its prestigious Gold Medal; the crowds swelled to 100,000; and Farrini counted the money. The final seal of approval came when, no doubt to the dismay of the *Court Circular*, its 'mob' was joined by the Prince and Princess of Wales who took their daughters to watch Tom Baldwin's final appearance in London that summer. It has been said that the Prince took a diamond ring from his finger and presented it to the parachutist, but this was not recorded at the time, and surely the press would not have missed such an occurrence! Nevertheless, it's a good tale, and we shall keep it in the folklore file . . .

After taking his show to northern England and Scotland, Baldwin sailed on the SS *Oroya* to give a series of exhibitions in Australia. The following summer he was back again at the Alexandra Palace, and once more toured the Far East. By 1890 he was richer and thirty pounds heavier, and gave up the trapeze bar to concentrate on the organization of what was now a well established business. His place under the parachute was taken by a circus performer with whom Baldwin had worked many years before, christened William Ivy but renamed Ivy Baldwin when he came to work for Tom, who knew the trade value of what had become the most prominent name in parachuting.

But the 'Baldwins' were not alone in the skies. Tom had opened a door, and a host of imitators rushed through it, close on his heels. How had he opened it? What had prompted this sudden revival of parachuting?

Firstly, there was the man himself. Tom Baldwin was an outstanding performer, with an outward show of nonchalant dare-devilry that appealed to the public, and a behind-the-scenes professionalism that attracted the promoters.

Secondly, the frequency and safe conclusion of Baldwin's jumping confounded the most vociferous opposition. Almost before they could draw breath for another tirade and a further forecast of imminent disaster, Baldwin had made another successful jump.

Parachuting would still have its critics and would never lose its 'dicing-with-death' label, but Tom Baldwin brought it out of its dark ages.

Thirdly, the simplicity of his parachute and of his method of using it greatly reduced the complexity and cost of parachuting exhibitions. The 'limp' parachute was easily copied and constructed by the do-it-yourself jumpers of the time, who weren't put off by such nonsense as patent rights. The 'overheads' were reduced and the options widened even more when Baldwin — and others — replaced the gas balloon with a simple hot-air bag. The parachute was at last free of the big cities.

The 'hot-air bag' was not new. It was a simple derivative of the 'Montgolfière' of a hundred years before. A huge 'bag' made of thick cotton fabric or canvas would be suspended from a wire slung between two poles, with its open mouth held over the downwind end of a covered fire-trench. When the balloon was full of hot air and 'on its feet', the poles were removed, the mouth closed, the passenger attached, and the whole smoky business released into the air. Before the jumpers adopted it, the hot-air bag had already served as a means of transport for aerial trapeze artists, who would perform their act as they drifted into the sky, then stay with the balloon as it cooled and came down, hopefully not too fast. Miss Leone Dare in America and Blondeau in France were foremost amongst those who survived.

In America the new breed of jumpers quickly adopted this vehicle, which was independent of a gas supply, and cheaper to operate. 'Smoke Jumpers' they were called, or 'Riders of the Bag', and during the 1890s and beyond, no county fair in the United States was complete without one. Many were trained by Baldwin himself, for in 1891, faced with increasing competition for the overseas exhibitions, Tom and brother Sam concentrated their activities at Quincy, where they bought Singleton Park and opened it as a showground, with ballooning and parachuting as the main attractions. Tom appealed to the adventurous instincts of young America with advertisements such as the one that appeared in the *Quincy Journal* of 2 June 1892:

'Baldwin has more engagements for the Fourth of July than he has aeronauts. Any young man who desires to gain fame or an early death would do well consulting Mr Baldwin.'

The Baldwins ran the Park and an associated balloon manufacturing business for eight years before Tom moved to California. There he would make the first dirigible to fly successfully in the U.S.A., and later would make and fly his own aeroplane. A major but largely underrated figure amongst the American 'Early Birds', Thomas Scott Baldwin is one of the most significant of our parachuting pioneers.

Other Americans soon followed Baldwin to Europe, and beyond. The team of Williams and Young appeared at the Alexandra Palace in 1889, and Charles Leroux and the woman parachutist, Hattie Lawrence, were prominent amongst those who toured Europe. The Van Tassells re-appeared, with Parc now following in the steps of other aerial showmen by letting the rest of the family do the actual jumping, in this case his daughters Gladys and Valerie, who parachuted and gave indoor trapeze shows in the Far East and Australia. One of Van Tassell's team, Joseph Lawrence, met a particularly unfortunate end when he was swept into the sea when making a descent in Hawaii, and killed by sharks.

British aeronauts were also quick to follow Baldwin's example. The Spencer brothers, grandsons of Edward Spencer who we last met bidding 'good night' to Robert Cocking from the basket of the 'Nassau' balloon, incorporated the Baldwin style of parachuting in their well-established aeronautical activities. By December 1888, Stanley Spencer was parachuting from the rafters of Olympia Palace, whilst brother Percival left for India and Ceylon where he blazed a trail for other show jumpers to follow. The Spencers were soon administering a 'team' of parachutists who appeared at fetes and shows throughout Britain during the 1890s and 1990s. A similar 'team' was established by Auguste Gaudron, a celebrated balloonist and himself a competent parachutist who had appeared at the re-opening of the Alexandra Palace in 1898 with Mademoiselle Alma Beaumont and Captaine Charles Lorraine in a three-sided 'parachute race', and who subsequently jumped there regularly, sometimes astride a bicycle. His 'team' was to include the famous Dolly Shepherd. We shall hear more of Dolly, when we consider the show-jumpers. In Birmingham, Lieutenant Lempriere also presented 'parachute races' between himself and his 'charming lady pupils'.

Amongst the young adventurers of this parachuting revival were those who were to take parachuting out of the pioneering age and into the era of the aeroplane. This was particularly so in America, where Charlie Broadwick, Leo Stevens, 'Dad' Coughlin, Ed Bolan, Albert Berry, Leslie Irvin, and William Morton were amongst those who began their parachuting careers under a balloon and continued them into the age of the aeroplane. We shall meet them all, later.

The technical advances in parachuting that came from this period of revival and transition were initiated by the jumpers themselves, for the scientific mind was understandably pre-occupied first with the imminence and then with the momentous actuality of heavier-than-air flight. Because parachuting advances were made by showmen, and because showmen tend to guard their trade secrets, little publicity was given to new discoveries, and there was no co-ordination of effort. Trying to establish exactly who was the first to introduce a particular technique or piece of equipment

into the world of parachuting is sometimes a fruitless exercise. There was, however, a logical sequence in the improvement of the parachute during this period, and we can identify the major contributors.

The first step was to stow the limp parachute in a container — a bag, or a sack, or even an inverted bucket with a laced covering. This container would be attached to the balloon or to its basket. When the parachutist, gripping his trapeze bar, dropped away, his falling weight would pull the canopy from the container, streaming it into the airflow. This novelty was introduced entirely in the interest of spectacle. It hid the parachute from sight, increased the impression of free drop, and added greatly to the 'will-it-or-won't-it-open?' drama.

Orde Lees with pilot Captain Saunders before jumping in a 40 mph wind at Gottenburg. (page 40)

It is believed that Baldwin was the first to introduce the bag, and it is likely that the did so in America, but at the same time and quite independently, Katchen Paulus was developing the system in Germany. Early in her parachuting career, the attractive Katchen had watched her instructor and fiance, Hermann Lattemann, fall to his death. Having despatched the girl for a descent from 5,000 feet above Krefeld, he endeavoured to follow by 'ripping' the balloon in anticipation that the collapsed material would as usual gather in the netting to form a canopy. Alas, on this occasion, it didn't. It streamed and flapped uselessly above him as he hurtled earthwards. Katchen Paulus went on to become Germany's most celebrated parachuting pioneer, making 147 jumps before she retired in 1909. Most of these were with the canopy and lines stowed in a bag, and sixty-five of them were with a second 'chute rolled in a bundle and attached to the first. When safely suspended beneath the first, she would open the bundle by pulling a wooden pin from a metal cone, and as she fell the length of the streaming lines and canopy, the shock load would break the ties that bound the second parachute to the first. It was a novelty that many other show jumpers adopted, and a fore-runner of the 'cut-away' descents that still feature in the air shows of today.

The American J. J. Coughlin refined the bag system by folding the parachute inside its container and separating it from the rigging lines in a way that would reduce the risk of entanglement. Others dispensed with such niceties altogether: Ed Unger and Ed Boland were amongst those who merely attached the apex of the 'chute to the balloon rigging or basket, then bundled the canopy and lines in their arms, and jumped. It gave the same dramatic effect of apparently unsupported free drop before the parachute appeared, and opened, although the likelihood of the latter must have been lessened.

The trapeze bar was usually combined with a simple sling-seat, and sometimes with a safety belt that was comforting for novice jumpers but mostly scorned by the true professionals. This system was quite adequate when dropping beneath a fully extended 'chute, but when canopy and lines were stowed in a container, the preliminary free drop before opening imposed a much heavier shock-load on the parachutist. It was this that prompted the introduction of a body-harness. Crudely made harnesses of belly band and shoulder straps, made of leather or webbing, appeared on the American showgrounds in the early 1900s, although most aerial entertainers, for effect, still clung to their trapeze bars. In Europe, the development of a body harness received a major impetus when the military began to take a practical interest in the parachute as a means of escape from balloons. By the close of the nineteenth century the balloon was established as a military observation platform, a role in which it had served in Napoleonic campaigns, in the American Civil War, and in the Boer War. The introduction by the Germans of the more stable 'Drachen' balloon had greatly increased this potential.

In 1909, Captain Maitland of the Royal Engineers, serving with the Balloon Section, was considering the use of parachutes as a means of escape from British observation balloons. Only one way to find out: do it. Captain Maitland made his first jump under the tutelage of Auguste Gaudron and Dolly Shepherd, and declared himself well pleased with the experience, although he didn't like the trapeze bar. 'I could not allow my men to do that,' he said to Dolly Shepherd. 'It is too dangerous, and they must have their hands free.'[10] The subsequent introduction of the parachute

harness in Britain was largely his doing, and parallel developments took place in Germany and France.

At that stage, the simple and extremely uncomfortable harnesses were independent of the parachute container. They were worn on the body, and attached to the parachute lines as and when required. The next step was to combine harness and parachute; to have the jumper actually wearing it. The American Charles Broadwick is credited with being the first to do so. A balloonist since 1886 and a parachutist since 1892, Charlie Broadwick in about 1905 made his first body-pack parachute. Attached to a body harness and worn on the back in the manner of a knap-sack, it comprised a cover portion in which the canopy was folded, and a base portion which held the lines, the two components fastened with break-ties. The pack was connected to the balloon or basket by a 'static line' which, as the jumper fell away, would break the ties and allow the canopy and then the lines to deploy in a regulated sequence. It was the fore-runner of today's widely used static-line operated parachutes. Charlie Broadwick would subsequently incorporate the harness into a waistcoat-like garment to produce the 'Broadwick Coat-Pack'. It should be emphasized that this back-pack was operated by static-line: no 'ripcord' yet.

Moving in that direction, however, was yet another American pioneer, Leo Stevens. A celebrated balloonist with a balloon manufacturing business in New York, Stevens also developed a body-pack during the late 1900s. The main difference from the Broadwick design was in the method of operation: the back pack was opened when the static line pulled out a locking pin that allowed spring-assisted flaps to fly open and release the canopy into the airflow. A form of 'ripcord', yes, but a ripcord that was designed to be operated by static-line, not by hand. However, although at first his 'chute was used solely by show jumpers leaping from balloons, Leo Stevens was looking ahead: he called it a 'Life Pack'. The time had come to introduce the parachute to the aeroplane.

The euphoria with which the earliest balloon flights had been greeted had lessened with the gradual realization that although man had at last entered into the upper air, he had by no means conquered it. Fanciful notions that the balloon might be propelled and steered came to nothing. Man was not really flying: he was drifting. So the search for controlled and sustained flight had continued, mostly in theory and occasionally in practical endeavours that were sometimes comic, sometimes tragic, and which sometimes marked a step in the right direction. Major advances came when emphasis turned from 'flapping' flight to gliding flight, as developed by Otto Lilienthal in Germany and Percy Pilcher in England. Both of these pioneers of flight died in the wreckage of their 'hang gliders', but they had shown the way. Also towards the end of the nineteenth

In 1913, the American 'Tiny' Broadwick sits in her sling-seat before becoming the first woman to jump from an aeroplane. The static-line operated parachute is stowed above her head. The pilot is Glenn Martin. (page 38)

century, the new automobile industry provided a petrol motor to replace the clumsy steam engines with which some would-be aviators had tried to bully their way into the air.

The threads came together in Wilbur and Orville Wright, bicycle mechanics of Dayton, Ohio. They concentrated first on the achievement of flight control with biplane gliders, then on the application of power, and after much painstaking experiment, on 17 December 1903, they made the first powered, sustained and controlled flight in a heavier-than-air machine. The momentous event amongst the remote sand hills of Kittyhawk did not shake the world. In fact the world heard little of it, and what it did hear it didn't believe. Sheltered by their own reticence and a disinterested press, for the next four years the brothers developed their 'Flyers' in virtual seclusion in a ninety acre field east of Dayton. Meanwhile, the European pioneers went their own way. By 1907, Santos Dumont, Farman, Bleriot, Voisin and Delagrange had struggled a few feet into the air, but with little control over what they could do once there. In 1908, shortly after Cody made the first tentative flight in Britain, the Wright brothers astonished the public and their fellow aviators in the first series of displays given by Wilbur in France and Orville in America. Their demonstrations of flight control opened the skies. Whereas in 1908 they, Glenn Curtiss in America, and a handful of adventurers in

Europe had been the only fliers, by 1909 there were forty licensed aviators spreading flimsy fabric wings over the earth. In that year, Bleriot's crossing of the English Channel, and the first great international aviation event at Rheims, firmly announced that the aeroplane had arrived.

Where was the parachute? It was still securely attached to its original partner, the balloon. It had no place in that first powered scramble into the sky. The early assemblies of fabric, wood and wire did not have the capacity to carry a parachute, nor — even if the notion had occurred — did they have a need for one. Oh yes, aeroplanes crashed and aviators were killed, but early flight was rarely far enough from the ground for a parachute jump to have been feasible. At the Rheims meeting of 1909 the altitude prize was won by Hubert Latham when he managed to coax his Antoinette monoplane to a height of 505 feet. Even with the rapid improvement in aircraft performance over the next few years, there was no cry for a life-saving parachute. It was still seen as an instrument of dare-devilry, associated entirely with the balloon.

When, in 1912, the parachute was at last introduced to the aeroplane, it was primarily as a promotional stunt, with only vague notions of more practical purpose. Anthony Jannus and Bud Morriss were two young fliers working for a showman and maker of aeroplanes called Tom Benoist, operating at Kinnoch Field, St Louis. To Tom Benoist came a request from China for a two-seater aircraft with trap doors under the seats in case either of the crew was wounded and became an embarrassment to the other. Tom Benoist didn't take the idea seriously, but his two pilots were intrigued by it. In such an event, what would happen to the man? And what would happen to the aircraft? The man was easy: put a parachute on him. But the aeroplane? It was widely held that if suddenly relieved of weight, an aeroplane would leap upwards as did a balloon, and that control, often marginal at the best of times, would be lost altogether. There was only one way to find out. From a Benoist 'pusher', the aviators dropped a succession of increasingly heavy loads, first without support, then beneath small parachutes. They were relieved to discover that the aircraft appeared not to mind. A live trial was the next logical step. They approached the boss:

'Prior to this,' comments Morriss, 'we had agreed on the result of a flip of a coin that Tony would pilot and I would jump. Explaining this to Benoist, he disagreed with our plan, stating that we could only carry them out if we obtained the services of a professional jumper. Honestly, the feeling of relief that flooded my soul was so great, and I can tell you that that is as near as I have ever been to jumping in my life of flying.'[11.]

Good fliers were hard to come by, and Tom Benoist surely wasn't going to have one of his men risk his neck in any damned parachute! But he supported the drop because he saw it as excellent advertisement for his aeroplane. The idea of saving wounded aviators appears to have been abandoned. The main objective was now the immediate well-being of Tom Benoist.

An advertisement was placed for a professional parachutist, and was answered by a local 'smoke jumper', Albert Berry, son of the well known balloonist 'Captain' John Berry of St Louis. Albert brought along his parachute. It was one of the standard 'limp' variety, made of unbleached muslin, and still employing a trapeze bar. A cone of galvanized iron was attached to the forward strut of the aircraft undercarriage, and the parachute canopy was folded inside it, each fold separated by sheets of newspaper. Break-ties held the canopy inside the container, and another series of ties across the mouth of the cone held the rigging lines and trapeze in place.

It was cold, with flurries of snow, on the afternoon of 1 March 1912. Dressed in rubber coat, boots, cavalry trousers, and stocking-cap pulled down over his ears, Albert Berry took his place alongside Anthony Jannus in the open seats of the fragile biplane. From Kinnoch Field they climbed laboriously to a height of about 1,500 feet above Jefferson Barracks, where Albert clambered onto the axle, grasped the trapeze, and launched himself into space. The parachute opened amidst a cloud of newspaper, and Albert Berry landed cold but safe some two minutes later, the first man to parachute from an aeroplane. He repeated the act a few days later at Kinnoch Field, where it was still bitterly cold, and where he declared that he wouldn't do it again unless there was a lot more money in it.

The event caused no great stir. Army officers who witnessed the descent at Jefferson Barracks saw no military merit in the act, and politely declined the suggestion by Bud Morriss that the system could perhaps be used for seeding poison gas from containers suspended beneath parachutes. Aviation circles attached no life-saving significance to the demonstration, and were more concerned with the effect of the drop on the aircraft and its pilot. The *Aero Club of America Bulletin* said that:

'. . . it demonstrates a moot matter — that it is possible in time of war for an aviator to drop a heavy load of explosives without excessive risk to himself'.

In its brief report of the event the British magazine *Flight* thought that:

'In a feat of this kind it is rather open to doubt as to whether the pilot or the parachute jumper is running the greater risk. In our opinion we should be inclined to attach the greater courage to the aviator.'

This concern for the pilot rather than the parachutist was effectively demonstrated when, shortly after the Berry jumps, another stuntman called William Morton also leapt from an aeroplane. Morton was a veteran showman, fifty-four years of age, who, in his lavender tights, jumped regularly from the captive balloons that were a feature of the permanent 'fairground' at Venice Beach, California. He could see no problem in jumping from an aeroplane other than finding a pilot willing to take part in the venture, but eventually Phil Parmalee was persuaded to fly his Wright model 'B' for the show. Morton stuffed his canopy into an inverted can tied beneath the pilot's seat. Clutching the trapeze and a bundle of rigging lines to his chest, and wearing his lavender tights, Morton took his place on a plank lashed to the front skid. The first attempt failed when the strangely burdened aeroplane ran into the sea on take off, to a mixture of cheers and boos from the crowd. A week later they tried again. A reporter from the Los Angeles *Examiner* was there:

'With a deafening roar of engine and propellers the plane started down the strand at a speed of fifteen miles an hour, then rose lightly into the air. Parmalee made a long turn to the right, sailing over Venice, climbing higher all the time. He turned again over Del Rey and shot straight down the ocean front nearly half a mile out at a height of 2,300 feet . . . a black dot and a white thread dropped from beneath it and the great crowd gave a gasp as they saw Morton take the plunge. As a plummet, man and parachute dropped 300 feet and then, like a giant gull unfolding its wings, the parachute opened wide and the man, hanging to it seemingly by the slenderest of threads, swayed back and forth in the air to the rocking of the canvas support . . .'

Morton was drifted across the beach by the on-shore wind, to land on Trolley Way, where his parachute caught in the power lines and dropped him heavily onto the tracks. Not many were there to see his arrival: they had all rushed along the sands to Fraser's Pier to congratulate the pilot.

At the time, neither Albert Berry nor William Morton received recognition for what was a considerable act of pioneering, primarily because their jumps were professional exhibitions and not intended for the advancement of aviation.

In the strict sense of the word there are still many 'pioneers' to appear in our story of the Sky People. By our definition, however, Albert Berry and William Morton, in leading parachutists into the world of the aeroplane, led them out of their pioneering age.

CHAPTER TWO
The Show-Jumpers

Almost without exception, the pioneers of parachuting — as we have defined them — were show-jumpers. Some, such as André Jacques Garnerin, John Hampton, and the Spencers, were primarily balloonists who took to the parachute to improve their public appeal and augment their income. Others, such as the ill fated Robert Cocking and Francois Letur, were obliged to become showmen as the only means of testing their parachutes and beliefs. Others, such as Tom Baldwin and Leslie Irvin, began as show-jumpers before progressing to wider fields of aviation. And others, such as Elisa Garnerin, Katchen Paulus, Albert Berry and William Morton, were full-time professional show-jumpers who operated either independently or for 'managers'. We have seen how, for more than a hundred years, the parachute served no purpose other than exhibition, and how the advances in equipment and techniques during that time were inspired by showmanship rather than scientific interest.

The show-jumpers ended the pioneering era with a flourish. In Europe, and particularly in England, the first decade of the twentieth century saw a major resurgence of interest in ballooning, which still provided the only means of flight for most enthusiasts at a time of great aeronautical expectation. For those who could afford it, ballooning became a sport, encouraged in England by the foundation of the Aero Club in 1901, and finding expression in balloon races, cross-country pleasure flights, and balloon meetings such as those at Hurlingham and Ranelagh. The balloon's little friend, the parachute — itself revived by Baldwin and his imitators — had its place in this renaissance:

'This was the age of the balloon, before the aeroplane captured the skies. It was an age of great elegance and serenity, perhaps symbolized by the balloon itself, so majestic and unhurried. It was an age when the parachutist, smartly attired, would spend an hour or more strolling amongst the crowds as they gathered to watch the inflation and preparation of the balloon, making friends and establishing a personal relationship with the spectators before the event, then returning to the arena to celebrate with them afterwards. It was altogether a more leisurely time.'[1.]

Thus spoke Dolly Shepherd, the most celebrated of those parachutists who thrilled the Edwardian crowds in those tranquil years before the world went to war. Dolly was a professional, but she didn't jump just for the two pounds and ten shillings that was the fee for her performance: she jumped for the excitement and joy of it. The story of her days as an Edwardian lady parachutist conveys that joy, and serves as an admirable illustration of the techniques and hazards of early parachuting. In 1904, when Dolly was seventeen years old, Auguste Gaudron invited her to join his well established team of parachutists, who gave performances at fetes and fairs throughout Britain. Dolly didn't know it at the time, but she was replacing another girl called Maude Brooks, who had recently sustained serious injuries while parachuting in Dublin. Dolly made her first jump from the edge of the basket of a gas balloon, with the apex of the parachute tied by a break cord to the netting. No pack. No harness. The balloon carried passengers, who paid well for the privilege of watching a pretty girl launch herself into space. It was piloted by 'Captain' Gaudron:

' "We were over 2,000 feet. Get ready to jump." The Captain's calm voice broke into my reveries. It was like a piece of ice being dropped into the pit of my stomach.
' "There's a nice green field over there," he was saying, pointing outwards and downwards at what looked like a green pocket-handkerchief set amongst roads as narrow as string, and clumps of trees like pieces of moss. "Remember how to land," he reminded me, then uttered a loud: "GO!"
'Gripping the trapeze bar tightly with both hands, I took a deep breath and launched myself into space . . .
'Oh, that first fall! What a heady mixture of fright and sheer exhilaration it was! My heart rose into my mouth as I plummeted for what seemed far too long, dropping like a stone. I could hear the rapid flap-flap-flap of the silk streaming after me as the canopy broke from the balloon netting and sucked at the rush of air, and then at last there was a big whooooooosh . . . the sling tightened, and the trapeze bar tugged at my arms . . . the parachute was open . . . !

'I looked up. The canopy was stretched over me like a beautiful silken dome, billowing softly as though it were breathing — as though, like me, it was glad to be alive, glad to be free. It was, at that moment, the dearest friend I had in the world. I gave it a joyful smile.

'Suspended there in the clear, warm air, high above the land of mere mortals, I experienced a sense of elation such as I had never known. But the wonderment passed as, dangling beneath my gently swaying friend, I turned my attention to the scene below. I still had to land!

'Just as the earth had seemed to slip away beneath us as we had ascended in the balloon basket, now it was drifting back to meet me. Gradually the fields and the houses and the trees began to assume their rightful proportions. The Captain's aim had been good, for the field that he had chosen as my landing place was approaching, slowly at first, then appearing to pick up speed as it came closer, until with a final rush, as though trying to grab me by the legs, the grass suddenly leapt up at me . . .'

After several jumps from the basket, the next progression for Dolly was to be suspended beneath the basket of a manned balloon, from which she liberated herself on the command of the good Captain. After several descents in this fashion, she was ready for her first 'solo', using a smaller, unmanned gas balloon. It was at Ashby-de-la-Zouch:

'I stepped into the sling and took up the trapeze bar.

' "LET GO!" I cried, in a firm voice.

'Up went the balloon, and away I sailed beneath it, waving my little flag as I went. Up and up and up I soared, leaving behind the cheers and the faces and the waving hats, rising rapidly into a world of utter and incredible silence. The sounds of the crowd, the barking of dogs, and the songs of the birds were lost, for with increasing height all nature becomes silent. Nor is the stillness of a balloon ascent broken by the sound of the wind, for the balloon becomes part of that wind. It moves with it. It belongs to it. There was not even the creaking of the basket or the muffled voices of its occupants that had accompanied my previous ascents. I was alone. Alone in the immensity of the sky. Alone in its silence.

'Yet I was not frightened. On the contrary, I was enthralled . . . There was just me and my friend the parachute, and our balloon lifting us higher and higher into the blue . . . into the silence . . .

' "Here goes . . ." I said aloud to the silence, and gave an almighty tug on the ripping cord that simultaneously released the parachute and ripped the valve of the balloon open. There was the now familiar drop of some 250 feet before the canopy opened and slowed my fall . . . Hoping for a soft landing, I enjoyed as always the gentle, swaying descent under the big silk umbrella. Within minutes I was picking myself up from the corner of a field. As I bundled my parachute, I was conscious of the songs of the birds, which for a short while I had left far behind me.'

The final stage in Dolly's parachuting education was a solo drop from a hot-air balloon at Pickering in Yorkshire:

' "LET GO!" roared the Captain.

'Thankfully, the crew let go. Equally relieved, the balloon headed for the sky, dragging me after it. In answer to the jubilant cheers, I waved my little flag as I was born aloft, swinging beneath my bag of hot air. The sensation was much the same as that of an ascent under the gas balloon, apart from the smell of the smoke that lingered in my nostrils, like the childhood scent of bonfires in my father's beloved garden.

'The crowd and the park and the town itself dwindled, and there was the broad sweep of the moorland rolling away to the north, and the verdant pastures of the Vale of Pickering to the south. I had little time to admire the scenic grandeur, however, for I knew how important it was for me to part company with my hot-air friend before his enthusiasm cooled and he collapsed on top of me. At the same time, I had to be high enough to give my parachute ample time to open fully. The Captain's words hammered in my brain: "Take no chances — you must pull away at fifteen hundred." So my attention was occupied more by my aneroid than by the scenery.

'As I neared the crucial height, I looked below for a suitable landing spot. "There — that beautiful piece of green velvet will do," I said to myself, and gave a hard pull on the ripping cord. Away we went, my parachute and I, leaving the poor balloon to wonder what was happening as the sandbag tied to its crown promptly turned it upside down, spilling out its hot air in a great belch of black smoke. Swinging beneath the opened canopy, I watched it make its ungainly way back to earth. I was very grateful to it, of course, but decided that I preferred my little gas balloon. Somehow it was more elegant . . .'

For eight years Dolly thrilled the Edwardian crowds. She became a firm favourite at the 'Ally Pally' and with the working class audiences of the Midlands, and at the same time enjoyed the attentions of the rich and

A U.S. Navy jumper demonstrates the manually operated parachute. Military 'show-jumpers' played an important role in persuading fliers that parachutes actually worked! (page 77)

famous. She and the other prominent aeronauts were the pop-stars of the age. But it was fame without fortune, and fame gained at immense risk. At the time Dolly joined Gaudron, there were four others in his team. Three of them — Violet Kavanagh, 'Captain' Smith, and 'Professor' Fleet — were to die on the showgrounds of Britain. Dolly herself came close to disaster on many occasions. Performances were never cancelled because of a little wind. If the balloon could fly, the parachutist could jump. In Scotland, Dolly descended from a hot-air balloon amidst flashing lightning and crackling thunder — to land in a cemetery. There were landings in trees, upon roof-tops, and once almost on top of an express train. There was an occasion when she fell for almost 5,000 feet under a streaming canopy before it banged open at tree-top level, and another when her 'chute was apparently sabotaged and she crashed down into the crowd under severed lines as the balloon hauled her into the air. And there were times when, hanging beneath a solo balloon, the release mechanism jammed.

37

The first time she was alone, and clung to her sling and trapeze bar for over three hours as she was carried above the clouds and into the night, until the balloon tired of the deadly game and deposited her, close to exhaustion, into the pitch darkness of a field.

The second time it happened not to her, but to a friend, Louie May, who was to make her first parachute descent as part of a 'double act' with Dolly. The two girls ascended, hanging to their separate parachutes beneath a free gas balloon. When Louie May pulled her liberating cord at 3,000 feet, nothing happened. It was jammed, and no amount of pulling and jerking would free the 'chute. As the balloon rose into cloud, and through it into cold loneliness beyond, it became apparent that Louie May could not hang on for long, so Dolly pulled her friend across to where she herself was hanging, and two miles above the earth directed the terrified girl to relinquish her own trapeze and sling, and twine her body to her own. She then released her own parachute, and the two fell beneath a grossly overloaded and only partially opened canopy. It opened fully before they hit the ground. Louie May was unhurt. Dolly broke her back. She was told that she would never walk again, but two months later she was not only walking — she was parachuting once more.

That first mid-air rescue in the history of aviation was widely publicized, and attracted the customary indignation. In the correspondence column of the *Staffordshire Sentinel*, the Reverend Edmund Pigott announced:

> 'These and all similar performances, such as tight-rope dancing and trapeze work without nets, only appeal to the lowest instincts of a man's nature, and are in a sense educationally degrading. My own opinion is that all matters such as this need most careful supervision. Parachute descents should be forbidden.'

A Mr Caleb Hackney added: 'Can not public opinion, perhaps supported by some exalted personage, put an end to parachute descents by females? As a last resort there is Parliament.'

As Dolly said, 'What a dull world it would be if it were full of Reverend Pigotts and Caleb Hackneys!'

Dolly Shepherd made her last descent in 1912. She flew with the 'Red Devils' display team in 1976 at the age of ninety, met 'The Falcons' in 1983, and died two months later just short of her ninety-seventh birthday, within a few days of correcting the final proofs of her autobiography.

America had its own 'Parachute Queens'. In the 1890s there had been Ruby Deveau, known as 'Queen of the Clouds'. She began jumping in 1892 at the age of fifteen, and made 175 exhibition drops, mostly from hot-air balloons, until she landed on a roof in Ontario in 1895, broke her back, and retired.

Then in 1908 appeared the jumper whom Americans remember as their 'First Lady of Parachuting', a slip of a girl, less than five feet tall, called 'Tiny' Broadwick. Billed as the daughter of Charles Broadwick, the balloonist and parachutist, she was in fact no relation. She was born Georgia Thompson, and story has it that in 1907 at the age of fifteen she saw Charlie Broadwick, in spangled tights, jump from a hot-air balloon in Raleigh, North Carolina, and asked if she could make a descent herself. She got her wish from the wise Charlie Broadwick who saw a showman's dream coming true in this pretty, diminutive girl. What a crowd-puller she would be! When he left Raleigh, the fifteen-year-old 'Tiny' went with him, for jumping from balloons was surely more fun than working in that cotton-mill. Charlie dressed her in a frilly bloomer suit and white stockings, framed her cherubic face in a leather helmet, billed her as his daughter, and within a few years, with only slight exaggeration, could claim in his publicity hand-outs that Miss Tiny Broadwick was 'The Biggest Drawing Card in America'. She was sometimes called 'The Doll Girl', which was a name that Tiny privately hated but publicly encouraged.

For five years the Broadwicks parachuted only from balloons, then in 1913 Tiny became the first woman to jump from an aeroplane. By that time, Charles Broadwick was developing his 'back-pack' parachute and had been joined in the venture by California's foremost aviator and plane-maker Glenn Martin, who was one of the first of the great fliers to appreciate the life-saving potential of the parachute. In fact Glenn Martin has sometimes been credited as the inventor of this back-pack, for the only relevent patent (US Patent 1,165,891 of December 1915) is in his name, but this is no more than a slightly refined version of Charlie Broadwick's work. Martin's interest in the Broadwicks also had a lot to do with the popularity of Tiny, for his association with her brought welcome publicity and cash to the youthful Martin Aircraft Company. He first dropped Tiny on 21 June 1913. It was not intended as a major public exhibition, but the press were there in force. The Los Angeles *Tribune* reported:

> 'At the base of the northern slope of Griffith Park, Glenn L. Martin, Southern California's contribution to the ranks of the world's greatest aviators, and Tiny Broadwick, a winsome little eighteen-year-old with a national reputation as a parachute jumper, yesterday made aviation history in thrilling fashion. At a height of 1,000 feet Miss Broadwick released herself from a trap seat set in the front of Mr Martin's speedy biplane and dropped to earth uninjured — the first woman to make a parachute drop from an aeroplane.
>
> 'Nor was the handful of spectators thrilled alone by the feat of the daring bit of femininity that dashed earthward from the great man-made

bird. As the parachute sped down from the great height, Aviator Martin, with consummate skill, drove his monster aeroplane hither and thither around and about the falling bit of silk and its precious freight of record-making girlhood . . .'

They don't write them like that any more!

Tiny repeated the performance before a larger audience in Chicago when she jumped from Martin's 'hydroplane' into Lake Michigan. These first two jumps from an aircraft were made with the parachute stowed in a container attached to the aircraft, but by early 1914, Charlie Broadwick's 'Coat Pack' was ready for demonstration, and Tiny displayed it effectively to the public and to military observers in a series of jumps from aircraft in Los Angeles and San Diego. After appearing at the San Diego World Fair in 1915 and 1916, Tiny's jumping became less frequent, and she made her last descent in 1922, also in San Diego, from an aeroplane piloted by the famous stunt flier 'Upside-Down Pangborn'. Tiny never counted her parachute jumps, but reckoned to have made more than a thousand.

Although Tiny was not a Broadwick, parachuting was in the family, for Charlie's wife Ethel was a jumper. Sadly, she died in 1920 under high twists and a streaming canopy.

Although Tiny Broadwick grabbed the biggest headlines, there were many other show-jumpers in the American skies during this period of transition from balloon to aircraft. Prominent on the West Coast was young Leslie Irvin, who defied well-meaning parents to gain his FAI Balloon Pilot's Licence at the age of fourteen, and to become a parachutist under Ed Unger at fifteen and a full-time professional aeronaut at seventeen. With the veteran Glenn Morton he was a regular jumper at Venice Beach, and on one occasion in Los Angeles when Tiny Broadwick could not appear for a billed exhibition, the slightly built Leslie Irvin put on the bloomer suit and the white socks and the leather helmet and jumped for Charlie in her place — making sure to land well away from the crowd. He also worked as an assistant casting director for Universal Studios in Hollywood, and whenever an aerial stuntman was called for, he cast himself in the role. It was when parachuting into the sea off Long Beach from Earl Daugherty's aeroplane for a film called Sky High that he earned his nick-name: throughout an illustrious and profitable career in parachuting he would be 'Sky High Irvin'. In 1914 he really did go sky high when he parachuted from an aircraft at 8,200 feet to establish an unofficial world altitude record for a drop from an aeroplane — unofficial because nobody at that time was keeping the score. It was fitting that the jump was made over Elsinore, which fifty years later would become one of America's major skydiving centres.

On the east coast, one of the foremost show-jumpers was Rod Law, who in an eventful life had been sailor, circus rider, steeplejack, and — according to his wife — 'general darned fool'. His first jump was from the upraised arm of the Statue of Liberty on 2 February 1912. He break-tied the apex of a borrowed 'chute to the top rail of the observation platform, climbed over, and jumped. The canopy opened just before he hit the stone pedestal 151 feet below, and Rod Law limped off to collect $1,500 from the Pathe Motion Picture Company. Film was also shot of him parachuting from the 170-foot high Williamsburg Bridge into East River, and from the roof of the 173-storey Bankers Trust Building on Wall Street — to land on another roof a mere two storeys high. Deciding that jumping from aeroplanes was probably a lot safer, he became one of the first to make an aircraft descent when he parachuted from a 'hydroplane' at Marblehead in April 1912, using a Leo Stevens back-pack with the ripcord tied by static-line to one of the aircraft struts. For the next two years he parachuted throughout the eastern states, piloted on at least one occasion by his sister Ruth, but mostly, as the hand-bills said, by ' . . . Harry Bingham Brown, English Pilot, elevating Frederick Rodman Law in his Wright Aeroplane to a Height of 4,500 feet, Disposing of his Human Freight at a Dizzy Height, Who descends by the Aid of a Parachute. No Other Act Like It in the World!'

In 1913, seated in a small chamber on top of a twenty-foot rocket loaded with fifty pounds of slow-burning black powder, Rod Law attempted to have himself blasted into the sky, whence he would return by parachute. When the fuse was lit, the rocket exploded on the ground like a bomb. 'What happened?' asked Rod Law as they lifted him from the smoking debris. Rod Law survived such stunts to serve with the US Army Balloon Division during World War One, but he couldn't survive fifty cigarettes a day, and died of lung cancer in 1919 at the age of thirty-four.

As the age of parachute pioneering came to a close with the advent of aircraft jumps, the popularity and frequency of show-jumping waned. In Europe by 1910, the aeroplane had become a practical vehicle for private owners and young adventurers. Ballooning declined accordingly, and parachuting, not yet fully adapted to the aeroplane, declined with it. Exhibition jumping retained its appeal a little longer in America, but by 1915, as Leslie Irvin said 'The parachute game was pretty stale and there was so much competition.'[2] The final blow to this great period of show-jumping was dealt when the world went to war, and aeronautical interest was diverted to more deadly purpose.

By that time, our pioneers and their almost total association with show-jumping had established a concept of parachuting that was to have a marked influence on its subsequent role in aviation history. Three basic principles of exhibition jumping had been firmly established. Firstly, there must be a constant pursuit of novelty. Secondly, the most attractive novelty is a pretty face. Thirdly, the greater the real or imagined danger to which that pretty face is exposed, the better the show. The danger element was not, of course, limited to the pretty parachutist: it was an attraction in its own right, and as such it was in the interests of the show-jumpers themselves to foster the image, if not the reality, of extreme hazard. One might think that it was hardly necessary to exaggerate the dangers. The numbers of dead and maimed parachutists, and the sad fact that most of them received more publicity in death than they did in life, widely advertised the nature of the trade. So it was that, at the close of the pioneering age, parachuting was not only associated entirely with showmanship, but with a form of showmanship that was at best foolhardy, and at worst irresponsible. The 'dicing with death' label was firmly tied to the parachute. It was an association that would, as we shall see, long delay the acceptance of the parachute for more purposeful use. It was one that the next generation of show-jumpers would continue to foster most energetically.

During the First World War and for several years after it, show-jumping became a means of promoting the parachute itself. The audience was no longer that of the fairground, but of military observers and reporters, for this was a time when the more far-sighted could anticipate the need for a parachute as an aerial life-saver, and when the most astute manufacturers of parachutes could anticipate handsome contracts. Not that there were many 'manufacturers', for the making of parachutes had long been a 'do-it-yourself' industry practised by the show-jumpers themselves. Charles Broadwick and Leo Stevens in America; the Spencers and Everard Calthrop in Britain; Katchen Paulus and Otto Heinecke in Germany; and 'Pere' Robert in France — these were foremost amongst the few who produced parachutes for sale before 1919, although there were other 'inventors' with a parachute to produce if they could find a market. The only way that these actual and potential manufacturers could effectively demonstrate their goods was to 'show' them. This was particularly the case in England and France, where at this time there was a flurry of parachuting endeavour, mostly theoretical, sometimes practical.

Everard Calthrop, in his almost obsessive endeavours to persuade the British government to accept his 'Guardian Angel' parachute as a life-saver, was a great believer in live demonstration. The 'Guardian Angel' was a complex system, incorporating a silk canopy packed between metal discs stowed in a canvas container that was attached to the aircraft. The deployment was initiated by the falling weight of the jumper and controlled by a series of break-ties. It was to demonstrate the 'positive opening' characteristics of

this 'chute that Calthrop sponsored the famous Tower Bridge display of 11 November 1917. On that day, before an invited audience of reporters, Major Orde Lees and the Hon. Lieutenant Bowen leapt from the upper parapet of the Bridge only 150 above the Thames. Orde Lees had an aversion to that sinking feeling that comes from jumping feet first into nothing, so insisted on a head-first dive. Bowen's departure was more orthodox. Their parachutes opened dramatically just before they splashed into the water. It was a convincing and well publicized piece of commercial showmanship.

Orde Lees became a regular demonstrator of Calthrop's 'chute, in England and abroad, and his many descents from aircraft included at least five from heights below 300 feet. He was an impressive jumper, but an unpopular man. As a member of Shackleton's 1914 Expedition he had been one of those stranded in Antarctica. As they awaited rescue, other members of the party agreed unanimously that if they had to resort to cannabalism, Orde Lees would be the first to go. So Calthrop was probably only too happy to follow show-jumping tradition by adding a pretty face to his 'display team'. The face belonged to a seventeen-year-old who one day in 1919 turned up at Richmond Park where the 'Guardian Angel' was being jump-tested, and asked if she could have a go. She gave her age as twenty-one, and because she didn't want her parents to hear of such unladylike behaviour, gave her name as Sylvia Boyden — which in fact was that of her grandmother. She got her jump — and some 150 more, most of them 'showing' the 'Guardian Angel' at air shows and before military observers, and all in the name of Sylvia Boyden. She demonstrated the 'chute in America in 1919, and in Denmark in 1920, where she jumped at Copenhagen in a wind of 60 mph. Also in 1920 she was the only woman to perform at Hendon's first RAF Pageant. *Flight* reported the show:

> 'As one of the Handley Pages approached over the enclosure, Miss Sylvia Boyden, with knees tucked well under her chin, dived head-first from her seat near the tail, followed by a red and white Guardian Angel parachute, which opened with its usual exceptional quickness and brought the diver swaying violently, but gracefully, to the ground. After releasing herself from the harness and gathering in the parachute, Miss Boyden, who is but twenty-one, and pretty at that, there and then celebrated her thirteenth descent, in true aviator's style, with a cigarette, and then faced the ordeal of being photographed and filmed.

'Professor' William Newall, a professional show-jumper since 1912, also demonstrated the 'Guardian Angel' during the early 1920s. Newall had been the first to jump from an aeroplane in England when he leapt from a Grahame White biplane at Hendon in 1914,

Sylvia Boyden was the prettiest of several British jumpers who regularly displayed Calthrop's 'Guardian Angel' parachute during the early 1920s.

using a bundled 'chute and trapeze ring in traditional style, and with the assistance of another parachutist Frank Goodden to push him off the improvised seat attached to the skid. Newall died in Denmark in 1922 when his 'Guardian Angel' hung up, to leave him dangling beneath the aircraft. Although he was eventually able to release himself from the harness and drop into water from sixty feet, he was dead when recovered by boat.

America did not witness the same degree of commercial showmanship, for there the development of a life-saving 'chute became a matter of military trial rather than privately sponsored advertisement. However, it was in America that show-jumping as pure entertainment was so vigorously revived in the 1920s.

During World War One, American industry had been slow to respond to the demands of aerial warfare, and although large numbers of aircraft did eventually roll from the great Standard and Curtiss factories, they were nearly all training machines. At the end of the War, thousands of these aircraft stood idle. Also idle were thousands of newly trained pilots, back from the War, still with a yen to fly. They could buy one of the surplus biplanes for as little as $300, or a brand new one still in its crate for $600 — which is why, some say, aeroplanes came to be called 'crates'. All America was there waiting for them, just dying for a ride in one of these new-fangled flying machines, and there were no more Fokkers coming out of the sun, and no tiresome flying regulations. So throughout the United States, surplus aircraft and surplus pilots came together in an explosion of exuberant, uninhibited aviation. These young gypsy pilots roamed the country in their battered biplanes, bringing aviation to urban and rural America long before the air mail and the passenger routes arrived.

They would appear unannounced out of the sky, roar down the main street, then perhaps pull a few stunts over the town. If people came running and looked upwards as though they had never seen a 'plane before, it would be a good town, but if they continued about their business with no more than an upward glance, the flyer would know that someone had been there before him, and would move on. At the good towns he would look for a field that was close to the road and not too green, for green was wet and soft, and if there were cows they would tell him which way to land, for cows eat facing into wind. The farmer would probably be the first to come running, and he would get a free flight, and he would tell the others how marvellous it was up there, and the pilot would fly dawn to dusk until there were no more people queuing with their dollars. He would carry out running repairs on the old biplane, and sleep under its wing, and if there was a barn he would stake the aeroplane beside it for shelter. That is why he was called a 'barnstormer'.

As more young flyers joined the ranks of the barnstormers, competition grew, and they had to devise means of luring passengers out to the landing fields and the cow-pastures. Now, when they buzzed a town, they had someone standing out on the wing-tip, waving, or hanging upside down from the spreader-bar: a 'wing-walker'. Wing-walking had developed in California in response to Hollywood's thirst for visual drama. A former Air Service mechanic called Ormer Locklear was the first and most famous. He used the aeroplane in flight as a piece of gymnastic apparatus, and pioneered the mid-air change from one aircraft to another. He was a pilot too, and died in 1920 when he spun his aeroplane into the ground — with the cameras rolling, of course. A host of others had followed him onto the wings, and there were many pretty faces amongst them: Gladys Roy, Mabel Cody, 'Princess' Elly Jonescu, Gladys Ingle, and Ethel Dare, known as the 'Flying Witch'.

The wing-walkers performed their aerial gymnastics without 'chutes, but it was not long before the parachute became part of the act in its own right, and it was through this association with the American barnstormers that show-jumping experienced a major revival. These itinerant parachutists became known as 'Gypsy Moths'. Some were veteran jumpers, but most were young stuntmen and wing-walkers who merely added the parachute to the show. One-eyed Wiley Post, who would gain aviation fame in the 1930s with his round-the-world flights, was one who began his flying career as a wing-walker and show-jumper. Another was a tall, quietly spoken youth from Minnesota, called 'Slim' Lindbergh.

Five years before he burst into the 1927 headlines as the first man to fly solo across the Atlantic, Charles Lindbergh began his aviation career amongst the mid-western barnstormers. To earn cash to buy an aircraft of his own, the young Lindbergh worked first as a wing-walker for pilot Erold Bahl, then decided to add parachuting to the act after watching veteran Charlie Harden make a descent at Lincoln, Nebraska, with a container-chute of his own design. Even after his momentous pioneering flights, Charles Lindbergh would look back on his early parachute jumps as being amongst his most notable aviation experiences. He wrote:

'When I decided that I too must pass through the experience of a parachute jump, life rose to a higher level, to a sort of exhilarated calmness. The thought of crawling out onto the wing, through a hurricane of wind, clinging on to struts and wires hundreds of feet above the earth, and then giving up even that tenuous hold of safety and substance, left in me a feeling of anticipation mixed with dread, of confidence restrained by caution, of courage salted through with fear. How tightly should one hold on to life? How loosely give it rein? What gain was there for such risk? I would have no pay in money for hurling my body into space. Nor was there any scientific objective to be gained. No, there was a deeper reason for wanting to jump, a desire I could not explain. It was the quality that led me into aviation in the first place, when safer and more profitable occupations were at hand, and against the advice of most of my friends. It was a love of the air and sky and flying, the lure of adventure, the appreciation of beauty. It lay beyond the descriptive words of men — where immortality is touched through danger, where life meets death on equal plane; where man is more than man, and existence both supreme and valueless at the same instant.'[3.]

He persuaded Charlie Harden to let him make a jump — not just a straightforward drop, but a 'double', with the first 'chute being operated by the static-line as he fell away, then being cut away to pull out a second canopy:

'I watched in amazement the transition of my daydream into the reality of me, my mind, my body, in the front cockpit of an airplane climbing up through empty space into which I was going to throw myself against the instincts of a thousand generations. The stiff, double-canvas straps of the harness dug into my legs and pressed down onto my hip-bones. The big parachute bag lay awkwardly out on the right wing, its top lashed to the inner-bay strut's steel fitting. To the uninitiated eye, it might have contained a bushel of potatoes. It was a long way out along that panel, but you had to be sure the parachute would clear the 'plane's tail surfaces as you jumped . . . It's hard to see safety in that dirt-smeared canvas sack bulging on the wing. My heart races. My throat is dry. Minutes are long.

'The nose drops, the wing lowers, the plane banks toward the field. The nose dips, rises, dips again. That's my signal. I look back. The pilot nods. Thank God, the waiting time is over! Unbuckle the belt . . . get a firm hold on center-section struts . . . rise in cockpit . . . leg over side . . . lean into the slipstream's blast.

'Now, out along the spar . . . Nothing but wires to hold onto . . . I reach the inner-bay strut . . . Remember to hang on to top and bottom — never at center, lest it snap.

'I sink down on the wing, legs dangling on top of patchwork fields . . . I unsnap a parachute hook from the landing wire . . . snap it onto my harness . . . now the other . . . I let myself down on drift and flying lines . . . they bite into my fingers . . . Nothing but space, terrible, beautiful . . . swinging free beneath the wing.

John Tranum sets off on one of his many journeys back to earth.
(Photo: RAF Museum)

'The roar of the engine dies . . . the nose drops slightly . . . NOW! I force my hand to reach up and pull the bow's end . . . Tightness of harness disappears . . . the wing recedes . . . white cloth streaks out above me . . . I'm attached to nothing . . . I turn in space . . . I lose the sense of time . . . My body is tense in a sky which seems to have no place for tenseness . . . Harness tightens on legs, on waist. My head goes down . . . muscles strain against it . . . tilt it back . . . The canopy is pear-shaped above me . . . it opens round and wide . . . There's the plane, circling . . . There's the field below . . . I swing lazily, safely on the air. The sun is almost setting. Clouds have reddened in the west.

'But there's a second jump to make. I must leave plenty of altitude. The ground has already risen — fields are larger. I reach over my head for the knife-rope; a pull, and it will cut the line lashing the second chute to the first. I glance at the earth . . . back at the chute . . . YANK! . . . The white canopy ascends . . . I'm detached from old relationships with space and time . . . I wait . . . I turn . . . but my body is less tense . . . I have experience . . . I know what to expect . . . The harness will tighten . . . and . . . but why *doesn't* it tighten? . . . It didn't take so long before . . . Air rushes past . . . my body tenses . . . turns . . . falls . . . good God . . .

'The harness jerks me upright . . . My parachute blooms white . . . Earth and sky come back to place . . .

'Life changed after that jump. I noticed it in the attitude of those who came to help me gather up my chute — in Harden's acceptance of me as a brother parachutist. I'd stepped suddenly to the highest level of daring — a level above even that which airplane pilots could attain.'

With a parachute that he bought from Charlie Harden for $125, 'Daredevil Lindbergh', as he was now billed, toured the Midwest with pilot Cupid Lynch. By the time that he had made another seventeen jumps, he could afford to buy his own Curtiss 'Jenny', and came in off the wing. As we shall see, he was by no means finished with the parachute.

The new breed of jumper did not altogether replace the 'smokemen' of the previous era. 'Smoke-jumping' from hot-air balloons was still an effective and cheap means of thrilling the carnival crowds. Indeed, as it became more of a rarity, its very novelty held a great attraction for a new generation of upturned faces. It had become almost a family art, and was handed down as such. When 'Mile-High' Oscar Ruth died in 1926, he left his business to his assistant Claude Schaeffer, who was still jumping some forty years and 5,000 descents later! Charles Dame was one who kept the tradition alive on the eastern side of the USA, whilst on the west coast, the Australian veteran 'Captain' Penfold — who in 1913 had jumped in England for the Sandow Chocolate Company dressed as Father Christmas — smoked his way into the sky regularly at Santa Cruz.

Like Lindbergh, most of the 'Gypsy Moths' used a container parachute, attached to the aircraft and deployed by their falling weight. By 1919, however, a revolutionary means of thrilling the audience was available to the show-jumper: the manually operated parachute. Worn by the man and completely independent of the aircraft, it provided the jumper with the opportunity to fall freely through the air for as long as altitude and nerve allowed, before pulling the ripcord. The development of the manually operated 'chute by Floyd Smith, and the first jump with it by Leslie Irvin at McCook Field in 1919, belong to the next chapter, for it was designed primarily as a life-saver for aircrew. But what an opportunity it also offered the show-jumper! Even with an automatically operated 'chute, it was that short plunge through space before the canopy blossomed fully into life that thrilled the crowd. How much more sensational to see that tiny figure, black against the sky, fall from the 'plane completely unsupported and come hurtling earthwards! Would he pull it? Would it open? Would it . . .? Then a great letting out of breath as there was a flash of white above the plummeting body and the loud whack of the canopy as it opened only a few hundred feet above the ground. What a golden opportunity for the show-jumpers to tie that 'dicing-with-death' label a little tighter to the parachute.

So why didn't the barnstormers all rush to buy one of the new Irvin 'chutes? Partly because they couldn't afford one: it cost almost as much as an old 'Jenny'. But that wasn't the main reason why the show-jumpers didn't hurry to add free fall to their repertoire. Free fall? Not on your life! Didn't the doctors and the scientists and the old-time jumpers and just about everyone else say that free fall would kill? That you would lose consciousness before you could ever reach for that ripcord? Sure, Les Irvin and Floyd Smith and some of the other jumpers at McCook had dropped short distances before yanking the ring, but perhaps they had been lucky. The belief in the fatal consequences of free drop was deeply ingrained. It was not easily budged.

One of the first show-jumpers to ignore advice and to equip himself with a manually operated 'chute was a big Iowan called 'Kohley' Kohlstedt. Floyd Smith said of him:

> 'One day a booking agent called me up and asked if I knew a crazy guy by the name of Kohlstedt. I told him I did and he wasn't crazy. He said he must be because he wanted to make a contract for exhibition parachute drops of 5,000 feet or more delayed, open the chute less than 500 feet from the ground, and land in the infield or no pay. When he was first doing delays he jumped one day, 1,200 feet, counted for a 900 foot drop and released about seventy feet from the ground.

John Tranum, one of the great barnstorming sky people of the 1930s.

His count was correct, but the altimeter of the 'plane from which he jumped was off, so he learned something about altimeters at the cost of two stoved-up legs.'[4.]

Only slowly did the show-jumpers adopt the new 'chute, and begin their hesitant exploration of free fall.

By 1925 the individual barnstormer was finding the going hard. Competition had increased and had driven passenger-charges down at a time when the cost of maintaining the ageing biplanes was going up. There was some public opposition too, as the uncontrolled nature of the flying took an increasing toll. The ex-military flyers had been joined by other sky-struck youngsters who did not have the benefit of formal training. In aircraft that were often poorly maintained and whose flying and stalling speeds were dangerously approximate, they were a hazard to themselves and to their passengers, and too many died. The fliers began to drift together to operate out of fixed bases, or to join the itinerant 'air circuses' that would largely but not completely replace the individual barnstormer and his 'Gypsy Moth'.

The greatest of the American travelling air shows was the Gates Flying Circus, which brought its 'Death Defying Aerial Acts' to cities throughout the States from 1922 to 1927, before settling for a further two years in a permanent base in New York. During that time it claimed to have hauled 750,000 passengers without losing one. It attracted those passengers through its aerial stunting, and the menu inevitably included wing-walkers and parachutists. The first of these was Thornton 'Jinx' Jenkins who used an old balloon-type parachute until it failed to open at San José in February 1922, in front of 20,000 people. A few months previous to that, a stuntman called Wesley May had sent a telegram to Ivan Gates saying, 'When your present wingwalker bumps off, wire me.' Gates sent the telegram, and Wesley May took the place of the late 'Jinx' Jenkins, and lived for another three months. He used one of the new 'chutes, and his free falls from 3,000 feet were advertised as 'bullet drops'. A favourite Wes May stunt was to roller-skate too and fro along the top wing of a 'Standard' reinforced with beaverboard, then skate right off the end into free fall, to the consternation of the crowd who hadn't been aware that he was wearing a parachute. He also carried out the world's first in-flight refuelling when he clambered from Frank Hawk's 'Standard' onto a 'Jenny' flown by Earl Daugherty, with a five-gallon can of gasoline strapped to his back — all as part of the show. Three months after joining the Gates Circus, he jumped at Cressey Field, San Francisco, and hanging by his hands from the harness, landed in a tree, in a cemetery. Trees were an accepted hazard for the show-jumper, but this one wasn't playing fair. The branch broke, and Wesley May fell onto a tombstone, and died.

Faced with the expense of changing the name on his posters every time his jumper was killed, Ivan Gates decided to call them all 'Diavolo'. His foresight paid off in the case of the first 'Diavolo', for Red Kiehl died at Cheyenne in 1923. Two 'Diavolos' who survived were Aaron Krantz and Art Starnes — the latter destined to become one of the pioneers of high altitude free fall.

Occasionally, the 'Circus' had guest jumpers. At Ellington Field, Texas, a local showgirl called Rosalie Gordon was allowed to jump, purely in the interests of publicity for herself and the 'Circus'. She got more publicity than she bargained for. The lines of her container-chute fouled the landing gear when she jumped from Clyde Pangbourne's 'Standard', to leave her dangling helplessly beneath the fuselage. Stuntman Milton Girten, who was also in the 'plane, climbed down onto the spreader-bar, but was unable to pull the girl to safety. Yet another stuntman, Freddy Lund, climbed onto Pangbourne's 'Standard' from another aircraft, to take over the controls while the powerfully built Pangbourne joined Garten. Between them they managed to haul the girl onto the spreader-bar and back into the cockpit. The event attracted almost as much nation-wide publicity as it would have done had the girl been killed.

There were other great air circuses, all with their wing-walkers and jumpers. 'Dale And Seitz' featured King Joe Leboeuf, a previous smokeman and now billed as 'The World's Oldest Parachute Jumper' with some 2,000 descents to his credit. 'The Five Blackbirds' — an all-black circus — had a girl jumper called Marie Daughtry. 'Mabel Cody's Flying Circus' had Buddy Plunkett who began jumping at fourteen and whose favoured crowd-teaser was to open an old, torn parachute after a lengthy free fall, plummet down beneath the trailing tatters, then yank the ripcord of his 'real' 'chute some 300 feet above the ground.

The search for aerial sensationalism reached its peak amongst the sky people of California, where not only were there the audiences of the pleasure beaches and showgrounds to be thrilled, but Hollywood directors with a thirst for outrageous stunts. The 'Dog-fights' of World War One, recreated for films such as *The Dawn Patrol*, *Hells Angels* and *Wings* provided a marvellous opportunity for the fliers and the jumpers to show their paces and risk their necks. A sequence much sought after by directors but less popular amongst the performers involved an aircraft that had been doused with oil and petrol being set on fire during flight, requiring the pilot to make a hasty and very realistic leap for life. John Tranum and Buddy Plunkett were amongst those who survived this particular stunt. One of the most durable of the west coast stuntmen was 'Speedy' Babs. At Venice Pier he used to jump with a sackful of

Above: British show-jumper Harry Ward with flexible wings was one of the few 'birdmen' to survive the experience. (page 50)

Left: Leo Valentin, preparing to make a test jump with his rigid wings, in which he was later to die at Speke airport in 1957. (page 56)

fireworks that he would set off as he descended. It was always a toss up, he said, whether he would burn to death or drown. He claimed to have been the first to ride the top wing of a biplane and drop from it into free fall while upside down at the top of a loop — without the audience knowing that he had a parachute, of course. 'Speedy' reckoned that he had broken fifty-six bones during his stunting, ' . . . but only a few at a time.'

It couldn't last, this wild era of unregulated flight and extravagant stunting. The beginning of the end came in 1926 when Congress enacted the Air Commerce Act, which required for the first time that mechanics and pilots be licensed, and aircraft be registered and certified. Lindbergh's Atlantic crossing in 1927 inspired a resurgence of interest in aviation and joy riding, but the new legislation ended the heyday of the individual barnstormer and the early and unfettered flying circus. Their place was taken by slightly more respectable outfits, operating mostly within the law, and with a new breed of aeroplane to replace the old 'Jennies' and 'Standards'. Groups such as the 'Inman Brothers Flying Circus' and 'The Flying Aces' would carry on the old traditions in more restrained form, and most air shows would continue to feature parachutists. Even they, however, were becoming subject to regulation in the USA. By 1931 all parachutes had to have an 'Approved Type Certificate'; riggers had to be licensed; and those making 'premeditated' jumps had to wear a reserve 'chute as well as a main.

This eventual gesture towards safer show-jumping in America did little to change its public image. The 'Gypsy Moths' and the circus jumpers of the 1920s had set out to confirm the widely held opinion that parachuting was a hazardous and foolhardy business. They had succeeded admirably.

Europe did not experience the same explosion of aerial exuberance that marked the barnstorming era in the USA. The skies were not as wide and not as free, and the grim reality of aerial warfare had been much closer. Flying was nevertheless in its exciting adolescence. Young men wanted to fly, and people wanted to watch them, and to take a 'flip' themselves if possible. Retired military aviators attempted to establish 'flying companies' primarily for selling joy-rides, but the pickings were lean, and few could afford to employ a wing-walker or jumper. The larger European air pageants of the 1920s, although comparatively sober affairs by American standards, were immensely popular, and they usually did feature a parachutist, often 'showing' a particular make of parachute on behalf of its manufacturers.

In England, Sylvia Boyden and Orde Lees continued to display the 'Guardian Angel' into the 1920s, and a 'Miss June' became another popular exponent of Calthrop's 'chute. The first team of military show-jumpers made their appearance at the annual RAF Pageant at Hendon in 1927, when six airmen made simultaneous 'pull off' descents from the wings of three Vickers Vimy biplane bombers.

Restrictions on parachute descents from civil aircraft came early to England. One of the few flying companies who used parachuting to attract the paying passengers was that of Captain Muir, with his Surrey Flying Services. He did it the cheap way, by inviting members of the public to make a descent. Brave Mrs Cain volunteered at Leicester on 9 September 1926. She was fitted with a harness, to which the static-line of a container chute was attached. Somehow it became detached again, for when she jumped from 1,000 feet, she fell straight to her death wearing only the harness. Five days later the Air Ministry issued a 'notice to airmen' stating that parachute descents from civil aircraft were prohibited unless a formal application giving full details of the proposed descent had been submitted fourteen days in advance, and approved by the Ministry.

During the 1930s, show-jumping in Europe, as in America, became concentrated at the major air pageants and at the displays given by the itinerant air circuses. Lola Schrotter, Richard Kohnke and Meister Knecht in Germany, and the Frenchmen Jean André and Jacques Marget, under his distinctive dome-shaped canopy, were amongst the foremost 'continental' show-jumpers. In England, a number of professional parachutists of varying proficiency operated either independently or as regular performers for the major air circuses.

Ben H. Turner attracted a little publicity when he missed the proposed site of the Kingston-and-Surbiton aerodrome to land instead upon the lion cage at Chessington Zoo. He was one of many European jumpers who combined public appearance with the demonstration of specific parachutes for promotional purposes, and in 1937 he enjoyed an eventful tour of South America showing the 'GQ' range of manually operated 'chutes. Benno De Greeuw was another who in a six-year career of some 125 jumps demonstrated the 'GQ', and also jumped for the film industry.

A more prolific jumper was Ivor Price, who parachuted for three seasons with the Cobham Air Circus — the most famous of the travelling aerial shows of the '30s. In 1934, purely for publicity. Price created a record for jumping frequency by making eight descents in fifteen minutes fifty seconds, leaping from a Tiger Moth at 800 feet and opening at 400. Far greater publicity attended his death. With more than 800 jumps behind him, he appeared with the Circus at Woodford on 3 May 1935, a few weeks after his marriage. He was a tidy-minded man, and when he was packing his 'chute he would tie a handkerchief round the gathered rigging lines close to the peripheral hem to keep the canopy neatly closed while he folded it. At Woodford, he omitted to untie the handkerchief. He jumped from an

Avro Cadet at 2,000 feet and pulled the ripcord at 1,000, which would have given him five seconds to realise his mistake and perhaps curse his forgetfulness as he hurtled to the ground beneath the streaming, sealed canopy. A stunned commentator, lost for words, played the National Anthem over the loudspeakers.

Ivor's partner on the show circuit that season was Naomi Heron-Maxwell, who in showbiz tradition carried on the act with a jump at Retford the following day. Naomi survived her parachuting career to become a record-breaking glider pilot. In 1939 she set out to walk to India. She had reached Yugoslavia when war broke out, and after being attached to the British Mission at Zagreb for some time, found her way back to England to become a ferry pilot with Air Transport Auxiliary. Naomi was what, in the 1930s, they would have called a 'game girl'.

Ivor Price's place with Cobham was taken by a Canadian called Marsden, who also fell to his death shortly afterwards. Of Cobham's show-jumpers, the most successful was a young Yorkshireman called Harry Ward, who became the leading British parachutist of the 1930s. As a parachute rigger in the RAF, Harry made his first descent by means of a 'pull-off' — standing on the outer wing of a Vimy biplane, yanking the ripcord to stream the 'chute into the airflow, and being snatched bodily into space. That was in 1926, at RAF Northolt, where Harry then joined a small team of jumpers who toured RAF Stations to demonstrate the new Irvin 'chute to sceptical aircrew. Leaving the Service in 1929, he drove a London bus for three years, learnt to fly, made a few exhibition jumps with the 'Russell Lobe' parachute, and in 1932 became a full-time pro jumper. For the next five years he jumped regularly for several of the air circuses, notably Cobham's. In the winter of 1934 he toured India with 'Captain Dalton's Air Display'.

It was not easy money. During the English seasons with the travelling circuses it was usually two performances a day, almost every day, on "no jump, no pay" terms — which meant that if the jumper was to earn his keep, he could not afford to take much notice of wind speeds and cloud base. If the aeroplane could fly, he could jump. In fact there was little profit for anyone in the air circus trade. In the face of rising costs, Cobham gave up the game after three seasons. In 1937 when Harry Ward was touring with the 'Aircraft Demonstration Company' of Henry Barker and James King, the company's total income from thirty-two shows in England averaged £89 per day, with £119 from each of eight shows in Northern Ireland, after which the company was bankrupt and Harry was out of cigarettes. He was lucky to be alive at all, for on one of the last jumps of that tour, at Greystones in County Wicklow, a strong wind blew him into the sea. Landing in deep water 100 yards from shore, he became entangled in his 'chute and almost drowned. As he struggled to keep his head above water while rescuers formed a human chain from the beach, he would have taken little comfort from the knowledge that 'a priest and doctor were in attendance' as the following day's *Irish Press* reassuringly reported.

The stunts that Harry did for the film companies of Pinewood and Denham in 1936 helped his dwindling finances, but show-jumping remained his principal source of income, and in order to draw bigger crowds, Harry tried two things. Firstly, in the good old show-jumping tradition of putting a prettier face than his own at risk, he trained two girls in the hope that they would brighten his displays. Josephine Anne Stainton Nadin smiled engagingly for the cameras before she made her first descent at Doncaster, but the grin disappeared when it actually came to jumping, and she soon decided that parachuting was no career for her. 'Speedy' Pepper, who used to ride the 'Wall of Death' with a lion in the side-car of her motorbike was next. She made one jump. 'Too bloody dangerous,' she said, and went back to her lion. So Harry gave up on girl jumpers, and turned instead to wings. He had heard of Clem Sohn.

Prior to 1936, Clem Sohn had been just one of many American show-jumpers who carried only local fame with them from aviation meeting to aviation meeting, but in that year he broke from the pack and hit the headlines when he began jumping with 'bat-wings'. Made of treated canvas and stiffened with metal rods, these flexible wings were fastened to his body and arms, with a separate canvas vane between his legs. Thus equipped he claimed that he could 'glide' for considerable distances before opening his parachute, and the publicity that both preceded and followed the descents that he made before crowds of up to 100,000 at Dayton Beach in Florida gave the impression that the day of the birdman had truly arrived. In 1936 he came to Europe, where the same extravagant claims greeted his shows in England. When he jumped at Hamworth, although he dropped from only 3,000 feet, journalists solemnly declared that he had "swooped like a bird for a mile" before opening his parachute. Clem Sohn, like the wise professional that he was, did not refute the claims made on his behalf by those with a capacity for imagination, but the known fact is that wings such as his, although theoretically capable of providing limited lateral movement during free fall and of slightly retarding vertical speed, would have been almost impossible to control effectively, and any movement across the sky would have been largely accidental.

After his appearances in England, Clem Sohn travelled to France, preceded by growing excitement and intense publicity. On 25 April 1937, at Villacoubly, at 10,000 feet and almost directly above an expectant crowd of 50,000, he made his customary head-first dive, and spread his wings. From the ground there was no visual evidence that he was going anywhere other than straight down. At less than 1,000 feet above the ground he operated his parachute. Like a fluttering white banner the canopy streamed above him, but failed to open. He reacted instantly, and pulled his reserve. It flashed upwards, to snake round the main in a fatal embrace. Some said that it was a classic 'Roman Candle', and had nothing to do with the bat-wings. Others reported that the main canopy had fouled the left wing. Whatever the cause, Clem Sohn was very dead.

He had several imitators in America, all seeking to improve their show-jumping image and audience. Amongst them, Manos Morgan and Tommy Boyd claimed that they had been able to glide for long distances with their respective designs of flexible wing. There was nobody up there with them to say that they couldn't.

In England in 1936 it was Harry Ward who climbed onto this latest show-jumping band-wagon. With a caravan manufacturer of Gargrave in Yorkshire, called Cecil Rice, he designed a set of wings which were duly constructed with the help of the village seamstress and bootmaker. With a nine-foot span, they were made of linen with wooden stiffeners, and a separate vane between the legs. Unlike Clem Sohn's wings, Harry Ward's were detachable. He could let them go and grab for that ripcord if he ran into trouble. The only 'test' to which they were subjected was when the fully equipped birdman had himself suspended from a railway crane at Gargrave station, to the dismay of passing passengers.

Harry Ward made no extravagant claims for his device. He let the press and the public do that for him, and viewed the whole experience with a jovial sense of humour:

'First time I was shovelled out with the kit on — locked to me with a stainless steel band and wing-nuts — I spread my wings and came down on my back like a bomb. I went into a flat spin over a housing estate, opened my parachute just in time. When I got down I just lay on the field. The crowd were tickled to death — they thought I'd copped it!'[5.]

He subsequently devised a unique means of leaving the aircraft that would reduce the risk of fouling his equipment on exit: 'They shovelled me out of the 'plane at 11,000 feet on a plank — like a corpse going over the side.'[6.]

Eventually, during the nine jumps that Harry made with his wings, he gained a measure of control over them, and was able to stabilize, turn, and achieve some degree of lateral movement. The Air Ministry was obviously puzzled yet impressed by this aerial novelty, for they insisted that Harry register his wings as a light aircraft.

On the death of Clem Sohn, Harry offered to complete the American's show programme, but the French had seen enough of birdmen for the time being, and said no thank you, and shortly afterwards, Harry hung his own wings up. Ask anyone who might just remember the aviation scene of the 1930s if they can recall any of the great birdmen of the time, and the chances are that they will name Clem Sohn, but not Harry Ward. The difference between them was that Clem Sohn killed himself, and Harry Ward didn't. That's show-jumping!

Another name that might be remembered from amongst the sky people of the 1930s is that of John Tranum — partly because he deserves to be remembered as one of the great international show-jumpers, yet partly again because of the manner of his death.

Danish by birth, Tranum had learnt the trade of stunt pilot, wing-walker and parachutist during the wilder barnstorming days of California. For the Hollywood cameras he had crashed 'planes into buildings, abandoned others in mid-air after setting fire to them, parachuted from the 154-foot Pasadena bridge and from the seat of a motorbike after driving it over a cliff. He barnstormed through South America, and in 1930 came to Europe to demonstrate the 'Russell Lobe' at air displays and before military audiences. The promotion of a parachute that is being advertised as a life-saver obviously requires the performer to demonstrate how safe and reliable it is. This wasn't John Tranum's style. He had been brought up in the hard school of American barnstorming where the whole object was to show how *dangerous* this jumping business was. Nor did routine exhibitions pull the crowds. He appears, during a series of shows with the 'Lobe' at Reading, to have run out of patience, for after a display that attracted only a sparse audience and a passing mention in the local press, he purposely landed in the middle of the Thames for his next exhibition. 'Airman Falls in River! Almost a Tragedy!' screamed the headlines, and the public rolled up in their thousands for his next performance. He was reprimanded by the Air Ministry, subsequently gave up his association with the Russell Company, and joined Barnard's Air Circus to do some real stunting.

After touring South Africa, he returned to England to work as test-jumper and exhibition parachutist for Leslie Irvin, who encouraged John Tranum to take a crack at the world record for a free drop — wearing an Irvin 'chute, of course.

Looking back at the early '30s for a moment, we see that by then most show-jumpers had at last taken to the manually operated 'chute. It had by that time become a proven life-saver as well as an exciting display tool, and the fears and mysteries of free fall had been lessened by the example of military test-jumpers and by a handful of showmen who had progressively extended the duration of free drop. Most of the show-jumpers still preferred to jump from heights at which the crowds could see their tumbling bodies leave the aircraft and

The Royal Air Force Parachute Display Team was one of the first of the military teams that took over the show grounds from the professional jumpers in the early 1960s. Launching themselves from a Beverley at 9,000 feet at the 1961 Farnborough Air Show are from left to right: Johnny Thirtle, Jake McLoughlin, Doug Peacock, Peter Hearn, 'Snowy' Robertson, and Tommy Maloney. (page 58)

come hurtling earthwards for a few breath-holding seconds before they set the life-saving silk free; but there were those who went for the longer drops, usually as a one-off jump to gain prestige rather than as a regular feature of their displays. Amongst them was a young jumper called Joe Crane, who as we shall see would become a key figure in the development of sport parachuting, and who, in 1925, had established a world record for a free drop when he fell 2,250 feet before pulling the ripcord. A short while later he extended it to 3,500. It is likely that other professionals like Kohlstedt or Wes May or Harry Eibe or Art Starnes had fallen just as far or even further, but if so, they didn't claim any records.

A close friend of Joe Crane — Spud Manning — was the first to go for the really long one that would pave the way for the high altitude jumpers of the 1930s. On 1 March 1931 he jumped from 16,665 feet above Los Angeles and opened his 'chute 15,265 feet and some seventy-five seconds later — as measured by barograph. Not only did Spud Manning fall a long way: he also fell in a stable position. Those who believe that free fall stability and basic 'skydiving' techniques were a product of the late 1950s might look up the February 1934 copy of *Popular Mechanics*, in which Floyd Smith describes the aerial manoeuvres that Spud Manning had mastered in his long free falls. It is all there — basic stability; lateral turns; back loops; a vertical head-down dive for increased speed; and even what the modern skydiver calls 'tracking'. 'While coming out of the head-first dive', wrote Floyd Smith, 'the high velocity causes a considerable horizontal movement, the body acting as a gliding plane against the air. Manning often thus executed a spiral glide coming out of his high-speed, head-first position.'[7]

Spud Manning didn't need 'bat-wings' to achieve body flight. Nor did he need a stopwatch, nor a counting system like Kohlstedt. 'He would spot landmarks on the horizon and calculate his altitude by angular observation,' wrote Floyd Smith. As a professional wishing to keep his trade secrets to himself,

Above: The RAF 'Falcons' exit their Hercules aircraft en masse at 12,000 feet. (Photo: RAF Falcons).

Opposite: 'Falcons' above Sydney Harbour in 1988.
(Photo: RAF Falcons).

this modest pioneer of body flight did not advertise his skill. When Floyd Smith wrote of it, Spud Manning was dead, killed when his 'plane crashed into Lake Michigan in 1933.

Other professionals may have gained some basic mastery over free fall, but if so, they also kept quiet about it. Richard Kohnke, the 'father of German sport parachuting' and another high-altitude jumper, also had some body control. But most of them were content to let gravity drag them earthwards as it wished, trying only to keep their eyes on the ground or on a stopwatch. That was the way John Tranum fell when on 23 May 1933 he leapt through a gap in the clouds above Netheravon from a Hawker Hart, at 21,000 feet:

> 'I carried my stopwatch strapped to the palm of my left hand and started it as I stepped off. Down I went, somersaulting continuously for the first mile. As the somersaults got fewer, I found myself in the attitude of a diver, at an angle of about forty-five degrees. It is true that I carried a stopwatch, but I used my eyes too. These gave me some bother, for, although my goggles fitted well, my eyes would water. My stopwatch told me that I had fallen 17,250 feet, and the ground looked very near, so I pulled the ripcord.'[8.]

Tranum had indeed fallen 17,250 feet, which beat Spud Manning's record by 2,250 feet. Two years later, the Russian Ievdokimov fell 26,000 feet before opening his 'chute, and John Tranum was persuaded to regain the world record. It appears that he was not over-keen to do so. After his first high-altitude drop he had written, 'I have learnt all I want to know about free drops, and am satisfied.'[9.] He was coming towards the end of a great parachuting career. He had become a heavy drinker, and a nervous jumper. On 7 March 1935 he climbed into the cockpit of a Danish military machine at Kastrup airport, intending to regain that record with a free fall from 30,000 feet. The 'plane, piloted by Captain Laerum, circled out high above Copenhagen, climbing slowly into the cold, thin air. At 27,000 feet, the parachutist began to make frantic signals to the pilot. Something was desperately wrong. Captain Laerum put the nose down, diving fast for Kastrup. When they lifted John Tranum from the cockpit, he was dead — of heart failure, resulting from 'nervous strain', concluded the official enquiry. The real cause of his death was perhaps the pride of a great parachutist who wouldn't admit that he'd had enough.

In March 1938, the Frenchman James Nieland (sometimes called James Williams) dropped from a Mureaux monoplane at 27,560 feet, fell for over two minutes, and opened his 'chute a mere 1,064 feet above the ground, to break Ievdokimov's record by a small margin. Nieland died that August when jumping from a mere 3,000 feet.

The following year, the parachute, and many of the show-jumpers, went to war.

Only slowly did the flying shows come back to life after World War Two — more slowly in Europe than in America. World War Two had done nothing to lessen the public's association of the parachute with matters deadly, daring and death-defying. Even though it had proved itself so effectively as a life-saver, the image of desperate fliers baling out of disintegrating bombers and flaming fighters encouraged a sub-conscious association with disaster. So the crowds were ready to savour the death-defiance of the show-jumper, and to admire his seeming nonchalance, and to get his autograph on their programmes, and touch his white overalls as though that would bring them a little of the luck that he surely lived by. But where was he? And if there was one, who was he?

Few of the pre-war jumpers came back. Many had left the business as it declined during the late '30s, and others had given their lives in the fighting. If there was a jumper at those early post-war shows, the chances are that he was an ex-airborne man, who had learnt to jump amongst the ranks of the paratroopers of World War Two, and in whom the jump-fired adrenalin still flowed. This young ex-paratrooper would have learnt his parachuting on the end of a static-line, and now he would have acquired an aviator's back pack or a seat-pack or a 'training main', and would be trying free drop and manual operation for the first time, and there wouldn't be much that he knew about it. In America, too many of them died. It was as though the War had swept away a whole heritage of show-jumping: as though it had hidden from view a generation's experience of free falling and exhibition skills. Our young show-jumper was starting again, with nobody to teach him, and only one way to learn: by trial and error.

The experience of four jumpers who performed in Britain as 'The Apex Group' during the late 1940s and early '50s illustrates this virtual return to parachute pioneering. Ollie Owen, Johnny Rallings, John Fricker and Chuck Thompson were ex-RAF Parachute Jumping Instructors who were keen to continue parachuting after they left the Service, and to explore the new thrills of free fall. They decided to finance that ambition through displays. It is significant that this earliest group of post-war and part-time show-jumpers were motivated by parachuting itself rather than the profit that might derive from it.

They bought back-packs with plain twenty-eight-foot canopies for £86 each, and with no reserve 'chutes, no stopwatches, no altimeters, and wearing their round PJI helmets of canvas-covered rubber, they began to free fall — Ollie in 1948, the others early in 1949. They rarely jumped together, but appeared individually at air shows throughout Southern England, and took an additional 'fiddle' whenever they could afford it. In RAF PJI parlance, a 'fiddle' was a jump of which the sole purpose was pleasure. In verb form, 'fiddling' meant some pretty nifty steering of a plain canopy. In both senses, The Apex Group were prime 'fiddlers'. To maintain their group identity, they circulated amongst themselves detailed reports of every jump they made, to build up from practical trial an unrivalled dossier of parachuting experience. Thus Johnny Rallings in his Jump Report No. 5, relating a descent with Ollie Owen from a De Havilland Rapide at Southend airport in 1949, the aim of which was to 'impress local blokes of the importance of our parachuting — and to have a good long fiddle . . .'

> 'I went No. 1 with leg vane, OO No. 2 with streamer. On leaving the aircraft I opened my legs and rapidly assumed a head-down position. After a few seconds a violent spin set in which I was unable to control by any arm or leg manipulation. The rate of this spin was timed and estimated by a reliable observer at just over 100 rpm. After about fifteen seconds I decided to bunch to break up the spin. Before I did so, however, one side of the vane tore away from the leg attachments. I somersaulted once or twice and assumed a very head-down position without spinning for the remainder of the delay. I opened at about 2,000 feet and had three twists. My left cheek was smacked by the liftwebs, during opening, sufficient to bruise it and break the skin. The opening shock was not very violent. The rest of the descent was normal, except that the pilot had ignored our request for dropping point, and, as a result, I had to spend my time fiddling back onto the airfield. Stand up landing.'[10]

By his Jump Report No. 15, Johnny Rallings could conclude:

> 'In the last two or three fiddles I have concentrated on body position during delay. For what it is worth, gents, in case you didn't know, here is what I have to say:
> If the parachutist wants a steady head-down position he should:
> (a) Open his legs wide immediately after exit.
> (b) Arch his back to the full and throw back his head.
> (c) Keep his arms still and crossed over the breast, right hand on ripcord ring.[11]

The 'leg vane' — a piece of fabric attached between the legs — was subjected to much experiment by the Group in its search for stabilized fall. After one such trial, which resulted in the expected and speedy head-down dive, the after-effects worried Ollie Owen a little. He reported indistinct vision, headache, bodily stiffness,

and general fatigue, but admitted that ' . . . these conditions should not be taken as potentially representative as I did jump on an empty stomach and had some beer immediately afterwards.'[12]

In November 1949, Ollie circulated a detailed and far-sighted proposal to establish a civilian parachute training centre. The others were less enthusiastic, and the idea came to nothing. In retrospect, what a loss to British parachuting! Such a centre, run by these four adventurers with their teaching ability, their inquiring minds, and their wealth of carefully documented experience could have put Britain in the forefront of the era of sport parachuting that was about to dawn. By 1952, this unique band of sky people had broken up and gone their separate ways, leaving their accumulated knowledge in that bulky file of 'jump reports'.

A contemporary of The Apex Group on the British air show circuit was ex-paratrooper 'Dumbo' Willans. Like the Group, Dumbo was also a product of the static-line who had to feel his own way into free fall. He combined exhibition jumping with test-work for the parachute industry, in which capacity he made the first live tests of the Irvin barometric automatic-opening-device that was to be incorporated in Martin-Baker ejection systems. For these trials, knowing nothing of stabilized free fall, he tumbled and spun earthwards from 15,000 feet and then from 25,000 feet. Later, he would make live trials of the Folland ejection seat, but in the late 1940s and early '50s — as with The Apex Group — it was love of parachuting rather than profit that led Dumbo round the show circuit, piloted in a Tiger Moth called 'Greensleeves' by Hawker's test pilot 'Doc' Morrell:

> 'Squatting on the trailing edge of the wing, waiting to jump, became a familiar occupation. Out there in the wind — one eye on the altimeter and the other on the ground — and a general picture of silver wings and flying wires and Doc grinning behind his goggles with a tattered scarf streaming behind him — that was the life! Hand signal left . . . left a bit more . . . hard left . . . steady. Upwind fence below . . . look back along the line of drift — plenty of room below now. "OK Doc, — thanks for the buggy ride!" Over the edge into fresh air with the orange fuselage of the Tiger leaping into the blue above and Doc's goggled face peering down over the cockpit rim.
>
> 'There was something about those air displays. The white marquees, the wind sock blowing in the wrong direction and much too fast, the small boy who put his foot through the wing; the eternal ham salad and the blaring public address system. Walking back across the fields with the warm, grass-smelling bundle of nylon fluttering up against my face, looking up at the next act and

tripping on a dangling rigging line; Doc taxiing across in the Tiger to give me a lift back . . .

'Perhaps the best part of all was flying back in the evenings with the work done and the motor purring happily under its polished cowling. That was the time to relax and let old Greensleeves head into a misty horizon, towards home, while the scent of a bonfire drifted up through hundreds of feet of still air from the toy landscape below.'[13.]

Dumbo Willans was subsequently to gain recognition as 'the father of British sport parachuting', but of that we shall hear more later.

In France, it was another ex-paratrooper who was to dominate post-war show-jumping, and to become the last of the great international stars. Leo Valentin made his first parachute descent in 1938 at the age of nineteen, as a trainee at the French military centre at Bakari, in Algeria, and subsequently joined and jumped into action with the French Special Air Service during World War Two. His early training at Bakari had involved free drops, and after the War and whilst still serving with 'Les Paras', he returned to free falling. But it was free falling of a completely uncontrolled nature:

'Like a sack being hurled out of a window, like a bomb being released at night, but not like a human being. In any case, not as a human being ought to jump. Any old how! With no style! Flung about in all directions, head over heels, making involuntary loops, rolled about like a barrel, on your back, on your belly, on your sides, in a spin . . . We used to call that "making a mayonnaise" . . .'[14.]

After some 150 jumps, deciding that there was no future in 'making a mayonnaise', Valentin set out to find the key to stabilized and controlled free fall. After trial and error he found that key in the simple theory of convexity-and-symmetry:

'Let me see: if I jump with my body extended, i.e. with hollow back, extended neck, chest thrust out, arms and legs splayed and slightly backwards, I present to the air a symmetrical surface, so to speak, of a more or less convex form. I already look more like a bird than a common sack of sand.'[15.]

We know now that his discovery was not new: that Spud Manning and other jumpers of the 1920s and '30s had been there before him, but to Leo Valentin and other parachutists of the time if was new. It was revolutionary! And when, after more trial and error, he flew stable for the first time, he experienced in full the wonder known to those of us who had to fight for our stability, instead of being led to it by gentle and modern progression:

'I dropped once more from 9,000 feet. Immediately on leaving the aircraft I took up the position. I was a little tense and ill at ease like a man who is learning to drive a car. However, suddenly I had a sensation of great well-being. Had it not been for the wind I might have been motionless in the sky, reclining face downwards on the cushions of air through which I was plunging almost without stirring . . . it seemed impossible that it could be so easy, so agreeable, so intoxicating in its smoothness. This revelation — for this is what it was — left me at one and the same time numb and yet deeply moved in spirit". . . I fell stable. I was gliding. Now there was no reason for me to envy the buzzard.'[16.]

To stability he soon added the full range of basic free fall manoeuvres, and then he told the rest of the parachuting world of his discovery. This disclosure was Leo Valentin's greatest contribution to parachuting, for everyone else had also forgotten the lessons of the free falling pioneers, and Spud Manning's secrets lay hidden in those old copies of *Popular Mechanics*. The Frenchman passed on his knowledge to other French jumpers, then spelt it out in his 1955 biography, called *Bird Man*, for Leo Valentin was not content with the skills and sensations of unaided flight. He wanted to fly with wings, like a bird. He still envied that buzzard, after all.

He foresaw a time when, with wings attached to his body, man would be able to leap from an aircraft and glide to earth unaided by a parachute, and he left the Army to devote himself entirely to that dream. He experimented at first with a series of non-rigid wings, came close to disaster with them on several occasions, and concluded that they could do nothing more than slow the rate of fall. He studied more closely the aerodynamics of gliding flight, and designed rigid wings with a nine-foot span, hinged to a steel corset round his chest, with a locking device to prevent the air pressure folding them behind his falling body and breaking his arms. The first time he jumped with them, they flipped him onto his back and slammed together in front of him as he spun earthwards from 4,000 feet. He managed to free an arm and yank the ripcord of his 'chute with only four seconds separating him from the ground. He went back to the drawing board and the wind tunnel.

It was to fund these experiments in winged flight that Leo Valentin became one of the most prolific show-jumpers in France — with and without his wings. He specialised in delayed drops from 9,000 feet, marking his fall with a trail of talculm powder. He paired up for

Opposite: The free falling cameraman has brought parachuting to a wider audience through still and cine film. One of the first in the sky was American professional jumper Bob Sinclair. Jim Hall, founder of 'Para Ventures' is on the left, preparing a USAF pupil for a 'buddy jump' at Elsinore in 1961.

a while with another great French parachutist, Pierre Lard, and with several women jumpers. He didn't enjoy his partnership with Monique Laroche, who at that time was not up to his own exacting standards. With Odette Goegel and Baby Monetti he made linked jumps, holding to their harnesses in a free-falling threesome, but that partnership also ended when Baby Monetti fell to her death at Maubege.

At Gissy Les Nobles, outside Paris, on 13 May 1954, Valentin tried new wings, made of balsa wood, weighing twenty-eight pounds, and with a new locking device to hold them open, whatever his position in relation to the airflow. They worked. From 9,000 feet he was able to direct his fall in a controlled spiral. He continued his experiments, and to finance them he also continued his show-jumping — although with growing reluctance and some forboding:

> 'All these experiments were very costly. The aviation meetings represented my only possible source of income until I had perfected my Bird Man number . . . I could only subsist until then by entering full tilt into the 'circus' . . . For a time I found I was the prisoner of my sudden reputation as a Bird Man and could not withdraw from the demands of the public . . .'[17.]

It was the demands of the public and his need for cash that brought Leo Valentin to the annual air pageant at Speke aerodrome, Liverpool, on 21 May 1956. In the morning he made a twenty-second free drop, without his wings. Then, in the afternoon, the Bird Man climbed into a Dakota with his latest set of wooden wings. For once he was without his usual friends and helpers. He had difficulty making himself understood, and the organizers had to call for an interpreter from the crowd. Valentin seemed unhappy, unprepared. On the long flight to altitude, strapped in his wings, he was a solitary and silent figure. At 9,000 feet, with apparent reluctance he readied himself for the jump. With his wings folded inwards and held out in front of him, he approached the open cargo-door. He seemed to hesistate, then launched himself into space. There was a crash of splintering wood. His left wing had smashed against the rear edge of the door. Falling, strapped to the rotating remnants of his wings, he endeavoured to release his main parachute. The canopy flared free, then tangled in the whirling wreckage of wood. He managed to pull the chest-mounted reserve. Like a shroud, it wrapped itself round his face as he spun to his death.

Leo Valentin died because he was too proud to shake his head and say, 'Sorry folks — not today — it doesn't feel right.'

Others tried on wings during the 1950s, but with little thought of scientific development. Their main aim was to add spice to their displays. Lyle Cameron, Red Grant and Don Molitar were amongst the American pro jumpers who used flexible wings and leg vanes, but to no great effect except on their publicity. Bohelm of Switzerland wore ten-foot wings of canvas with rigid ribbing, and died in them in Spain. The Italians Rinaldi and Canarrozzo also jumped on occasions with flexible wings.

They were wild jumpers, those two. Scorning helmets, goggles, stopwatches, altimeters and reserve parachutes, they fell usually in a fast, head-down dive with legs apart and hands across the chest, that became known to a generation of skydivers as the 'Canarrozzo Position'. They would fall thus until the ground loomed large enough, then they would pull, usually below 500 feet. 'Too close to the daisies', Leo Valentin would say with a shake of his head, for he appeared often at shows with the Italians, and would watch their flirtation with death with sad foreboding. It has been said that the Italian pair vied with each other to see who could delay his opening the longest. If that were so, Salvator Canarrozzo eventually won, for at Venice in April 1953 he didn't open at all. His friend Rinaldi hung up his jump-boots shortly afterwards. There wasn't so much fun in it with Salvator gone . . .

With the death of Leo Valentin in 1956, the era of the full-time professional show-jumper virtually came to an end. Show-jumping would continue, and so would professional parachuting, but the two would no longer be synonymous.

At the prestigious Farnborough Air Show in 1961, a team of six parachute jumping instructors of the Royal Air Force, gripping each other's parachute harnesses to form a closely linked line-abreast formation, stepped from the freight-bay of a Beverley transport aircraft into 9,000 feet of air. Trailing smoke from flares attached to their ankles, they fell as one body for twenty seconds, then broke away to dive into their own air-space, thus creating a dramatic inverted bomb-burst effect. Opening steerable canopies (a 'TU' blank gore cut into a standard twenty-eight foot canopy), they tacked over the upturned faces in Farnborough's public enclosure to land in a close group about the orange cross laid on the airfield. I remember it well. I was one of them.

During that same year a team of French Army instructors from Pau were making public appearances throughout France, and in America, the US Army's 'Golden Knights' were establishing themselves as the foremost parachute display team in the country.

Those early military teams were soon joined by others. In America, the US Navy put its 'Chuting Stars' into the air, and the 'Golden Knights' were expanded into three teams — one for competition, two for display. In England, Army teams followed the RAF into the sky, with the 'Red Devils' appropriately coming to the fore, and the Navy subsequently joining the act with its Royal Marine teams. Some justification for this military involvement lay in the adoption of free fall parachuting as a means of delivering special forces to their objectives, but primarily the military teams — either officially funded for their recruiting and publicity value or operating as a 'sporting activity' — rode into show jumping on the crest of the wave that accompanied the rapid development and popularization of sport parachuting during the 1960s.

The sportsmen themselves — this new generation of sky people who came to parachuting for the sheer joy and exhilaration of it — also began to appear on showgrounds throughout the jumping world, either individually or in small groups. They came to the shows not primarily to make a living, but to make a little cash to pay for the cost of their sport, a spirit pioneered by The Apex Group in the late 1940s. The willingness of these enthusiastic 'amateurs' to jump for sometimes no more than their expenses brought show-jumping within the budgets of the smaller promoter, and the great advances in equipment and skill that accompanied the growth of sport parachuting brought the jumpers themselves into the smaller drop-zones. Parachute display was no longer the preserve of the major air show. Just as in the late nineteenth century the solo hot-air balloon and the 'limp' parachute had brought show-jumping to wider audiences, so the skilful young jumpers and the steerable parachute of the 1960s brought it to the County fair and the City park and the sport stadium and the village fete.

Amongst this proliferation of military teams and enthusiastic skydivers, what room was there for the professional jumper? On the showgrounds, precious little. A few kept going, but to stay in the parachuting business, most professionals had to turn entirely or partly to other forms of parachuting-for-pay. A demand for instructors had its beginnings in the state-aided parachute schools of France, then spread to the commercial centres of the USA and other European countries. As the numbers of sport parachutists grew ever larger, providing them with parachutes and accessories became a minor industry for current or ex-jumpers. A welcome revival of professionalism came in the mid-1960s with the introduction in the USA of cash prizes, instead of two-foot high statuettes, for accuracy competitions. The first National Professional Parachuting Championship was sponsored by the Hotel Thunderbird in Las Vegas in 1965, with a first prize of $2,000 collected by Bob Holler.

The various forms that professional parachuting might take were uniquely brought together in the 1960s by a Californian company, 'Para Ventures', later to become 'Parachuting Associates Incorporated', formed in 1959 by Dave Burt and Jim Hall. After serving as a paratrooper, Dave Burt had joined the US Forest Service as a 'smoke-jumper', that hard breed of men who parachute into remote mountain country to fight

forest fires. During four years and nineteen actual fire-jumps, Dave said that the only injuries he received were blisters on his hands from digging fire-breaks. He was lucky. Three of his fellow jumpers broke their backs on those jumps, and twelve of them were incinerated in the fire that swept Mann Gulch in Montana in 1949. Another smoke-jumper at the time was Jim Hall, a graduate mining engineer, and he and Dave Burt decided to team up as full-time professional parachutists.

They pioneered 'parachute exploration' in the remote mining regions of Alaska and Mexico, and also in Mexico they made advertising jumps onto the beaches and into the fairgrounds with Corona beer and Coca Cola banners. In 1959 they formed 'Para Ventures', and equipped it with a formidable gathering of Californian parachuting talent — including Verne Williams, big Bud Kiesow, and former paratrooper, smoke-jumper, and Alaskan barnstormer Bob Sinclair. Based in Los Angeles and doing most of their jumping out at Elsinore, they at first offered a full range of parachuting services: exhibitions, instruction in sport jumping, parachute rigging and sales, exploration and supply dropping, trials of equipment and techniques, and film work. As they expanded, they set up an office in Hollywood Boulevard, and concentrated on the trials and the filming.

Under contract to the US Air Force, the team made a valuable contribution to aviation safety in the 1960s, with their realistic testing of aircrew survival equipment; production of an award-winning aircrew training film called *Passport to Safety*; and development of the 'Buddy System' of accelerated free fall training for aircrew and astronauts. In 1963 the 'Buddy System' won for Jim Hall the highest award in the field of parachuting safety — The Leo Stevens Parachute Medal. He would later go on to live-test the zero-zero ejection seat.

Through its film work, Para Ventures led show-jumping into its major expansion onto the screen. Aerial stuntmen had always featured in the 'movies', but the growth of the television industry greatly increased the potential market, and fortuitously coincided with the development of air-to-air photography during free fall and parachute flight. One of its earliest exponents was Bob Sinclair who, for Para Ventures, filmed with his fifteen-pound helmet-mounted camera the aerial rescues, mid-air pursuits, and free-falling fist-fights between the goodies and the baddies of the early *Ripcord* television series. Following the success of *Ripcord* there was a spate of imaginative TV commercials, sequences for other television and large-screen productions, and a film for NBC's *Tonight Show*, featuring its presenter Johnny Carson making his first jump — from 12,000 feet under Jim Hall's 'Buddy System'. That film took skydiving to its largest ever audience.

Opposite inset: Notable amongst this group of modern aerial cameramen are: extreme right, Gus Wing; third from right, Mike McGowan; fourth from right, Leo Dickinson; fifth from right, Norman Kent; third from left, Skip Kniley; kneeling on right, Simon Ward. (Photo: Mandy Dickinson)

Opposite: Leo Dickinson captures the freedom of the skies in his 'Stand up Wally Gubbins' portrait. (Photo Leo Dickinson)

Above: Falcon's-eye view of the San Diego Stadium, in which they are about to land. (Photo: RAF Falcons)

Other and perhaps better cameramen were to follow, but Para Ventures and Bob Sinclair showed the way into this new form of show-jumping.

A group led by Lyle Cameron took over the *Ripcord* filming, with Lyle himself and Doyle Fields as cameramen. Doyle Fields was also the jumper who, for ABC Television's documentary *The Bold Men*, captured on film one of the most daring show-jumps of all time. On 1 January 1965, skydiver Bob Allen dropped from an aircraft at 14,600 feet over Arvin, California, holding a bulky package at arms' length in front of him. He was followed one exact second later by another figure. This second jumper wore all the accoutrements of a skydiver — except for a parachute. His name was Rod Pack. His parachute — a chest type reserve — was that bulky package in the hands of Bob Allen. Rod Pack had less than ninety seconds in which to catch the falling figure beneath him, take the 'chute as they both fell through the sky at 120 mph, clip it to the harness that he wore, and pull the ripcord. Adjusting his position and rate of fall, he flew down to Bob Allen and that life-saving package — not too fast, for it he overshot and dropped beneath the other man, that *would* have been a problem. The two figures closed. Above them hovered cameramen Doyle Fields and Bob Buquor, whose role was not only to film the event, but also to dive in and clip Rod Pack to their own harness if the mid-air pass failed. But it didn't. With time and height to spare, this strange transaction was completed, and Rod Pack pulled his ripcord and parachuted down to a ploughed field, fame, and the wrath of the Federal Aviation Administration. Their regulations quite clearly stated that a pre-meditated parachute jump should be made with two 'chutes, and here was a guy jumping without even *one*! They fined him, but didn't stop Rod Pack from parachuting. A motorcycle crash and a leg broken in three places did that some sixty-four jumps later.

Rod Pack was a professional stuntman, and made his reasons for the 'chute-less jump quite clear. They were those of show-jumpers since André Garnerin: 'Where there's a first', he said, 'there's always money involved. It was to further my career as a stuntman and also to make a few coins on it.'[18.]

Whilst operating the mid-air camera or performing in front of it were ways for the pro jumper to 'make a few coins', the cameramen had to be good, for there was room for only a few at the top. Up there in the 1960s were Americans Bob Buquor and Carl Boenish. They were foremost amongst those who took air-to-air photography from a mere recording medium to an art form. Bob Boquor set the standards for still-photography in particular, until he drowned off Malibu Beach, dragged under by the weight of his cameras when he landed in the sea during the filming of *Don't Make Waves*. Carl Boenish, with Jay Gifford, filmed the parachuting action for Burt Lancaster's *Gypsy*

Moths, the first major film to feature show-jumping as a central theme. Cleverly, Boenish heightened the dramatic impact of that film's aerial sequences by shooting at twenty-four frames per second, instead of the slower speeds normally used for free-fall action. A great influence on young skydivers of the early 1970s was his second parachuting production, *Masters of the Sky*, a stunning compilation of free fall and canopy shots, with the action spliced to driving rock-music. Sadly, Carl Boenish was also to die, parachuting from the great mountain face of Trollveggen, in Norway.

Skydiving film today reaches an ever larger audience through the medium of video. Artistic standards have reached new levels in the work of cameramen such as Norman Kent and Leo Dickinson, and video serves too as a valuable parachute-training aid.

While the camera still attracts some of the more extreme forms of exhibition, live display out on the showgrounds has, with the advent of the military teams and the sport jumpers, been presented in a new light. The object is no longer to portray parachuting as a particularly foolhardy means of risking one's neck. Just the opposite. The modern show-jumper seeks to emphasise the safety of leaping from aeroplanes, not the danger. This is not only because he is required to perform to prescribed standards of safety, but because this attitude is inherent in the training and the philosophy of today's military and sport parachutist. Yet his displays have lost nothing in dramatic impact through this reversal in role. The 'novelty' that was constantly being sought by the old-time stuntman, and the real or apparent perils that he portrayed, have been replaced by the sheer skill that can be demonstrated by the modern jumper with a modern parachute. When Loy Brydon and Dick Fortenberry first performed their 'Max-track' in the 1960s as part of the 'Golden Knights' display — trailing smoke from 12,000 feet as they left the aircraft together then diving in opposite directions across the sky to open their parachutes nearly two miles apart — who needed bat-wings? The smoke patterns woven during free fall by teams of skydivers; the 'canopy stacking' with ram-air parachutes; the precision landings on minute drop zones — these are skills and spectacles that need no exaggeration.

So the modern generation of show-jumpers is at last endeavouring to loosen that 'dicing-with-death' label tied to the parachute by exhibition parachutists since André Garnerin first thrilled the crowds. Exciting skills rather than death-defiance is what today's skydiver offers. 'Look!' he is saying, as he flares out his ram-air canopy for a feather-light stand-up landing a few yards from the crowd line, 'This is great and exciting fun — but by no means as dangerous as it might appear.'

But those crowds — they're not really convinced, are they? Those old-timers tied that label *really* tight.

CHAPTER THREE
The Caterpillars

On the afternoon of 20 October 1922, Lieutenant Harold R. Harris, chief of the Army Air Corps flight testing section at McCook Field in Ohio, took to the sky in a new high-wing Leoning monoplane, to carry out aileron trials. Also airborne was Lieutenant Muir Fairchild, flight testing a Thomas Morse biplane. What better way to test their fighting 'planes than in mock combat? In classic 'dog-fight' style they twisted and zoomed through the sky above Dayton. Chasing the biplane into a turn almost 3,000 feet above the confluence of the Mad and Miami rivers, the Leoning was suddenly shaken by violent lateral vibrations. The stick was torn from the pilot's clutch and began to thresh from side to side, battering his thighs. Fabric tore from the wings, and the wings themselves began to disintegrate. Harris undid his seat strap and pushed himself upright into a wind blast of some 200 mph that slammed him backwards and dragged him from the cockpit of the plunging aircraft. He wrote in his report:

> 'After clearing the 'plane, an attempt was made to operate the parachute ripcord, but I was unable to locate the ring for some considerable time on account of repeatedly grasping the leg strap fitting, thinking it was the release ring. Three separate attempts were made before the ring was finally located, and it is believed that during this time my body was spinning, head downward, and I distinctly remember looking at my feet three times, with the knowledge that they were pointing up towards the sky.
>
> 'Upon the operation of the ripcord the parachute opened almost immediately, but with a considerable jerk. From the time of opening to the time I landed was an extremely short period. Fortunately no trees or houses were encountered, but the landing was made on a fragile grape arbour, which easily gave way and nicely broke the fall to the brick pavement below.'

For the first time an American military pilot had saved his life with a parachute.

Lieutenant Harris was not the only one to take comfort from the event. The Army Air Service Type-A

Parachute that had saved him had been devised and developed by the Parachute Section of McCook, whose staff were now delighted to see their belief in the manually-operated 'chute so effectively demonstrated. Two of the staff — Milton St Clair and John Mumma — commemorated the occasion by mounting on the wall of the Section's parachute laboratory a piece of the Leoning's fabric, with photographs of Harold Harris standing beside the wreckage of his machine, and of his parachute draped from the grape arbour. This exhibition caught the attention of two air-minded visitors, Maurice Hutton, the aviation editor of the *Dayton Herald*, and his photographer, Verne Timmerman. In discussing with St Clair the likelihood of other fliers having to 'take to the silk', Timmerman suggested the formation of a roll of honour — even a club — for those who saved their lives with a parachute. Less than a month after Harris baled out, a second military flier became a candidate for that proposed roll of honour.

When Lieutenant Frank Tyndal's biplane shed its wings during a flight test above Seattle, the pilot in turn parted company with the little that was left of his machine, to land unharmed on Harbour Island under his silken life-saver. Mementos of that escape were added to the wall at McCook, and the idea of forming a club gathered momentum. A name was sought. Milton St Clair told how one was chosen:

> 'I received literature about the Caterpillar Tractor Company from a relative, showing a design for their advertisements, that is a wavy streak with 'Caterpillar' written across its face. I immediately got in touch with Hutton and Timmerman, and suggested to them that the organisation be called 'Caterpillar Club' for several reasons, namely: the parachute main sail and lines were woven from the finest silk. The lowly worm spins a cocoon, crawls out and flies away from a certain death if it remains in sight of the cocoon. A better example of what a pilot or passenger should do in the case of an uncontrollable 'plane could not have better figurative depiction. Hutton and Timmerman gave enthusiastic support to this name.'[1.]

The 'Guardian Angel' parachute being tested from the basket of an observation balloon in 1916, by former show-jumper 'Professor' Newell. (Photo: RAF Museum) (page 68)

Enthusiastic support also came from Guy Ball as technical head of the Parachute Section, but he was unable to persuade more senior officials at McCook to allocate funds to the administration of the proposed club and the printing of certificates for its members. The idea may have become no more than a list of names and a collection of photographs on a wall at McCook had not Leslie Irvin, the first man to test the Type-A, and now its primary manufacturer, heard of the idea. He offered to administer the scheme, and to present a certificate and a caterpillar-brooch to each person who saved his life with a parachute — not just an Irvin parachute: any parachute. The staff at McCook readily agreed.

Thus, the 'Caterpillar Club' was born.

Although other parachute manufacturers have subsequently introduced similar schemes and alternative mementos, the term 'caterpillar' has become firmly attached to anyone who has leapt for life from a disabled aircraft, whatever type of parachute he happened to be wearing — just as Leslie Irvin intended. Little did he realize how many of those little brooches he was going to distribute around the world.

The story of the 'caterpillars' would not be complete without mention of the parachute designers and in particular the test-jumpers who made it possible for those leaps for life to be undertaken with a comforting expectation of success. They will feature prominently amongst this particular category of sky people.

Top: Corporal Garland Cain of the U.S. Army, one of many military test jumpers who pushed back the free fall frontiers during the 1920s, takes to the air. (photo: U.S. Air Force) (page 76)

Above: Floyd Smith, inventor of the first manually operated parachute. (page 74)

The parachute was being considered, if not actually used, for the purpose of saving life long before Lieutenant Harold Harris strapped one to his backside on that day in 1922.

The first conjectured use of the parachute as a lifesaver was as a means of escape from fire. It has been suggested that the parachute designed by Sebastian Lenormand and tested by several livestock in 1783 was intended for this purpose. This is a reasonable supposition, and the idea would probably have crossed the minds of previous 'tower-jumpers' and their audiences. Had any of those jumps been successful, the idea might even have advanced beyond conjecture, but there is no record of any such fire escape being developed in those distant days.

What is recorded is Joseph Montgolfier's suggestion that a parachute as designed by Lenormand and copied by himself could provide a means of escape from a balloon. In a letter dated 24 March 1784 to General John Meusnier, who had published a design for a steerable balloon that was far ahead of its time, Montgolfier wrote, 'An idea has come to me and I hasten to inform you of it, because it may be of use to you in connection with your air ship. It concerns the construction of a parachute with which one could, if necessary, descend from a balloon to earth in a simple and safe manner.'

Montgolfier was showing great foresight, for he wrote this before any man had yet made a parachute descent, but he did not put these thoughts into practice.

Jean Pierre Blanchard is credited with a similar notion when, in 1784, he rigged a large umbrella-type parachute, well braced and already open, between his hydrogen balloon and its passenger car. There was no suggestion, however, that this was to be cut free and used as an emergency escape system: it was intended solely to guard against too rapid a descent of the balloon itself. Blanchard soon dispensed with the idea, which is a pity, for even a cumbersome device such as this might have saved his wife Sophie. By 1819 Madame Blanchard was one of the foremost aeronauts in France, well known in Paris for her aerial firework displays. On 7 July 1819, her audience at the Tivoli Gardens gave a particularly loud cry of delight as high above their heads and beyond the gently descending parachute-flares and 'silver rain', a sudden burst of flame lit up the night sky. Alas, it was not part of the show. It was the fatal ignition of the hydrogen spilling from the balloon. Applause turned to shrieks of dismay as Sophie Blanchard fell from the night in her balloon car, crashed onto a roof, and was pitched to her death on the street below.

Two days later a proclamation was issued by the Prefect Of Police, the Comte d'Angles, forbidding further ascents by balloon unless the craft was equipped with a parachute. This might be seen as the first attempt to legislate for aerial safety, but nobody took any notice. This was not because aeronauts were disinterested in their own health, but because it was by that time accepted that in the event of a balloon bursting or otherwise losing its gas, the fabric would normally gather in the top of the netting to form a canopy sufficient to bring the passengers back to earth with a good chance of survival. Arnold junior had been one of the first to survive a burst balloon when he came down in Execution Dock after that ill-fated attempt to make a parachutist of George Appleby in 1775. The Italians Paolo Andreani and Carlo Broschi survived a collapse of their balloon in this way at Padua in 1808. Later, the American John Wise was to make a habit of it. His first such descent was unintentional, when his balloon lost all its gas in a thunderstorm in 1838, but he was then so confident of the outcome that he deliberately 'ripped' his balloon on several occasions, purely for show.

To set the record straight, mention needs to be made of the Polish aeronaut, Kuparenko. He is often credited with having saved his life by parachuting from a disabled balloon over Warsaw in 1808. There is, however, no contemporary record of the event, and we do not know of a parachute of that era that could have been used for such a feat. It is far more likely that Kuparenko landed beneath the remnants of his balloon as did other aeronauts, and that this was misinterpreted by subsequent reporters of the 'escape'. The Polish Aero Club confirms this view. Sorry, Kuparenko . . .

The deliberate ripping of the balloon remained a risky business, as Katchen Paulus' fiancé, Hermann Lattemann, had discovered when he crashed to his death in the streets of Krefeld. The risk was greatly reduced by Louis Capazza who contained his balloon inside a huge silk canopy instead of the usual netting, so that when the balloon was deflated either by accident or intention, the canopy would remain in place to form a parachute. A system of cords and pulleys was used to haul down the gas envelope and thus prevent it from fouling the canopy. Between 1892 and 1920, Capazza demonstrated the device on fifty-one occasions with his balloon 'Caliban', but it was never used in an emergency. It was a showman's vehicle, rather than a serious attempt to provide aviation with a life-saver.

In fact, during the nineteenth century, the parachute attracted more attention as a potential means of escape from fire rather than from balloons. Amongst a number of patents for fire-escape parachutes was one in 1879 by the American, Oppenheimer, which incorporated a five-foot stiffened canopy attached not only to the escapee's arms and neck but also to the head by means of a screw. In 1839, tests on fire-escape parachutes were actually carried out in Brussels, but the results were said to be disappointing, which is not surprising if they were anything like Oppenheimer's design.

For more than 100 years, while the balloon ruled the skies, only the show-jumpers had a use for the parachute. Other aeronauts didn't need it, and they didn't like it. Their view is summed up in the words of the great French balloonist, Tissandier, who wrote in *La Nature* in 1892 that 'the parachute, which to this day has served no other purpose than that of a curious device for exhibitions, has no practical use for the aeronaut.'

The arrival of the aeroplane during the first decade of the twentieth century did nothing to change that attitude.

We have already seen that the capabilities of the earliest aeroplanes restricted them to such low altitudes that a parachute would rarely have offered a chance of escape, even had there been one readily adaptable for use from aircraft.

Those first parachute descents from aeroplanes in 1912 had been primarily in the interests of showmanship, and the equipment and techniques used by sky people such as Albert Berry, Glen Morton and Rod Law had been designed for exhibition rather than escape. Yet by that time, aeroplanes were reaching heights where a parachute designed for the purpose could have saved some of the aviators who were dying in increasing numbers — twenty-nine in 1910; seventy-nine in 1911; one hundred and four in 1912. The aviation world was, of course, alarmed, but saw the remedy in better construction of machines and improved training of pilots, in tackling the cause rather than the consequence of accidents. This approach was undoubtedly influenced by the continuing attitude of aviators towards the parachute. It was an attitude of mistrust, fostered by over 100 years of show-jumping and purposeful exaggeration of the already considerable hazards of the act. Fliers considered that in an aerial emergency they would be far better off trying to crash-land their aircraft rather than entrust their lives to a bundle of silk.

The *Flight* editorial of 8 October 1910 represented the general view when it said:

> 'The idea of providing pilots with parachutes as a possible source of safety in the event of a mid-air calamity does not commend itself to us, because, in our opinion, the aeroplane itself is inherently the safest form of parachute that the pilot or his passenger can have, and they had much better trust their lives to it than abandon their posts, than rely upon an apparatus that might quite as easily fail them in an emergency.'

The same attitudes prevailed in America. The individual initiatives of pioneers Charlie Broadwick and Leo Stevens had produced static-line operated parachutes readily adaptable for use from aircraft. However, when 'Tiny' Broadwick demonstrated the 'Coat-Pack' to military observers at San Diego in 1914,

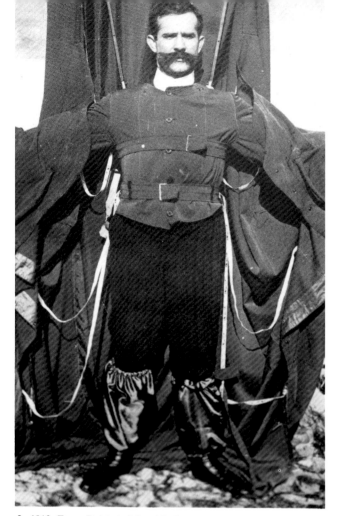

In 1913, Franz Reichelt fell to his death from the Eiffel Tower when demonstrating this 'parachute cloak', one of many futile endeavours to provide a life-saver for fliers.

— most of them, fortunately, bearing only dummy loads.

It was from the first level of the Tower in 1911 that Gaston Hervieu launched an aircraft fuselage, on the upper surface of which was attached a parachute, which when released from its stowage, snatched a dummy pilot from the falling 'aeroplane' and lowered it gently to earth. This demonstration won Hervieu the gold medal, with which he appears to have been content, for he developed the device no further. His was one of the first attemps to produce what became known as 'soaring parachutes', designed to extract the aviator forcibly from his machine rather than put him to the inconvenience of having to leap from it. Esnault-Pelterie designed a similar parachute but never put it to the test, and the Italian Pino filed a patent for a 'soaring' system whose complicated train of events was initiated by a small extractor 'chute released from the aviator's hat. Ridiculous it may seem, but to Pino must go credit for being the first to consider the 'pilot chute' that would feature so prominently in subsequent developments.

The only 'soaring parachute' to be successfully live-tested was that of Bonnet. His parachute, with lines already attached to the pilot, was stowed in extended form under hinged panels on the upper surface of a fuselage. When the panels were opened by means of a lever, the canopy would be inflated by the air flow, and would snatch the aviator from his seat. After successfully testing the apparatus with dummy man and fuselage dropped from a balloon — for which he was awarded the Prix Lalance — Bonnet sought someone to carry out a live trial. Nobody rushed forward. A year passed before noted aviator Adolphe Pégoud offered himself, and Louis Bleriot offered a rather worn out monoplane that could struggle to no more than 350 feet. At that height, over Chateaufort near Versailles on 19 August 1913, Pégoud opened the throttle of the Bleriot, put the nose down, and pulled the lever. There was a slight pause before he was dragged bodily from the cockpit to find himself suddenly and gratefully swinging beneath a fully opened canopy. The parachute suffered a few broken rigging lines and Pégoud cracked his shoulder against the tailplane, but the experiment was deemed a great success, and after the parachutist had been helped down from the tree in which he had landed, he was carried jubilantly to the chateau of Madame Quesnel for a celebratory glass. After the Bleriot had been abandoned, it had carried out a unique experiment of its own, executing what appeared to be a complete circle in the sky before making an unaided but reasonable crash-landing in a field. It is said that those evolutions of the pilot-less 'plane inspired the acrobatics for which Pégoud subsequently became renowned, for a few weeks later he became the first pilot to loop-the-loop and to fly upside down — intentionally.

the gentlemen had been more impressed by the petite parachutist than by the life-saving potential of her 'chute. They bought two of the packs, put them on a shelf somewhere, and forgot about them. The 'Life Pack' produced by Leo Stevens, although operated by static-line when used by show-jumpers such as Arthur Lapham and Rod Law, incorporated the ripcord system, and with further development could have become a viable life-saver. Such development was not forthcoming. The technical potential to provide a parachute for aviators was available in America: the will to develop and use it was not.

The French — well to the fore in European aviation by 1910 — were not quite so dismissive of the parachute. The Ligue Nationale Aerienne, in seeking to improve aerial safety, encouraged the production of a life-saving 'chute by offering a gold medal for the best design. A greater incentive to creativity was probably the 10,000 francs offered for a similar purpose by Colonel Lalance. As well as incentives, the French had the Eiffel Tower, from which during the next four years a succession of strange contrivances would be launched

Subsequent trials of Bonnet's parachute were less successful. It was inevitable that at some time the canopy would foul the aeroplane, and this happened in a demonstration near Vienna when it caught the tail surfaces of a Deperdussin. Pilot Lemaine was seriously injured in the crash-landing, and parachutist Le Bournis was lucky to escape with no more than a broken leg. The Bonnet system was abandoned.

Other attempts to 'extract' the pilot from his aircraft relied upon some means of artificial propulsion. The Austrian Odkolek, inventor of the Hotchkiss machine gun, used explosive charges to blast the canopy clear of the fuselage. He tested it with dummies from the Eiffel Tower, but there were no volunteers for a live trial. George Prensiel developed and actually tested at Hendon a 'chute that was propelled from a metal cylinder by compressed air to extract not only the pilot but the seat as well.

Compressed air to assist the opening of a canopy was also used by Frenchman Cayat De Castella. He was primarily a showman, and in the remunerative but somewhat ungallant tradition of that profession, it was Madame De Castella who did the actual jumping. For the descents that she made with her husband's invention, not only the parachute was stowed beneath the fuselage of the Goupy biplane: so was Madame De Castella. She was suspended in a prone, face down position just aft of the undercarriage, from which she would release herself, no doubt with profound relief, at a drop height of some 2,000 feet. This brave lady made two descents with the compressed-air chute at Nevers, then died beneath a streaming canopy on 21 July 1914.

Another who died bravely, yet foolishly, in this search for an aerial life-saver, was an Austrian tailor of Paris, called Franz Reichelt. He made an immense 'cloak' with metal stiffeners, with the idea that it could be worn by aviators who, after leaping from their doomed 'craft, would throw out their arms to extend the para-suit to its full eight square metres, and thus descend safely to earth. After testing it to his satisfaction by leaping from 15 feet into a pile of straw, he took his device to the Eiffel Tower on a cold Sunday morning in February 1912. He donned the weird garb, explained its function and his intentions to a small crowd, climbed to the first floor some 200 feet above the upturned faces, dropped a newspaper to assess the wind-drift, climbed onto a table, spread out his arms, and jumped. He fell like an over-dressed brick.

The European endeavours to produce a 'soaring' parachute or one equipped with some means of artificial propulsion were doomed to failure by their very complexity. It is significant that they were mostly designed by engineers and 'inventors', rather than practising parachutists, yet we must not dismiss their efforts too lightly, for in their designs were seeds that would one day come to fruition: Pino's pilot-chute; Prensiel's concept of an ejection seat; and ideas by Couade and others for 'chutes to lower a complete aeroplane and its occupant to earth that were impracticable in 1914, but would eventually be applied to the recovery of escape-modules and space-capsules.

In that flurry of parachute design that immediately but only co-incidentally preceded World War One, only the static-line operated parachute as developed by the pioneering show-jumpers showed any real promise as a life-saver, and foremost amongst these remained the 'chutes of Broadwick and Stevens in America, for they had grasped the basic concept of simplicity, and were aware that a plain round canopy cleanly presented to an airflow needed no further persuasion to open.

In France, in 1914, Jean Ors jumped with a static-line container-chute of his own design, but he also thought it necessary to assist canopy deployment with a central 'chimney' made of coiled willow. For a similar purpose, 'Pere' Robert used springs in the apex of his canopy, but his parachute was nevertheless the most promising in Europe at the time. It was worn on the back, incorporated a functional harness, and although designed primarily for static-line operation, it could be adapted to manual release — like Leo Steven's 'Life Pack'. In static-line mode it proved successful in several trials, including a jump by aviator Brodin from the bridge at Nantes.

In England, in 1914, Calthrop's 'Guardian Angel' was in the early stages of development. Everard Calthrop, a railway engineer, had been inspired to the production of an aerial life-saver by the sight of his friend the Hon. Charles Rolls crashing to his death in his Wright biplane at the 1910 aviation meeting at Bournemouth. At the low altitude at which the 'plane disintegrated, a parachute would not have helped Charles Rolls, but Calthrop foresaw a time when it would save the lives of many of his friend's successors in the air, and he devoted the rest of his life to that purpose. His parachute was a triumph of engineering, but of a complexity beyond the understanding of a simple parachutist. A silk canopy was pleated and folded between two metal discs, twenty-four inches in diameter. Each rigging line was individually folded and secured around the discs with a series of break ties. The discs were joined together and contained in canvas covers, and the whole assembly was attached to the aircraft, and connected to the aviator's harness with a single-point suspension line. When the parachutist jumped, this line would pull the canopy from its housing with the mouth already partially open, and would deploy the lines under constant tension to reduce the risk of them becoming tangled. For this latter contribution to parachute technology, Calthrop deserves great credit, and his 'chute certainly provided the 'positive opening' that he claimed for it. It was just so very complicated . . . !

Opposite: Leslie Irvin, whose demonstration of free fall and of Floyd Smith's manually operated parachute at McCook Field in 1919 was a milestone in parachute design and usage. (page 74)

Leslie Irvin preparing to land at McCook Field after his first free fall jump. He is about to break his ankle . . . (page 74)

The well-intentioned endeavours of the European parachute designers were to little immediate purpose. By 1914 the aviation world was no closer to equipping itself with a parachute than it had been in 1910 when the Ligue Nationale Aerienne had offered its gold medal. Aviators were still not convinced that it would work, nor that they needed one at all — an attitude once more summed up by *Flight* in September 1913:

> 'We see very little future for the parachute as a life-saving apparatus in emergency on aeroplanes.'

Few of the young military fliers would have argued with that when they went to War in 1914.

As a weapon of war, the aeroplane in 1914 was an untried novelty, and was not welcomed by most military gentlemen: it frightened the horses, damn it! Its sole purpose was artillery spotting and reconnais-sance, when the weather permitted. It carried no weapons and seemed to offer no threat to the enemy on the ground nor in the air. Nor were there many of them. When the Royal Flying Corps, formed in 1912, crossed to France to join battle in 1914, it could muster sixty-three assemblies of canvas and wood, propelled at low speed and no great altitude by engines of uncertain reliability. Another 116 were left behind, partly to cope with training, but mainly because they couldn't be trusted to get across the Channel. The French and the German air forces were only a little better off. In those circumstances it is little wonder that airmen shared the general attitude towards the parachute. It wasn't needed. And where would you put the damn thing, anyway? Far better to try and land the kite if the engine conked . . . Thinking thus, the young fliers went to war.

Then they started shooting at each other. Only with shot-guns at first, and to no great effect, but then the swivel-mounted machine gun appeared, and all the fun went out of flying. It became necessary to protect the reconnaissance aircraft with 'fighters', whose sole purpose was to shoot other aircraft out of the air. In 1915, Anthony Fokker improved the killing rate with an 'interruptor gear' that allowed a machine gun to be fired directly ahead through the propellor, and increasing numbers of 'planes fell from the sky — taking their crews with them, for there was still no parachute.

By the Battle of the Somme in 1916, British fighters had regained superiority, and the death toll rose on both sides. Still no parachute.

In 1917 the new Fokker and Albatross fighters were outflying the Allied aeroplanes, and in 'Bloody April' the average life-expectancy of RFC pilots on the Western Front was eight days. Still no parachute.

The slaughter in the air continued into 1918. Then, in the last summer of the war, from a disintegrating Albatross high above the trenches, a white streamer appeared, then blossomed into . . . a parachute! Lieutenant Steinbrecher was the lucky man on the end of it. German fliers had at last been given a means of saving themselves from a doomed aircraft. But not the British, nor the French, nor the Americans now engaged in the conflict. They would fight during the closing months of that war with the same choice that had faced a man in a flaming cockpit since 1914: should he leap, and fall to his death, or should he burn?

Why? Why were they not offered another choice? The choice of living, which a parachute would have given them?

It has been said that the denial of parachutes to the fliers of World War One was because of an 'official' belief that to provide men with a means of escape from a damaged aircraft would encourage them to do so before it became absolutely necessary. This may have been the personal view of a minority of staff officers sitting at comfortable desks, but it was never the declared policy of any of the combatant governments. The reason given, whenever the question was asked by press, public, or by the fliers themselves, was that no suitable parachute was yet available, but that development was proceeding. Sadly, by 'suitable', they meant a parachute that would not only be sure to function, but above all a parachute that would not detract from the primary purpose of the aeroplane — to out-fly and destroy other aeroplanes. The deadly and fluctuating struggle for air supremacy involved a constant search for optimum manoeuvrability, rate of climb, and ceiling, set against the limitations of engine power and payload. When a 'Guardian Angel' parachute was attached to a DH-4, the aircraft's top speed was reduced by three mph and its rate of climb by fifty feet a second. That was unacceptable.

Nor was the 'development' of a suitable parachute pursued with any vigour. Experimental units were given more urgent tasks, and those who should have been leading the search for an aerial life-saver were woefully ignorant of parachuting matters. 'I think that one parachute should be sufficient for both pilot and observer,' declared the Controller of the Technical Directorate in Whitehall.

The parachute used by the Germans was a simple design by Otto Heinecke. It comprised a twenty-one-foot cotton canopy packed into a canvas container, attached either to the aircraft or directly to the aviator's harness, and deployed in either case by an eight-foot static-line when he leapt for his life. It didn't always work. It wasn't perfect. But for the airmen who saved their lives with it — including Hermann Goering and the ace Ernst Udet — it was suitable enough! The parachutes of Broadwick or Stevens or Pere Robert or Jean Ors or Calthrop could have been made just as 'suitable' — with a little effort.

Whatever the practical reasons, it was primarily an attitude of mind that condemned so many fliers to death, just as it killed so many thousands on the ground. It was an attitude of mind that encouraged the use of the 'Guardian Angel' for the belligerent purpose of dropping spies, but denied it to aviators. It was an attitude of mind so pre-occupied with the infliction of casualties on a massive scale that the actual saving of life seemed an almost embarrassing irrelevancy.

An added irony is that, quite apart from those German fliers saved by the Heinecke, the parachute in World War One *did* save many hundreds of lives. It was allowed to so because the means was inexpensive and did not interfere with the killing of the enemy.

By the end of of 1915, all along the Western Front, flew the sinister, silent shapes of the tethered observation balloons, directing artillery fire onto the opposing trenches and gun emplacements and crawling columns of men. They themselves became targets for those enemy aircraft that braved intense ground-fire to pump tracer bullets into the hydrogen-filled 'sausages'. The French were the first to equip their 'Aerostiers' with a parachute with which to escape the subsequent inferno. Lieutenant Juchmès designed a parachute packed in a container that was attached to the rigging of the balloon, and from which it would be deployed by the falling weight of the observer when he jumped from the basket. Nothing new in this! It was exactly the same system that those long-disdained show-jumpers had been using for years. To persuade dubious 'Aerostiers' that the thing would work, Juchmès employed a jovial Marine called Constant Duclos to travel the length of the 'lines' and give demonstrations. He made twenty-three jumps, and the smile on his face as he did so impressed his military audiences even more than the twenty-three faultless openings.

The Germans also utilized show-jumping expertise when they equipped their observers with a 'chute designed by Katchen Paulus. Its canopy of unbleached calico provided a rate of descent that was fine for show-jumping, but a little slow for observers keen to outdistance the flaming remnants of their balloon.

British developments in this field were led by Colonel Maitland, whose first jump had been with show-jumper Dolly Shepherd in those more gentle times. Involved in early work with military airships, he had been the first to parachute from one when in 1913 he jumped from the 'Delta' with a Gaudron 'chute, to land in Cove Reservoir. Appointed to command the newly formed Balloon Unit at Roehampton in 1914, he urged the adoption of parachutes for his observers, and participated enthusiastically in the trials to find the most suitable. He chose a show-jumping 'chute. He found the 'Guardian Angel' too complicated, and in fact did not want its much vaunted 'positive opening'. He sought a prolonged deployment that would ensure healthy separation between the jumper and a probably burning balloon, and to achieve this he modified a simple Spencer container-chute by using a series of cotton 'ties' to regulate and delay the opening of the canopy.

Maitland's contribution to aerial safety has rarely been acknowledged. It would continue after the war, as would his personal involvement. In June 1921, at three o'clock in the morning, a night watchman at Cardington saw a parachute appear from a moonlit sky, and settle to earth close to the airship shed. In some trepidation he approached the aerial intruder. 'Good morning. Can I get a bed here?' the figure enquired. It was Air Commodore Maitland. He was making a return journey to Howden on the airship R33 after attending the Derby and had decided to 'drop off' at Cardington to attend a conference. Sadly, two months later when he really needed a parachute, it was just out of his reach when the R38 crashed into the River Humber, taking Maitland and forty-two others to their deaths.

Back to World War One . . . Amongst the many balloon observers who had cause to be thankful for a parachute was Leo M. Murphy, serving with the American Expeditionary Force:

'On the sixth of July 1918, some units of the United States Marine Corps were attacking Hill No. 204, located between Bellau Woods and Chatteau-Thierry. They were being pretty well splattered with machine gun fire from the top of the hill and were being shelled very heavily, and a call for counter battery fire was made.

'It being a very windy day and the clouds at 5,000 feet, there were no balloons up on either side of the front, but a chap by the name of Malcolm Sedgwick, a second lieutenant of Air Service, and I offered to see what we could do.

'From an elevation of about 1,700 metres, we were able to silence several of the batteries also many of the machine gun positions, thereby being of material aid in the success of the attack.

'About noontime, the usual anti-aircraft danger signal of two very rapid bursts in close proximity to ourselves told that something was wrong. At that moment, some of the rigging between the basket and the balloon itself was cut by machine gun bullets; I turned around and saw a D-5 Albatross which had come through the clouds with two spandau guns spitting tracers at a lively rate. The field glasses that were on my chest were hit, and a tracer bullet went through one of the fins, so Sedgwick and I decided this particular balloon was no place for us. I went first, and he followed. Needless to say, both 'chutes functioned perfectly and we thoroughly enjoyed the trip down. What was left of the balloon, mainly nothing, passed us on the way, and outside of the fact that the high wind was blowing toward the German lines, and that the German pilot followed us down, shooting bursts first at me and then at him, there was nothing particularly exciting about the event.'[2.]

How shameful that several thousand young fliers of World War One, for want of a parachute, did not live to tell similar modest tales.

When it was known in August 1918 that German airmen were being saved by parachute while 'our boys' were still dying without one, public indignation at last pressed the Allied governments into action. Five hundred 'Guardian Angels' were ordered, to be fitted into RAF SE-5s, and the American Air Service was promised 824 parachutes, including copies of the Heinecke. The war ended before any became available to squadrons at the Front.

In Europe the urgency immediately went out of the provision of parachutes, but in the USA a train of events had been set in motion that, fortunately for aviators throughout the world, was allowed to continue after the Armistice of November 1918. It had been initiated by General 'Billy' Mitchell, who as head of the American Army Aviation Service in Europe had, early in his command, asked Washington to provide para-chutes for his men, and had received the stock reply: none available. Making his opinion of Washington quite clear (he would later in his career be Court Martialled for his outspoken attacks on official policies, and later still exonerated and posthumously honoured) Billy Mitchell took it upon himself to establish a small team to evaluate all known types of 'chute and come up with the best one — fast! To this task was appointed James Floyd Smith.

Floyd Smith had been cowboy, orange picker, factory hand and a trapeze artist with a circus group called 'The Flying Sylvesters'. In 1912 he built an aeroplane, taught himself to fly it, and with his wife Hilder — another acrobat — barnstormed through southern California, where they made their first parachute jumps. They used Broadwick static-line 'chutes. Floyd thought they were fine for show-jumping, but his flying instincts told him that if the 'plane had been anything but well throttled back and flying straight and level when he had jumped, that line or even the canopy itself could have been snagged. In an emergency, he wondered, wouldn't it be better if the jumper could fall well clear of the machine before the 'chute opened?

It was an idea that he took with him when he joined the Bureau of Aircraft Production as an aeronautical engineer in 1918, and in July of that year he submitted an application for a patent on a design of 'chute that was to revolutionize parachuting: the first to be designed solely for manual operation. The design — there was no actual 'chute yet — was simple. It comprised a standard round canopy, to the apex of which was attached a small spring-assisted pilot chute. Canopy, lines and pilot chute were stowed in a fabric back-pack attached to an adjustable harness. The covers of the pack were held in a closed position by three metal pins, fastened to a wire ripcord and locked through metal cones. The ripcord passed through a flexible housing over the parachutist's shoulder to a circular handle, stowed in a fabric pocket on the front of the harness. A tug on that ripcord ring pulled the pins from the cones; strong elastics whipped the covers back; the pilot chute leapt into the airflow to act as an anchor and drag the main canopy and then the lines from the pack as the jumper fell.

Few of the components were new. Broadwick had designed the first back-pack; Leo Stevens the ripcord; Pino the pilot chute. Floyd Smith put them all together with a standard canopy to produce the first practicable manually-operated parachute. But if the components were not new, the concept was. In fact, the concept was revolutionary.

Fall freely, *then* open the 'chute? Impossible! Everyone said so. Everyone knew that a man would lose consciousness long before he could do anything about opening his own parachute. Scientists had calculated that a free falling human being would be unconscious by 100 feet, and dead by 500. Doctors agreed. Aviators agreed. In fact, hadn't the old-time jumpers themselves, like John Hampton, warned of the hazards of 'rapid descent'? This was the very reason why every parachute design had relied upon some form of immediate and automatic opening. There was no conceivable alternative, everyone was agreed on that — except Floyd Smith. He was not burdened with a degree in science, but he had been a fine trapeze artist, and he knew that whenever he had dived from the 90-foot board, or fallen from even greater heights into the safety nets, *his* brains hadn't been scrambled. Just the

opposite: they had been pretty damned clear! He didn't believe the scientists and the doctors. He was convinced that a man could fall and live and pull that ripcord.

In September 1918 he was appointed to head Billy Mitchell's 'team' at Wilbur Wright Field, Ohio. The 'team' comprised himself and former motor mechanic Guy Ball. They weren't made welcome at Wilbur Wright, and moved across to nearby McCook Field. They weren't much more welcome there. *Parachute engineers . . . ?*

Floyd Smith took with him his design and his conviction, and while they waited for parachutes from both Europe and America to be provided for the trials, he made his own, in the fabric loft of the Assembly Hangar at McCook. He made five, with canopies of silk put together for him by Mitchell Brothers, a dressmaking company in Chicago. 'We kept our 'chutes in two steel chests to prevent them being made into shirts and scarves,' said Guy Ball.[3]

By November, enough 'chutes had been submitted for the trials to begin. Floyd Smith's test programme was the most searching that parachutes had ever been subjected to. It sought answers to two questions. Could the parachute withstand the shock-load of high-speed bale out? And would it function without danger of fouling the aircraft in *any* flight situation? To find the answers, every parachute under trial, including his own, with the ripcord operated by a static line attached to the handle, was dropped with dummy loads ranging from 100 to 300 lb, at drop speeds from 100 to 130 mph. Those that survived were further tested in 'emergency' conditions — contrived spins, stalls, and full-throttle dives. Floyd Smith did the flying, in a DH-9 that had seen better days, and Guy Ball stood on the ground with a stopwatch. He became adept at dodging the weighted sandbags that hurtled regularly out of the sky beneath the streaming tatters of canopies and lines as parachute after parachute failed Floyd Smith's rigorous research.

When the war ended, instead of being disbanded, the team was increased. It came under the command of Major E. Hoffman, who was an engineer and pilot, but no parachutist. Wisely, he allowed Floyd Smith to carry on as he had been doing, and added to the team former show-jumper Harry Eibe, Army parachutist Ralph Bottreil, and engineers James Russell and Jimmy Higgins. The trials continued, and still the 'chutes came streaming down, offering little or no support to the big rubber dummy that soon became known as 'Whistling Billy'. The static-line 'chutes of Broadwick, Stevens, Ors, Kiefer Kline, Otto Heinecke, Leslie Irvin and the Omaha Tent Company failed the more demanding strength tests. The 'Guardian Angel' seemed strong enough, but on one trial it snagged the tail of the DH-9 and almost brought Floyd Smith to grief. His own 'chute, designed with these very tests in mind and modified as they progressed, performed well. But pull that ripcord by hand, during free fall . . . ? Major Hoffman wouldn't hear of it. He was on the side of the scientists and the doctors and just about everyone else: it couldn't be done.

Then Floyd Smith forced his hand. Based on the evidence that they had now accumulated from the dummy trials, he produced a list of design criteria for the ideal safety 'chute. One of the eleven requirements was that 'the opening means must not depend upon the aviator falling from the aircraft', which was another way of saying 'no static-line'. There was only one parachute that met all of Floyd Smith's design specifications: his own.

Hoffman, having approved the specifications, had no choice but to accept a live trial of the manually operated 'chute. But he certainly wasn't going to let one of his team risk his neck — certainly not Floyd Smith himself, keen though he was to be the first. Oh no! This was not really a trial of the parachute. This was a trial of the man. It was a test of man's ability to fall freely and pull a ripcord, against all scientific and medical and Major Hoffman's personal advice. So who would do it? How about that young jumper who was always across from Buffalo, and whose own parachute had been one of the best of the static-line bunch? He was crazy enough to do it. What was his name — Leslie Irvin?

When show-jumper Leslie Irvin had been rejected by the Air Service because of flat feet in 1915, he had moved from California to Buffalo to work on the assembly line at the Curtiss aircraft factory. Whilst there he had designed and made a static-line operated back-pack, and to promote it as an aerial life-saver had carried out several exhibition jumps along the Lake Erie shores, and one into the Lake itself that had almost cost him his life. His had been one of the first assemblies submitted to McCook for testing, and although he couldn't afford Company status, he thought that his parachute should have the dignity of being promoted on headed note-paper. He ordered some. 'IRVING AIR CHUTE CO.' it said. The 'G' added to his name was an error for which the printer disclaimed responsibility. Leslie Irvin couldn't afford a new batch. He couldn't, at the time, afford tram fares nor new shoes either, and walked to work with cardboard inner-soles in his boots, so the 'G' stayed. It stayed throughout his lifetime as the world's foremost parachute manufacturer.

When Hoffman asked if he would jump with the ripcord 'chute, Leslie Irvin didn't hesitate. He had come to share Floyd Smith's enthusiasm for manual operation, and he too had tried the high dives and the trapeze bar — never as a professional, but for the sheer hell of it when he had been working with the Hollywood stuntmen — and like Floyd Smith he had experienced that sharpening of the senses that gravity encourages.

That stuff about losing consciousness? That was all bunkum, wasn't it? There was only one way to find out.

On 28 April 1919, at McCook Field, wearing the manually operated parachute, Leslie Irvin climbed into the rear cockpit of Floyd Smith's DH-9, and at 1,500 feet above the airfield, he climbed out of it again.

> 'He climbed over the cockpit,' said Floyd Smith, 'sat on the edge with his legs hanging down and tried to leapfrog off. Instead he tumbled over and over. He pulled the ripcord without any trouble while falling. The 'chute opened almost immediately, in 1.4 seconds to be exact. His descent was steady. There was practically no oscillation. The demonstration of the 'chute was almost tame . . .'[4]

Tame it may have appeared. But that first pre-meditated jump with a manually operated parachute heralded a new era in parachuting. Oh yes — and Floyd Smith forgot to mention that Leslie Irvin broke his ankle on landing.

Important land-mark though it was, Leslie Irvin's jump at McCook attracted little immediate attention and only local and erroneous comment in the Press. Hoffman, fearful of the outcome, had invited neither reporters nor military observers to the event. On 9 May, however, he approved the detailed specifications for Aeroplane Parachute Type-A, and a few days later Floyd Smith, Higgins, Russell and Bottreil made further successful jumps with it. A contract was placed with the now formally established Irving Air Chute Company for the production of 300 assemblies, and with Mitchell Brothers for a further twenty.

It is ironic that Floyd Smith, although he now left McCook to become involved in the manufacture of his own design of parachute, was never able to do so. He was no businessman, and after an unsuccessful lawsuit against the Irving company, he sold the patent rights of what soon became known as the 'Irvin Chute'. Because it bore the Irvin label and because Leslie Irvin had been the first to jump it, most people would come to credit Leslie Irvin with the invention of the manually operated parachute. The canny ex-showman, whilst he never claimed so himself, certainly never denied it. Let us put the records straight: Floyd Smith invented the first 'free fall' parachute, and deserves more credit than he has had for the most significant advance in parachute technology.

Credit must also go to Guy Ball for the improvements made to the Type-A under his direction, for when he took over from Floyd Smith as technical head of Hoffman's team, the trials were far from over. There

Charles Lindbergh started his flying career as a barnstormer and show-jumper, then became a four-time 'Caterpillar' before gaining fame with his solo trans-Atlantic flight in 1927.

was still opposition to the concept of free fall, and there were still other designers trying to prove that manual operation was not the best answer. Calthrop was as persistent as ever, and sent a team of jumpers to America to promote his 'Guardian Angel'. After successful displays at Atlantic City, Orde Lees, Lieutenant Caldwell, Sylvia Boyden and Miss Boyden's chaperone came to demonstrate 'positive opening' at McCook. The 'chutes of Orde Lees and Sylvia Boyden opened positively enough, but that of Lieutenant Caldwell didn't open at all. As he jumped from the DH-9 at 600 feet, the static-line caught the elevator rocker-arm that projected from the fuselage, and broke under the shock-load of the falling man. As Caldwell plummeted to earth, he could be seen examining his harness, then raising a hand towards the dwindling aircraft where his parachute was still stowed. It was a tragic vindication of Floyd Smith's views of static-line parachuting.

As work on the Type-A continued, Guy Ball introduced bias-construction of canopies, and developed a slimmer back-pack, a chest-pack that could be clipped onto the harness when required by gunners and observers, and the seat-pack that was to become the primary life-saver for so many aviators. When the Army Engineering department introduced their own modification to the Type-A in the form of seven large vents in the crown of the canopy and a two-inch ring-slot all the way round it, Guy Ball objected. The scientists of the Engineering Department, however, had worked out that this modification would greatly reduce the opening shock, and they had Degrees and Guy Ball hadn't, so the modification went ahead. It reduced the opening shock all right. In fact it did away with it altogether, for when Sergeant Washburn jumped and pulled the ripcord of the new 'chute at Carlestrom Field in California, it didn't open at all. The air came in through the mouth of the canopy and went straight out through those scientifically designed holes. Sergeant Washburn's death was a brutal lesson in design and acceptance procedures.

The arrival of the manually operated 'chute was not received with wild applause by American aviators. They weren't keen on *any* 'chute, and least of all on this free fall idea. They were not at all convinced about that. What would happen, for instance, if you operated that thing at high altitude. Would it open? Or would the air be too thin?

There were brave young men prepared to find the answers by the only means possible. The first was Lieutenant John Wilson who at Kelly Field on 8 June 1920, jumped at 19,800 feet, and pulled his ripcord as soon as he was clear of the 'plane. The 'chute opened all right, but his subsequent account of his descent under the canopy through 'whirlpools of air' did not encourage confidence in the mode of transport.

The more experienced Sergeant Bottreil, veteran of some 300 show-jumps before he joined the cavalry in 1909, was the next, just ten days later. In a Lepare biplane, piloted by his friend Sergeant Strong Madan, he set out for the thin cold air above McCook. Madan could coax the 'plane to no more than 20,600 feet, which was just as well, for without oxygen, Bottreil was not his usual cautious self. As he stood up in the gunner's cockpit to struggle from the fur-lined coat that he wore over his parachute, he caught the ripcord handle on a projection, and the canopy was released into the 60 mph airflow. Bottreil was torn bodily from the cockpit and smashed through the tail fin with such force that he was knocked cold. When he recovered a few seconds later, he was swinging under an opened and slightly damaged canopy, but his left arm felt strangely numb. He couldn't move it. He looked. Blood was streaming from a torn sleeve and dripping from his fingers into the air. His upper arm had taken the full impact of the ash-framed tail fin, and had been gashed to the bone. He was a long time from the ground: time enough to bleed to death. Lifting his useless arm with his good one, he managed to wedge it into the suspension lines above his head, and loop one line round it to act as a temporary tourniquet. A better one was applied by the farmer in whose field he landed some 20 minutes later, and Ralph Bottreil survived. So did Strong Madan, for although the almost rudderless Lepare had been wrenched from his control, he had mastered it, and brought it back to McCook. A few weeks later he was unable to master the vicious spin of the Sopwith Camel that he was flight testing, and died in the wreckage. He had no parachute.

Lieutenant Arthur Hamilton made jump-and-pull descents from 20,900 feet in August 1920, and from 23,000 feet the following March, both without oxygen. Oxygen was first used for a high altitude jump by Sergeant Encil Chambers, who claimed 26,000 but had no barograph to confirm it, so the official record waited for Captain A. W. Stevens with his 24,200 foot jump at McCook on 13 June 1922, from a Martin bomber. It was a more scientific and well monitored attempt, and it was finally accepted that the parachute would open at whatever height the aeroplane of the day could reach.

Then in 1922 came those life-saving jumps by the first 'caterpillars', Harris and Tyndal. But, said those who still needed convincing, they too had opened their 'chutes pretty smartly. They hadn't fallen very far. *Nobody* had yet fallen very far. What would happen if you did? Say that you had even more trouble finding that ripcord handle than Harold Harris. What then? How long could you go on falling before you *did* lose consciousness? How fast would you fall? Faster and faster? And if you did manage to open your 'chute after a long fall, surely the speed would just blow it to pieces?

More brave men came up with the answers. Sergeant Randall Bose jumped at Mitchell Field from 4,500 feet

'Pull-off' jumps from the wing of a Vickers Vimy provided an early introduction to parachuting for those airmen brave enough — or daft enough — to volunteer for a practice descent. (Photo: RAF Museum)

and fell for 1,500 feet in twelve long seconds before opening, without damage to either himself or his parachute. A few days later he set out to better that one, but after dropping for thirteen seconds, 'things started to go black before my eyes. I was spinning very violently, and feared that I might lose consciousness.' He pulled, and came down to earth a shaken man. Randell Bose had experienced the flat spin that would trouble and sometimes terrify many a free faller in the years to come, but at that time it wasn't known if it was the spin or the twelve seconds of free fall that started to muddy the mind. Was that as far as a man could drop, and live? Was twelve seconds the limit of free fall consciousness?

A few months later, in early 1925, it was Sergeant Stephen Budreau who came up with the answer when he jumped from 7,000 feet and fell for 22 seconds before pulling the ripcord. That fall of over half a mile harmed neither the jumper nor the parachute. Also in 1925 it was becoming known that Joe Crane and Kohley Kholstedt and Art Starnes were making delayed drops, and although serious fliers considered them a bunch of crazy acrobats, they were showing that a man could survive the long falls. The mystery and the fear of falling free were being slowly eroded.

Whilst the work of the test-jumpers and the experience of the showmen undoubtedly pushed back the free fall barriers, this was not the main reason for the gradual softening of the attitude of American fliers towards the parachute in the mid-1920s. For them, a more convincing advertisement of its virtues were the lives that it was now actually saving.

Although the carriage of parachutes became compulsory for American military fliers and passengers in January 1923, it was not until a year later that more 'caterpillars' joined the company of Harris and Tyndal. Then they came in a rush. There were ten in 1924. One was Lieutenant Walter Lees, who unintentionally demonstrated the low-level opening qualities of the Irvin 'chute when he baled out successfully from only 150 feet above the ground. Another was the first US Navy pilot to join the 'club', 'Gunner' Cole. He joined in style, parachuting onto the well kept greens of the Coronado Country Club after abandoning his fighter when it lost a wing in collision with another at 1,200 feet.

During 1925, a further twelve aviators were saved. One of them baled out twice during that year. He was no stranger to the parachute: he was our former barnstormer, Charles Lindbergh. As a military flight cadet at Kelly Field, Texas, his SE-5 tangled with another, piloted by 2nd Lieutenant McAllister, whilst they were carrying out mock attacks on an old DH-4B. Both parachuted to safety, and two hours later were back in the sky in another pair of SE-5s, keeping well out of each other's way. Less than three months later, while flight-testing a 'plane for The Robertson Aircraft Corporation, Lindbergh again 'hit the silk', when the machine spun out of control from 2,000 feet.

Charles Lindbergh and the parachute weren't finished with each other yet. By 1926 he was one of that elite

Litigation between the Irving and Russell parachute companies in 1930 brought together many of those responsible for the development of the manually-operated parachute, including most of the 1919 McCook team. Back row, left to right: Erwin Nicholls, Mr Knight (attorney), Guy Ball, Floyd Smith, Lyman Ford, Frank Manson, Major Hoffman. Front row, left to right: Leslie Irvin, Hilder Smith, 'Tiny' Broadwick, James Russell, Ralph Bottreil.

band of pilots flying the US Mail, in open-cockpit biplanes, in all weathers, and at a time when a good pair of eyes were the main aid to navigation. But eyes can't see through a layer of fog such as that which hid the earth from Lindbergh on a night run from St Louis to Chicago. He flew until the engine coughed and died, then at 5,000 feet he went over the side, and opened his 'chute a few seconds later. Swinging in the darkness, he was surprised to hear the splutter of a Liberty engine coming back to life. He hadn't swiched off the fuel when it had died on him, and as the 'plane had nosed towards the earth, the last drops had run through to the motor. Suddenly the noise was growing louder in the murk, as though the unseen 'plane was coming straight towards him. The noise swept past him and faded, then came back again, from a different direction. It was as though, in the darkness, the aircraft was spiralling in search of the pilot who had abandoned it. Frantically, Lindbergh hauled on the lines to slip the canopy away from the sound, and after another pass it faded into the night. He landed safely, located the wrecked 'plane, and retrieved the mail bags. A month later, the mail was again a day late arriving in Chicago when the fog

rolled in once more, and again Lindbergh was forced to leap into the night, remembering this time to turn off the fuel before he did so.

Had it not been for the parachute, we would never have heard of Charles Lindbergh, for he would have died back in 1925. As it was, one of the few occasions on which this four-time 'caterpillar' flew without a 'chute was when in 1927 he traded it for its weight in fuel to fly 'The Spirit of St Louis' across the Atlantic, into instant fame.

By that time, through the bravery of the test-jumpers and the example of fellow fliers, American aviators were looking with more favour upon the parachute. They were even coining a maxim about it that would take its place in American air-lore: 'If you need one and haven't got one, you'll never need one again.'

Britain's second 'caterpillar' was Captain 'Tiny' Schofield, test pilot for Vickers. He poses beside the wreckage of the Wibault monoplane from which he had just baled out.

In post-war Europe, as in America, fliers had mostly reverted to their traditional disdain of the parachute. Unlike the US Army, however, the European air forces had not pursued the provision of one with any great effort. Certainly, there were no intensive test-programmes such as that undertaken at McCook. There were conferences and meetings and much production of scientific paper, but little came of it all. It was as though that flurry of invention that had preceded the war and had continued during it had left Europe confused. It couldn't make up its mind about parachutes, and in particular it couldn't decide between the merits of automatic and manual opening.

In England, a fierce argument was waged, mostly in the correspondence column of *Flight*, between Calthrop for his automatic 'Guardian Angel', and Colonel Holt for his manually operated 'chute. For another five years after the war the designers argued, the Air Ministry dithered, and British fliers died. Prompted at last by the rising death toll (seventy-one in 1924), public opinion, and a blistering attack in *The Aeroplane* by its influential editor, Charles Grey, an announcement was made in the House of Commons during February 1925 that parachutes were to be provided for the RAF. They were neither Calthrop's nor Colonel Holt's. They were to be the manually operated chutes of the Irving Company. Whilst the British designers had been arguing, the American 'chute had been going effectively about its business of saving lives, and that beat any number of letters to *Flight* and demonstration jumps at Stag Lane.

Two Flying Officers — Soden and Pierce — were sent to Buffalo to acquaint themselves with the Irvin 'chutes, and Major Hoffman brought US Navy jumper Lyman Ford to England to demonstrate them at RAF flying units. The first batch of parachutes were delivered in July 1925, and in 1926 Leslie Irvin came to Letchworth himself to establish a new factory, leaving the Buffalo operation to his partner George Waite.

As in America, British fliers needed persuading that this parachuting idea was not such a bad thing. To achieve this, Soden and Pierce formed a small group of 'instructors', drawn mainly from the parachute section of the Aeroplane and Armament Experimental Establishment at Martlesham Heath, a unit that under Flight Lieutenant John Potter and Sergeant Hawkings were known as 'the loonies'. Their early endeavours to promote the life-saving qualities of the new 'chute received a tragic set-back in June 1925. They had devised a system of jump-training from the Fairey Fawn which required the pupil to climb from the cockpit, descend to the bottom rung of the fuselage ladder, grasp the ripcord ring with one hand, let go of the ladder with the other, tumble into space, and pull. When Sergeant Wilson of No. 12 Squadron got as far as the letting go, he had a change of mind, grabbed with both hands for the ladder, and missed. Apparently unable to re-locate the ripcord as he fell, he died without operating his parachute. It was not the 'chute that failed: it was the training method. A first free fall can be a mind-numbing experience. It should not, ideally, be one's first introduction to premeditated parachuting. The American trainers had realized this, and had developed the 'pull-off' system, whereby trainees would be positioned on the outer wings of a biplane for take-off and flight, and when at drop height, on a given signal would pull the ripcord with one hand whilst holding on with the other. Released into the airflow, the canopy would open and wrench the pupil backwards into space, no matter how reluctant he might suddenly have become. It sounds quite mind-numbing itself, but it provided a safer introduction to the delights of parachuting, for it ensured that the ripcord was pulled and the canopy opened before the pupil left the aircraft. This system was now adopted by the RAF, whose Vickers Vimy provided an ideal slow-flying platform for pull-off jumps.

The Parachute Test Unit moved from Martlesham to Henlow in 1925, and under Flying Officer Soden, a small detachment was formed at RAF Northolt for the purpose of touring RAF squadrons to demonstrate the parachute to still-sceptical aircrew. Again as in America, it needed more realistic 'demonstrations' than this to convince British fliers that their seat-packs were something more than a rather uncomfortable cushion. These 'demonstrations' came in the summer of 1926.

Pilot Officer Eric Pentland was enjoying his seventh hour of solo flight in an Avro 504, high above the countryside near Chester. Half-rolls, his instructor at Shotwick had told him. He had completed four, and with growing confidence he threw the biplane into a fifth. Suddenly the world turned upside down and began to revolve, rapidly. As the aircraft fell from the sky in a deadly, inverted spin and the whirling green earth seemed to reach up for him, Eric Pentland pulled open his seat strap and yanked the ripcord handle almost at the same time. He was instantly torn from the terror of the cockpit into the unbelievable tranquility of flight under a fully opened canopy of white silk, 500 feet above Hemswell golf course. He landed close to the eighteenth green to become Britain's first 'caterpillar'.

Captain E. R. C. Schofield, as chief test-pilot for the Vickers Aircraft Company, was a more experienced flier, one of the foremost in Britain. Even so, there was nothing he could to do recover the new Wibault all-metal monoplane from a vicious spin when he was flight-testing it over Brooklands on 1 July, and he parted company with it to become the second British 'caterpillar' — all sixteen stone of him. That was the first time he had ever worn a parachute. Sadly, he wasn't wearing one on the day two years later when the aeroplane he was testing disintegrated in flight: as that American maxim said, he never needed one again.

Sergeants Frost and Steanes joined the 'club' three weeks after Schofield when they baled out of their Fairy Fox biplanes after colliding at 1,000 feet, flying out of Andover. That made it four: four lives saved in the space of six weeks. Perhaps, British fliers began to think, those seat-packs were not so uncomfortable after all . . .

Airmen throughout the world were beginning to come to the same conclusion. Leslie Irvin was a vigorous and persuasive promoter. He took on Lyman Ford as a full-time parachuting salesman, and the demonstrations that this most capable jumper gave — in any weather, for as he said, fliers wouldn't be able to choose just the good days — helped to persuade Russia, Sweden, Poland, Japan, Australia, Greece, Czechoslovakia and Romania to adopt the Irvin 'chute. France and Germany continued well into the 1930s with static-line operated parachutes of their own manufacture, but eventually they too 'went manual'. In its 'Salvatore' series, Italy produced a 'chute capable of either manual or static-line operation. Those who saved their lives with it still wrote to Leslie Irvin for their 'caterpillars'.

Although Europe benefited from the American experience, once equipped with manually operated 'chutes, its jumpers also had to come to terms with the lingering doubts and fears that still clung to free fall. In England, it was the men of the Parachute Test Unit who led the way. Amongst them were two jumpers called Dobbs and East, who made a largely unrecognised but significant contribution to British parachuting, and who would have contributed even more had they lived longer.

'Brainy' Dobbs, they called him, for he had an inventive mind — not entirely applied to the parachute, for he made a two-wheeled car, and an aquaplane, which he eventually crashed on the banks of the River Debden. Towards the parachute, he had the right attitude. 'A parachute', he would say to the men he trained, 'must be so simple that even the highest officer

To celebrate its 50th year of training Britain's paratroopers, No.1 Parachute Training School commissioned this painting by Tony Harold of a drop from a Whitley aircraft over Tatton Park in 1940. (page 107)

in the Royal Air Force can understand it.' His main contribution to parachute technology was the 'trapezoidal' ripcord handle. Remember the trouble that Lieutenant Harold Harris had in trying to find the ripcord ring as he tumbled through the sky? Others had experienced the same problem, particularly when wearing the heavy gloves required for open-cockpit flying. There were also occasions when the circular handle had slipped from its fabric housing to dangle free, which made the finding of it whilst falling even more traumatic. 'Brainy' Dobbs devised a trapezoidal-shaped handle (one side longer than the other) that not only presented a wider hand-hold, but also allowed the elasticated mouth of the pocket to grip the converging sides more securely. He had one made in the workshops at Henlow, where Leslie Irvin saw it on one of his frequent visits. Within months the American had patented it and produced it. So when you reach for your trapezoidal handle, all you sky people, think of 'Brainy' Dobbs.'

Dobbs was a good parachutist, but East was said to have been even better. The two of them, with no guidance, had tackled the mysteries of free fall, and it had been East who had quickly discovered that the normally tumbling body could be stabilized by spreading out arms and legs, and that even though this caused a tendency for the body to rotate like a propeller, that too could be controlled by adjusting the relative positions of the limbs. He hadn't fully mastered it yet, but he was close. He would surely have been amongst the first of the world's controlled free fallers had his bravery and confidence not killed him at the age of twenty-five. On 9 March 1927 he made a display drop from a Vickers Vimy at Biggin Hill. He was to have jumped from 5,000 feet and delayed his opening for twenty seconds, but Flight Sergeant 'Timber' Woods, the Vimy pilot, gave him an extra thousand without telling him, for he knew that it wasn't altitude but lack of it that killed people who leapt from aeroplanes. So East jumped from just above 6,000 feet. He was seen to be falling in a slow, head down spin, which then developed into an almost leisurely somersaulting, which continued until he pulled his ripcord only 100 feet above the ground. The canopy streamed, but he crashed onto the road that borders the airfield on its western side, and died instantly. Some said that he had been trying to dive into the valley and open his 'chute out of sight of the aerodrome 'to give them a real thrill'. What is more likely is that when that slow and not unpleasant somersaulting began, he became so intent on this novel sensation and on finding a means to control it, that despite the extra 1,000 feet that 'Timber' Woods had given him, he lost sense of time and of the looming earth until it was too late. He probably died — as other free fallers have died since — from sheer preoccupation.

Two days later, 'Brainy' Dobbs was practising 'balloon hopping' at Stag Lane aerodrome in North London. Harnessed to a small gas balloon, he was making gigantic leaps across the airfield, rising to over 100 feet, then settling back to earth before propelling himself once more into the air and the gentle wind. It was great sport! At the end of the 'field he made one final bound. He sailed over a tree, and came down the other side onto electric power cables. He, like East, died instantly.

The late 1920s and the 30s were known as the 'Golden Age' of aviation. It was the age of the great pioneering flights of Lindbergh and Cobham and Wiley Post; of the record breakers; of the air races and the coming of the speedy, snarling monoplanes; of Amy Johnson and Amelia Earhart; of the spreading air routes and the majestic flying boats that were built to serve them; of the French air-mail pilots celebrated by Antoine De St Exupery; of the flying circus and the 'joy-ride'. It was an age in which the parachute played its part; in which

it underwent further technical development; and in which it came of age as a life-saver.

Amongst the 'technical developments' was the continuing assault on the mysteries of free fall. In 1928, three US Navy jumpers made a series of carefully monitored free fall descents: Crawford fell 2,800 feet; Morgan for 3,000 feet; and Whitby for 4,400 feet. All were able to give lucid accounts of the experience. 'Despite the rolling and turning that took place at different moments, there was a curious calm throughout the fall. Everything remained clear; to my own inward astonishment I found myself picking out the barracks where I lived from the scrambling of buildings,' reported Whitby. No sign of failing senses there.

Also in 1928, The US Air Corps published the results of trials on 'Rates of Descent of a Falling Man'. which concluded that 'a man equipped with a parachute pack, but allowing it to remain closed, will fall at a maximum rate of between 160 feet per second (109 miles per hour) and 175 feet per second (119 miles per hour), and that he will gain this velocity in about twelve seconds time, having fallen about 1,400 to 1,500 feet.'[5.] This discovery of a constant 'terminal velocity' finally destroyed the myth that a falling body would continue to accelerate to speeds at which neither man nor 'chute could function.

New parachutes appeared in the sky to rival the plain round canopies of the Irvin packs. Jimmy Russell of the early McCook team formed his own Company to produce the 'Russell Lobe' with its distinctive flat top and tucked-in skirt, attained through shaped gores and internal rigging. It provided more stable flight, but although used widely by show-jumpers, it never became an accepted life-saver. Major Hoffman also became a manufacturer, to produce his unique 'Hoffman Triangle' — the first parachute to incorporate inherent 'drive'. It did so by directing the airflow from a flat triangular canopy out of one opened corner, thereby 'thrusting' the parachute in the opposite direction. It was 'thrust' at no great speed, and turning it was a slow process, but it was a brave try and foretaste of things to come, and the 'Triangle' found some favour amongst professional jumpers. In Sweden, Carl Lundholm's 'Robur' was a promising 'chute, that used elasticated vents to reduce opening shock, and incorporated a single-point quick-release system in its harness that was soon to be adapted and patented by Leslie Irvin — ever on the lookout for a good idea.

Those patents played an important yet restrictive role in parachute manufacture at the time, for in order not to infringe them, designers were sometimes forced to seek alternative and less simple means of achieving identical results. Indeed, it was through the very simplicity and effectiveness of Floyd Smith's basic design that the Irvin 'chutes maintained their supremacy throughout the 'Golden Age', during which some ninety per cent of all parachutes produced in the world bore the Irvin label. In England, the only competitor was the GQ Company, formed in 1934 from the association of James Gregory's immense technical talent and Raymond Quilter's money and enthusiasm. Even the intense lobbying of the Air Ministry by this former Guards Officer could not break the Irving monopoly, simply because the Irvin 'chute was doing its job with impressive consistency. Although the main aircrew life-saver remained basically unchanged, improvements were made in fabric technology, in packs, and in harnesses.

Many of the parachute patents of the 1930s concerned themselves with the lives of the growing number of airline passengers. Some contemplated the lowering of an entire aircraft under one or a series of giant 'plane-chutes'. Others suggested means of providing passengers with individual parachutes, often incorporated in their seats. The technical problems were immense, and so was the opposition from the airline operators. Not only would the carriage of parachutes reduce profitable payload and involve initial cost of equipment — if you gave a passenger a parachute, he was likely to ask what was wrong with the aeroplane. The problems were psychological as well as physical, and in face of them, the concept of passenger 'chutes faded.

While advances in parachute design and technology undoubtedly contributed to the safety of the 'Golden Age' aviators, the fliers themselves were — as always — more impressed by the actual performance of the parachute in real emergencies. There were plenty of new 'caterpillars' each year to testify to that performance: they were now being bred in their hundreds.

It was a time of ambitious and imaginative aircraft design. Aviation, however, had not yet reached the stage where the flight characteristics of a particular aeroplane could be calculated with assurance before it actually took to the air. The sometimes unknown structural limitations of old and new aircraft, together with a touch of the exuberant recklessness that was still abroad, often led to those aeroplanes being flown beyond their capabilities. It is not surprising that over thirty-five per cent of the 'Golden Age' 'caterpillars' were born of the structural failure of their machines.

American Fay Gillis, the first woman pilot to wear the 'caterpillar' brooch, was one of them. Actually, she wasn't piloting the 'plane when it happened. She was in the passenger seat and Sonny Trunk was at the controls of a biplane that had seen better days. When he put it into a power dive from 5,000 feet, there was a sudden and violent vibration as it began to shed its tail, and then its wings. Sonny made an unmistakable gesture to his passenger, and followed her from the earthbound remnants of the biplane. The three of them hit the ground in quick succession and less then fifty feet apart — first the aeroplane, then Sonny Trunk under a barely-opened canopy, followed by Fay Gillis a few

seconds later. She actually landed in a tree, and completed her journey by ladder. 'I wouldn't care to repeat the experience,' she told the reporters who flocked around her. They largely ignored a rather battered Sonny Trunk, who was not twenty years old and pretty.

Fanrick Billing of the Royal Swedish Air Force experienced a different form of structural failure as he took off from an aerodrome near Stockholm to give an aerobatic display. As he lifted the aeroplane from the ground he sensed that something was amiss: looking over his shoulder he saw his entire undercarriage bounding along the grass below and behind him. He had a choice: he could risk a belly-landing, or he could jump. He chose to jump. Before he did so, finding that the aircraft handled well in its more streamlined form, he gave the crowd their aerobatic display, and only then did he put the aircraft into a last spectacular dive towards the nearest lake, and bid it farewell. It was, everyone agreed, the most novel stunt they had ever seen.

Jimmy Doolittle survived two aircraft failures to continue his career as one of the world's greatest aviators — racing pilot, record-breaker, test pilot, and World War Two combat pilot. Whilst practising for a stunt routine at the 1929 National Air Races in Cleveland, he flew the wings off a Curtiss Hawk, parachuted to safety, demanded another 'chute and another aeroplane, and completed his rehearsal for the afternoon show. In 1931 he built a sleek, monoplane racer, powered by a massive 512-horsepower radial engine that he thought might take him to a new world speed record for land 'planes, which stood at 277 mph. When he flew it for the first time at St Louis, he could not resist a low-level speed-run across the airfield. The needle was touching 300 mph when the left aileron tore loose. With split-second reaction Jimmy Doolittle yanked the racer's nose up to get it away from the crowd and to give himself height; whipped it onto its back with what little control he had left; tore the seat-strap undone; tumbled from the cockpit; and tugged the ripcord. Five seconds later he was on the ground with white silk settling around him. 'Aeroplane Failed: Chute Worked' said his telegram to Leslie Irvin. As we shall see, this great flier had one more jump ahead of him.

Loss of control — not necessarily associated with mechanical failure — accounted for almost another thirty-five per cent of the 'caterpillars' of the time. In particular, 'spinning' was still a feared and not entirely understood hazard, which set many a novice pilot struggling out of a whirling cockpit and grabbing for that life-saving ripcord. Deliberate spins were a feature of test flying, and one which brought Geoffrey de Havilland junior and John Cunningham their 'club' membership when they were forced to abandon an experimental version of the normally inoffensive Moth

Minor, and thus prolong their illustrious flying careers. Geoffrey de Havilland would eventually die in the wreckage of the experimental DH-108 'Flying Dart' in 1946, whilst Cunningham would become a night-fighter ace and test pilot for the world's first jet airliner, the 'Comet'.

Those who survived mid-air collision were the next most numerous category of 'caterpillars' — some seven per cent. One of them was the first member of the British aristocracy to join this even more exclusive 'club'. Lord Malcolm Douglas-Hamilton was serving as a Pilot Officer in the RAF, and in 1930 was practising for the Hendon Air Display when his Bristol Bulldog collided with a Hawker Horsley during a mock attack on the bomber:

> 'It all happened in a flash. I hit the Horsley at the bottom of my dive, on the tail and through the starboard planes. The Bulldog just broke up and dived for the earth with both wings folded back, luckily not over the cockpit. It was half upside down and I pulled the harness pin, the shoulder straps flew apart, and I fell clear. I pulled the ripcord and my parachute opened in a flash. My height from the ground was said by watchers to be between 150 and 300 feet when I left the machine . . .'[6]

The pilot of the Horsley parachuted to safety as well, but his passenger baled out too late.

Fog continued to provide an occasional member of the 'club'. When flying instructor Tom Newbould and his pupil Pilot Officer Farnes were trapped at night above fog in 1937, Newbould came close to death three times in quick succession — a little closer each time. When his home base of RAF Wittering indicated its presence beneath the blanket of fog by firing signal flares through it, Newbould cautiously eased the Hawker Hart down into the murk. At 500 feet he was suddenly dazzled by the explosion of another flare just off his wing-tip. The Hart slipped from his control into a deadly spin. He kicked the rudder bar to kill the rotation, then hauled back the stick and slammed on throttle, and evaded death for the first time by some 100 feet. Climbing out of the fog, he decided that he wasn't going to take the 'plane back into it. He took it instead to 4,000 feet and told Farnes to bale out, and when his pupil had gone, he followed him into the night. He pulled the ripcord, and under the open canopy was stuffing the handle into his Sidcot flying suit (it would have cost him 2s 6d if he had dropped it) when he heard the Hart's engine and saw its navigation lights swinging towards him in the darkness. In almost identical circumstances to Lindbergh, he was being sought by his deserted aeroplane. Just the once it roared past him, and that time he was less than fifty feet from death. Shaken, he drifted down into the dense fog, which was suddenly lit by an immense flash and a

shower of blue sparks. He had fallen between five high-tension cables, which had then been caught and dragged together by his lines and canopy. Most of Northamptonshire, including RAF Wittering, was plunged into darkness, but Tom Newbould, suspended just above the ground, was unharmed. That time, death had come within inches.

Fire always has been one of the most dreaded of aerial mishaps. 'When fire leaps close to one's anatomy, it generates a certain amount of hysteria, and in the vernacular, possesses one of an irresistible urge to be long gone,' said Lieutenant Hutchinson, after being very rapidly 'long gone' from a LB-1 bomber loaded with six bombs and 2,000 rounds of ammunition when its engine burst into flames close to McCook Field in 1926. Fire also persuaded Lieutenant Nam Bhand Nagrob to join the 'club' in 1929. He was Siam's first 'caterpillar', and the little Irving brooch was presented to him in style when, before a parade of fellow aviators at Dom Muang, the commander of the Siamese Royal Flying Corps conferred upon him The Order of the Golden Caterpillar.

Finally, there were those who just fell out: like Flying Officer Vickers Eyre, who undid his seat-strap to bend forward and pick up a pencil from the floor of the cockpit of his Siskin fighter. He inadvertently pushed the stick forward, and the next moment found himself falling through the air on his back, looking up at his boots. Then there was the well known American flier, tiny Mildred Kaufmann — so tiny that she had to fly with a special seat or a lot of cushions. It was cushions on the day at Buffalo airport in 1930 that she set out to beat her own record of forty-six consecutive loops. The cushions slipped as she was going over the top for the thirty-first time, and she found herself hanging from the cockpit rim of an inverted aeroplane until she was flung clear. After taking off her heavy gloves as she tumbled earthwards, she pulled the ripcord, and landed safely in strong winds. She was most upset that she had muddied her overalls. Another who tumbled from his cockpit at the height of a loop was Dimitrije Ljumovich of the Yugoslavian Air Force, whose escape was described in a letter sent on his behalf to the Irving Air Chute Company:

> 'By making loop he fell from aeroplane and in this moment the propellor cut his leg over his knee and he without his leg but with a cigarette in his mouth, fell on one foot and with your 'chute saved his life. This happened on August 17, 1931. He is still in the Flying Service, but with one wooden leg.'

By the end of aviation's 'Golden Age', over 4,000 of its fliers had been saved by their parachutes. No longer did they scoff, nor doubt. No longer was the parachute just a showman's vehicle. Through its own example, it had won acceptance. As the world prepared for conflict

American aviatrix Mildred Kaufmann joined the Caterpillar Club when she accidentally fell out of her aircraft whilst attempting to establish a new loop-the-loop record in 1930. She is wearing her seat-pack — and extra cushions.

on a massive scale, the young fliers of 1939 no more thought of going to war without a parachute than the aviators of 1914 had thought of going with one.

Some 100,000 aircrew were saved by parachute during World War Two. Only 34,000 of them joined the Irving 'Caterpillar Club'. The remainder were German, Japanese, Italian, many Russians and a conservative estimate of the number of Allied fliers who did not apply for membership. But by our definition all 100,000 of them were 'caterpillars'. All 100,000 of them had a story. We can relate but a few.

The contribution of the life-saving parachute to the air battles of World War Two was not just humanitarian. The new belief in the parachute gave many the confidence to fight as they did. What perhaps has not been fully appreciated is the value of the large numbers of men that it returned to the combat. Might not the Battle of Britain itself have ended differently if,

at a time when 180 RAF fighter pilots were being shot down above Southern England each week, sixty-five of them were not landing uninjured under their silk 'brollies'? Oh yes, German pilots were drifting out of the summer skies as well, but they were being met by pitchforks and prison camp, whereas many of those sixty-five RAF fliers per week were climbing into another fighter and rejoining the Battle that same day. Shortage of pilots was more critical to Dowding's Fighter Command than shortage of aeroplanes — particularly shortage of pilots of the calibre of Al Deere, Stanford Tuck, 'Ginger' Lacey, 'Cobber' Kain, and other aces who were all saved by parachute and who all returned to the sky to take ample revenge for the indignity of having been shot out of it.

One young man returned to the epic Battle seven times. Three times he survived crash landings, and four times he was saved by parachute. He was twenty-two years old, a Hurricane pilot with No. 43 Squadron, and his name was Tony Wood-Scawen. He first jumped for his life in June, 1940. 'Dear Sir,' he wrote to Leslie Irvin:

'On the 9 June I was shot down in France whilst on patrol and was obliged to "take the silk" or alternatively to get cooked to a turn in my Hurricane. To my immeasurable relief the 'chute opened, despite the low altitude, and I touched down without injury. I understand that this entitles me to the coveted badge of the Caterpillar Club. I should be delighted if you would send me one, but if you have discontinued the award of the badge I still wish to offer you my profound thanks for saving my neck.'[7.]

What he didn't say in his letter was that after landing, he had bundled up his 'chute, carried it twenty miles through the land battle of France, and was still carrying it when he arrived back at RAF Tangmere eight days after being posted as missing. 'I know this one works', he explained to his surprised Squadron Commander. Three more times during the next ten weeks he 'took the silk', and returned to fight. Then on 2 September, near Ashford in Kent, he baled out of a Hurricane for a fifth time, but he was too low, and died before his streaming parachute could take a deep breath and save him yet again. The score was almost even: he had shot down seven German 'planes, and three 'probables'. His brother Patrick, fighting with 80 Squadron, destroyed nine of the enemy. He died in combat the day before Tony. Their father collected two Distinguished Flying Crosses from King George later that year, after the Battle of Britain had been won by Churchill's 'Few'. Without their parachutes, the 'Few' might not have been enough.

Shortly after the USA joined battle in 1941, a familiar name appeared once more amongst the American 'caterpillars', that of Colonel James Doolittle. Still smarting from the military humiliation inflicted upon them by the Japanese at Pearl Harbor, the USA needed a morale booster. Jimmy Doolittle provided it. On 18 April 1942 he led sixteen specially prepared and heavily laden B-25 Mitchell bombers from the pitching decks of the carrier USS *Hornet*, and turned towards Tokyo. The attack on the Japanese capital was totally unexpected, but the physical damage was less important than the blow to Japanese pride and confidence, and the subsequent delight created in America by 'The Doolittle Raid'.

After dropping their bombs the B-25s kept flying west, heading for mainland China. Only one of them landed safely, at Vladivostock. The others, with fuel running low, were trapped in the night skies over China. Four of the captains decided to crash-land, the other eleven, including Doolittle, ordered their crews to bale out into the darkness. Amongst the 'caterpillars' born that night was Lieutenant Jacob E. Manch, co-pilot of 'Whiskey Pete'. He was a big man, and had a thing about personal survival:

'I grabbed a box of Robert Burns cigars and a bunch of "Baby Ruths" and stuffed as many as I could inside my A-2 jacket. Then I bundled up my private arsenal, a 44-40 Winchester rifle, German Luger, two .45 automatics, and .22 automatic and axe and Bowie knife and got ready to go. I told Bob Grey that I would be walking west and I would see him in Chungking. I wished him luck and dropped through the escape hatch.

'As I went out, I watched the two exhaust stacks go over my head, then reached for the D ring on my chute and couldn't find it. Scrabbling frantically I finally found it dangling to my right side and pulled. I was aware of the weirdest sound as I continued to fall. It was the rubber shroud lines of my parachute pack twinging as they let go each bundle of lines.

'Since I only had a twenty-four foot 'chute which was too small for my weight, the opening shock was something I wasn't ready for. I saw red, and the impact jerked my Bowie knife, axe, canteen and all my guns away, except the one in my holster. The box of cigars disappeared out of my jacket and the "Baby Ruths" were shucked, leaving nothing but the wrappers.

'Coming down I thought I heard waves breaking on a beach and the horrible thought came to me that I had sent the rest of the crew out without their Mae West life-vests on. They would surely drown if we were over the ocean and not over land as we figured. Just as I struggled to release my leg straps to get away from the 'chute in case I landed in the water, I hit the ground with a thud. What I thought was waves slapping on a beach was wind blowing through pine trees.'[8.]

Jacob E. Manch, even without his cigars, candy bars, and private arsenal, survived. Eight of the 'Raiders' were less fortunate. They fell into Japanese hands, and three of them were executed. Jimmy Doolittle landed in a well fertilized paddy field, but otherwise found himself amongst friends. When he returned to America, one of the first things that he did was to send an anonymous box of cigars to J. H. Patton of the Sacramento Air Depot — the man who had packed his parachute.

Many other famous fliers owned their lives to their parachutes. Douglas Bader baled out over France, leaving one of his artificial legs trapped in the cockpit of his Spitfire. His adversary, and later friend, Adolf Galland, had to batter his way out of the jammed canopy of his blazing Messerschmitt-109 before leaping clear. American ace Chuck Yeager, having already made a low-level escape from his Airocobra during training, deliberately fell for more than a minute before pulling his ripcord when his P-51 Mustang was blown to pieces 20,000 feet over France by Focke Wolfe-190s.

But most of the 'caterpillars' were not famous, except to those closest to them. And not all of them joined the 'club' as a result of enemy action. Flight Sergeant Frank Hulbert was one of those. He was flying inoffensively between two layers of cloud, at 2,500 feet in a Miles Master trainer, when something grabbed the wing of the aircraft, wrenched it almost to a halt, and sent it spinning down into the cloud. It had run into the cable of a barrage balloon, part of the aerial defences of the city of Hull. Spinning through cloud with one wing about to disintegrate was no place to be, so Frank Hulbert parted company with the aeroplane and pulled his ripcord. His 'chute opened and he drifted down out of the cloud to find himself 400 feet above Hull's city centre, and an object of considerable interest. He landed safely on a bomb-site, where a gentleman from the crowd that quickly gathered invited him into his nearby office to use the telephone. Frank Hulbert found himself in the parlour of an undertaker, who asked politely if there had been any passengers in the crashed aeroplane and seemed disappointed that there was not. The crew of the barrage balloon that had so abruptly terminated his flight, however, were delighted with the performance of their balloon, and insisted on taking the pilot to see the smoking remnants of its handiwork. 'All that seemed to be left was one wheel, so I must have made the right decision,' concluded Frank Hulbert.[9.]

The lowest successful bale-out recorded during World War Two was that of Flight Lieutenant Dudley Davis, who piloted one of three Hampden bombers in a low-level attack on the German battleship Tirpitz, in Wilhelmshaven. None of the Hampdens survived the screen of flack, but Dudley Davis successfully planted his mine before clambering from a blazing cockpit onto the wing, where at a height of fifty feet, amongst a confusion of passing cranes, warehouses and tracer shells, he yanked his ripcord, to be torn into the air in classic 'pull-off' style and deposited on a stone jetty at the end of the first up-swing of the opened canopy. He suffered a badly singed moustache.

At the other extreme, the highest bale-out of the War is not recorded, but it must have been made by one of those bomber crews flying in the thin air above 30,000 feet during the later stages of the conflict — or by a pilot of one of the new breed of German fighters, propelled to those altitudes by 'jet' or by rocket. They were regions largely unknown to parachutists, but as always, there were men willing to explore them, and to pass on their hard-won experience and advice to those who flew regularly at such great heights. We have already met Art Starnes in his show-jumping days, when he earned himself the title of 'The Aerial Maniac'. In 1941 he put his free fall experience to more purposeful use when he undertook a series of six closely-monitored jumps from altitudes up to 31,400 feet, wearing eighty-four pounds of recording equipment.

He made no attempt to stabilize his body during those long drops, but fell as would an aviator making a first jump. As he tumbled and spun through the air, he analysed what was happening, sought simple corrective measures for the more extreme gyrations, and published his findings and his advice in a booklet called *Delayed Opening Parachute Jumps and their Life-Saving Value*.

'Mr Starnes takes the guesswork, the uncertainty, the mystery and the curse of fear engendered by ignorance, out of the delayed parachute fall,' wrote the commander of the US Army School of Aviation Medicine in his foreword to the book.

But what if the 'chute, for some reason, was operated at those extreme altitudes? What would happen then? Could the man and the 'chute survive? Lieutenant Colonel William Lovelace, a surgeon in charge of the Air Medical Laboratory at Wright Field, was keen to find out, so he tried it. Forty thousand feet, he thought, would be a fair test. Only one man had jumped from that height — the Russian, Major Kharakhonoff, from 40,813 feet. It had been the Russian's 599th jump. For Lovelace, it would be the first. And he was going to have his 'chute opened immediately, and unless it blew to shreds under the opening shock, he was going to linger in the thin air, whereas Kharakhonoff had fallen free and fast to more hospitable levels. There were some who thought Lovelace would die. He nearly did.

On 24 June 1945, a B-17 'Flying Fortress' took him to 40,200 feet, where the air slicing through the open bomb doors was seventy degrees below zero and where the lack of oxygen would kill him in ten seconds if his portable supply failed. He was wearing only standard Air Force survival gear. He stepped out through the bomb bay, and whirled down the slipstream as the static line tightened. The canopy slammed open. It was as though he had been smashed against a brick wall. The violence of the sudden deceleration drove the breath from his lungs and the consciousness from his mind, and ripped the leather glove and silk inner from his left hand. Eight miles high, he hung limp beneath a violently swinging canopy, but it was open, and undamaged. At 20,000 feet, he stirred. Coming out of broken cloud at 8,000 feet, he was able to raise a weak hand to the anxious pilot of the AT-6 chase 'plane. He landed in a wheat field, suffering from oxygen starvation, severe shock, and a badly frostbitten left hand. But he was alive. By example he had shown that if they *had* to, aircrew could operate their parachute at those great heights, and survive.

Although the test-jumpers and the 'caterpillars' themselves pushed back the parachuting barriers even further during World War Two, the life-saving parachute itself required little modification. There was much advance in fabric technology, and associated strengthening of components, and great development of parachutes for the dropping of heavy loads, the delivery of paratroopers, and the retardation of bombs

THE CATERPILLARS

87

and even of aircraft, but the 'chute that saved those 100,000 lives was in its basic concept the manually operated system designed by Floyd Smith, improved by Guy Ball, and made by Leslie Irvin, twenty years earlier. It proved its worth in situations that seemed to defy the rules of chance and aerodynamics alike. For example . . .

Flight Lieutenant Joe Hermann was the pilot and Flight Sergeant John Vivash was the mid-upper gunner of a Halifax of No. 466 Squadron of the Royal Australian Air Force. Turning for home after their bombing run over Bochum on 4 November 1944 the Halifax was hit by flak and set on fire. Joe Hermann gave the order to bale out, and held the controls while most of the crew leapt into the night. Before he could snap on his own 'chute and before John Vivash with a

Above: In his painting 'Lancaster Bale Out', Frank Wootton captures the sensations and the loneliness of escape by parachute.

Opposite: A zero speed, zero altitude test ejection with a Martin-Baker Mk.10 lightweight seat blasts this test parachutist through the cockpit canopy. (Photo: Martin-Baker)

leg full of shrapnel could crawl to the hatch, the bomber blew up. Joe Hermann was conscious of dropping through the night sky, in company with assorted debris, all rotating slowly about him. He experienced no sensation of actually falling. Yet he *was* falling, and he was falling without a 'chute, and he knew it, and when he suddenly crashed into one of those pieces of 'assorted debris' that was keeping him ghostly company in his earthward plunge, he clutched at it with all the desperation of a man who doesn't want to die. It wasn't a piece of debris: it was John Vivash.

The gunner had been flung unconscious from the bomber at the same time as his pilot, and had tumbled through the air for almost a minute before coming to his senses. In the split second before Joe Hermann grabbed him, he had pulled his ripcord. Even then, had the canopy opened at its normal speed, the sudden deceleration would have torn the second man away, but under its double load and as though knowing what was required of it, the parachute took in the air slowly, and Joe Hermann was able to cling to the thighs of his mid-air partner. For another four long minutes he clung there until, under the single 'chute, they crashed together to the earth. Hermann hit first, and suffered two broken ribs as Vivash landed on top of him. Small price to pay, he thought, for a life of which he had despaired.

There would have been an even greater number of World War Two 'caterpillars' had more men been able to get out of their stricken aircraft. Towards the end of the war, 'planes were flying at speeds of over 400 mph in level flight, and diving at more than 500 mph. Unless the aerodynamics of the situation were much in his favour, at such speeds it was almost impossible for a pilot to climb from his cockpit. Many died because they were glued to their seats by airblast or centrifugal force. When jet-propelled aircraft entered the closing stages of the conflict, the problems became even more critical.

In January 1944 Squadron Leader Douglas Davie of the Royal Aircraft Establishment was test-flying a Gloster Meteor when one of its two engines exploded. Although he was able to struggle from the cockpit, he was slammed against the fuselage with such force that he was apparently unable to open his parachute. Another test pilot died in similar circumstances shortly afterwards. The time had come for some form of mechanical assistance to be provided for pilots needing to escape from fast-flying aeroplanes.

Such a system had been in operation for several years, for in 1938 the Germans had begun experimenting with an 'ejection seat', powered by compressed air (remember George Prensiel in 1914?) and had subsequently installed such seats in their faster fighters. Some sixty German 'caterpillars' were blasted clear of their 'planes during the war, but the failure rate was high, and many who survived had suffered severe spinal injuries.

In 1944, Britain and America began their own independent experiments. To the fore of British development was Jimmy Martin, a strong-minded Ulsterman and head of the Martin-Baker Company. He soon abandoned an initial concept of a spring-operated lever that would catapult a pilot from his cockpit in favour of an ejection seat. Whilst the engineers considered the mechanical problems, both in America and Britain aviation-medicine experts studied the human factors, subjecting themselves to brutal accelerations on test-rigs and horizontal 'sleds'. It soon became apparent that the weak link in the whole system was the human frame, and the subsequent history of ejection has centred on the need to apply massive propulsive power as gently as possible to the aviator's backside. By July 1946 Jimmy Martin considered that he had done just that. He had put together the basic components of an ejection system: a seat, a power pack, a vertical guide rail, and a parachute. He also had the man willing to try it — Benny Lynch, one of his fitters, who had been the first and most frequent passenger on the test-rig at the Denham factory.

On 24 July 1946 Benny Lynch strapped himself into the rear cockpit of a Meteor. At 8,000 feet over Chalgrove in Oxfordshire he yanked down the face-blind that fired two explosive charges, to punch the seat and himself clear of the aircraft. Another cartridge blew a drogue parachute into the air to stabilize the seat while its occupant quickly released the straps, tumbled forward into free fall, and pulled the ripcord of his standard aircrew parachute. He landed none the worse for the experience. Later that year, USAF test-jumper Larry Lambert, who had begun his parachuting career as a show-jumper in the 1930s, made the first live ejection trial in America.

In 1947 the Martin-Baker ejection seat was accepted into service by the RAF and the Royal Navy, and 1949 saw the first 'caterpillar' ejected into the 'club'. He was 'Ossie' Lancaster, a test pilot for Armstrong Whitworth. He was test-flying the company's second prototype 'Flying Wing' at 5,000 feet over Coventry when it began to pitch with such violence that Ossie Lancaster was unable to control the 'plane. Close to losing consciousness he was barely able to jettison the cockpit canopy and pull down the face-blind. When he let go of it a few seconds later he was falling in the seat, tilted forward and looking down at Coventry. He undid his straps, fell free, pulled his ripcord at 2,000 feet, and landed alongside a canal — rather heavily, for it was quite windy and he weighed almost fifteen stone.

In 1951, ejection seats were put to the ultimate test when the new breed of jet fighters met in combat for the first time — in the skies over Korea. Flying Officer Ron Guthrie, an Australian, was the first of many to join the Caterpillar Club from that war, when MiG-15s shot his elevator controls away south of the Yalu River. He ejected at 38,000 feet, the highest yet, to find himself sitting quite comfortably in his stabilized seat, in utter silence and with little sensation of falling. It was as though he were suspended in the sky, seven miles above a seemingly motionless earth. He noticed that his oxygen mask had been blown sideways, and he dragged it back over his face and sucked deep. Then, looking down at the great map of North Korea spread below him, he decided that if he opened his parachute at altitude, he might drift out to sea where his chances of

This first live ejection with a Martin-Baker seat was made by Bernard Lynch in 1946. 'Benny' went on to make 30 test ejections during the long development programme for ejection systems.
(Photo: Martin-Baker)

being picked up by an American amphibian were better than his chances of evading capture on land. So he released himself from the relative comfort of the plummeting seat, pitched forward into space, and pulled the ripcord at some 30,000 feet. It took him half an hour to reach the earth, and that was his last half hour of freedom for two years, for he came down on land through a hail of ill-directed rifle fire, to be taken prisoner by the Communist forces.

Amongst the American 'caterpillars' of the Korean War was a young Navy pilot who ejected when his plane was crippled by anti-aircraft fire on a ground attack mission. He survived to become the first man to put foot on the moon: Neil Armstrong. That wouldn't be his last bale-out . . .

Those early ejection seats — British and American — did what had initially been asked of them: they blasted a man clear of his aircraft without breaking his back, then remained reasonably stable while he undid his straps, fell out of it, and opened his manually operated parachute. He was, in fact, baling out of his seat in good old-fashioned style, except that the seat was no longer in the aeroplane. But what if he was injured? What if he was unconscious? What if he ejected so low that there wasn't time for him to do all that? Then he would die in the seat when it hit the ground. That wasn't good enough. There had to be some means of completely automatic operation.

Jimmy Martin came up with the answer in 1951 when he produced a seat with a barometrically controlled mechanism that would release its occupant and open his parachute for him at a pre-set altitude (usually 10,000 feet) or immediately if he was already below that height. All that the aviator had to do was jettison his cockpit canopy and pull the face-blind. The seat did the rest, and only abandoned its occupant when it had ensured that his parachute was about to open.

To investigate survivability on the very edge of space, Captain Joseph Kittinger made a series of high altitude parachute descents, culminating in this leap from the gondola of a balloon at 102,800 feet in 1960. (Photo: U.S. Air Force)

The automatic seat came into RAF and RN service in 1953, and one of the first to be grateful for it was Pilot Officer Desmond Melaniphy. In October 1954 his Meteor was in collision with another at 30,000 feet. With a buckled wing-tip his aeroplane plunged into a spiralling dive, pinning Des Melaniphy to his seat with such force that he was in danger of blacking out, and unable to lift a hand to the hood-jettison trigger. By gripping his left elbow with his right hand he was able to force his fingers up to the face-blind and wrench it down. The seat smashed him head-first through the perspex canopy, gashing his skull and knocking him cold. He hurtled earthwards in the seat until, at 10,000 feet, Jimmy Martin's mechanical wizardry went to work: the drogue line of the stabilizer uncoupled from the seat, the harness sprang undone, another drogue

began to deploy the parachute, the unconscious man was tipped forward from the seat, and his parachute was opened fully. Of all this Des Melaniphy was unaware. Slipping in and out of consciousness, with blood running down his face, he drifted through cloud, vaguely aware that he was swinging beneath an opened parachute, but temporarily without any idea of how he came to be there. It all came back to him as they were putting twenty stitches into the back of his head in a Chelmsford hospital.

Much more was required of that 'mechanical wizardry'. The designers of escape systems were hard pressed to keep up with the rapid advances in aircraft performance. Higher altitudes and faster speeds placed constant demands on the 'seat' designers, and at the other extreme there was a need for escape at that time when an aircraft is most vulnerable — low and slow, taking off from a runway or the deck of a carrier. Aircraft design features such as higher tail units and lighter frames also influenced ejection technology.

The effect of ejection at supersonic speeds was first demonstrated in February 1955 when George F. Smith, test pilot for North American Aviation, blasted himself out of a F-100A with the controls locked in a vertical dive of almost 800 mph, at 6,500 feet: 'I don't remember actually pulling the trigger . . . the last thing I remember was seeing the Mach meter in front of my face, reading 1.05. I woke up in the hospital five days later,' he said.[10.]

What had happened was that George Smith had been ejected into an air blast that had the characteristics of a brick wall. That and the almost immediate and brutal opening of his 'chute smashed him into those five days of unconsciousness; stripped him of helmet, gloves, shoes and socks; ruptured his liver and lower intestine; pulled his knee joints loose; turned his whole body into one bruise; and blinded him for days. Yet he lived to fly again.

By 1959, such improvements had been made that when British test pilot Johnny Squire became the first to eject at over twice the speed of sound, he not only survived the 1,500 mph escape from his Lightning at 40,000 feet — he was able to spend two days and nights paddling his little one-man dinghy ashore in the Irish Channel.

These advances in ejection seat design had to be tested and approved before they were accepted into service. Benny Lynch and Larry Lambert had many brave successors. In England there were Squadron Leader John Fifield, 'Doddy' Hay, Jake McLoughlin, Arthur Harrison, Sidney Hughes; in France, Andre Allemand, Cartier, and Jacques Duborg. In America the task was undertaken primarily by the experienced jumpers of the military test-centres — men such as George Post who was involved in the early downward-ejection tests, and James Howell who was the first to live-test the supersonic ejection system.

The American test-jumpers were concerned not only with the proving of ejection systems, but also with investigating the full scope of survival by parachute, particularly at the higher altitudes. This work came to a climax with the stupendous leaps of Captain Joe Kittinger in 1959 and 1960.

On 19 September 1957, test pilot Kittinger had ejected successfully from a F-100C Super Sabre when it lost its hydraulics at 1,800 feet. He said of that bale-out:

> 'Never did I really question that the parachute would open, and bring me back to earth so that I would fly again. This is because of a heritage that I — and the many thousands of other military pilots who each day and night take to the skies — have been given. It is a precious thing; it is the knowledge that through the years dedicated and skilled men have risked their lives to give me the most reliable survival equipment, parachute and all the rest of it, that any pilot may have.'[11.]

In expressing the confidence that most aviators by that time had in their parachute and associated equipment, Joe Kittinger was paying tribute to the men that he was about to join, for in April 1958 he was appointed to Operation Excelsior. Its aim was to examine survivability at the very edge of Space. Kittinger had already been there. Suspended beneath a helium balloon in an eight-by-three space capsule he had been hoisted to 96,000 feet in 1956 to collect human data for America's 'Space Biology' programme. Provided with warmth, air, and pressure, man could go to that height — but could he come back down by parachute if he had to? Someone had to go up there and find out. With his previous high altitude experience, and already trained by Larry Lambert as a test parachutist, Joe Kittinger was the obvious choice. George Post was appointed as back-up jumper.

The jumps were to be made from an open gondola, using a parachute designed by test-jumper Frances Beaupre, who collated and added to existing technology to produce the Beaupre Multi-Stage Stabilization Parachute — a combination of timers and barometric triggers to operate a pilot chute, a stabilizing chute, and then the main canopy. Three jumps were planned. The first was almost the last.

When the parachutist rose to his feet at 76,000 feet in his bulky pressure suit and 150 lb of recording equipment, he inadvertently triggered the timer of his pilot chute, so that when he eventually plunged into space, the pilot and stabilizer deployed before his body had picked up sufficient speed for them to inflate fully. Instead of steadying his fall, the stabilizer wrapped itself round Kittinger's body and whipped him into a vicious flat spin as he hurtled through the air at 423 mph. He fought it desperately, trying to turn his body into the spin and kill it, but gradually the centrifugal force whirled the blood from his brain . . . When he recovered consciousness he was swinging down to the New Mexico desert under his reserve parachute. His barometrically operated main canopy had fouled the stabilizer. When his reserve had also been automatically deployed, its pilot chute had joined the threshing tangle of nylon, but Frances Beaupre had envisaged every conceivable hazard and had 'weakened' the pilot chute bridle-cord so that it would break if snagged, and allow the reserve canopy to burst into free air. His foresight — that of a practising parachutist — saved Joe Kittinger on Excelsior One.

Excelsior Two, from 76,400 feet, was fully successful. Then came the big one. On 16 August 1960, Joe Kittinger stepped from the open gondola 102,800 feet above New Mexico — nearly twenty miles high. The six-foot stabilizer held him steady in a face-down position, but only slightly retarded his rate of fall, which reached 614 mph at 90,000 feet, slowing as he dropped into thicker air. After falling for four-and-a-half minutes his standard twenty-eight foot canopy blossomed into life, and thirteen minutes and forty-five seconds after stepping out of his gondola he landed in the soft sand of the desert. No man has jumped from such heights before or since.

Nick Piantanida tried. He aimed not only to go higher than Joe Kittinger, but to dispense with a stabilizer. He would be the first free faller to break the sound barrier, for from his target height of 120,000 feet he would reach a maximum speed of 750 mph. With the backing of Pioneer Parachute Company and Jacques Istel's 'Parachutes Incorporated' the strato-jump project was launched in 1965. Three jumps from a balloon gondola were planned. The first ended when the balloon burst at 22,700 feet, and Nick Piantanida parachuted to safety onto the city dump of St Paul, Minnesota. In February 1955 he was carried to 120,500 feet and began his final preparations to jump. Almost his last action was to disconnect his main oxygen supply. It was frozen. He could do nothing to budge it. To sever the hose would have been instant death. He had no option but to ride the gondola down under its own parachute. On 6 May 1966 he made his third attempt. As he ascended through 57,000 feet, the listeners on his radio link heard a gushing sound and a choking cry, and immediately triggered the emergency release that brought the gondola swinging back to earth. Nick Piantanada was unconscious. The face shield had blown out of his pressure suit. He died four months later, without regaining consciousness.

As jet planes moved into the Mach-3 speed range, it became necessary to provide even greater protection for that 'weak-link' in the ejection system — the human body. The ultimate protection was for him never to leave the pressurized cocoon of his cockpit, but for it to be turned into a capsule that could be blasted away from the aircraft then lowered to earth under its own parachute. All the aviator had to do was trigger the sequence, then sit tight until the capsule was on the ground. Chief Warrant Officer Edward Murray was the first to live-test the concept when he was strapped into an aluminium capsule measuring five by two feet and successfully blown out of a B-58 Hustler in February 1962. When escape capsules came into USAF service, test pilot Al White was the first to save his life in one. In June 1966 he ejected from a triple-sonic XB-70 bomber at 25,000 feet over the Mojave Desert. His co-pilot Carl Cross failed to eject in time, and was killed in the aircraft.

The 'pilot escape module' of the F-111A swing-wing 'plane provided for both crewmen to be ejected in a single capsule that would be cut from the fuselage by linear charges, blown clear by 50,000 lb of rocket thrust, stabilized during its free fall, then lowered to earth under a barometrically operated seventy-foot canopy, with a shock-absorbing bag under the module to soften the impact. It first proved its value in 1967 when test pilot David Thigpen and engineer Max Gordon escaped in their module from an unco-operative F-111A at 27,000 feet.

When American fliers went to war in Vietnam, their retrieval after bale-out became an urgent requirement, and several means of snatching them to safety even before they landed were evolved. Charles Alexander, test-jumper for Pioneer Parachute Company, was the first live subject for mid-air recovery. At 8,000 feet a C-122 snatched a seventy-foot energy-absorbing line extended above his open canopy by an eleven-foot engagement 'chute, and winched him in over the tailgate.

Although the first generation of astronauts returned to earth beneath parachutes, they have not always qualified as 'caterpillars' in our sense, but their sighs of relief when those big 'chutes have unfurled above their falling capsules have echoed the sentiments of any sky person feeling the tug of an opening canopy. John Glenn, the first American in space, said it for all his successors as he emerged from the silence of re-entry after his three orbits to announce to his breath-holding listeners. 'Chute is out. In reef conditions at ten thousand eight hundred feet. Beautiful 'chute! 'Chute looks good . . . 'chute looks very good!'

The earliest Soviet cosmonauts in fact returned under man-carrying parachutes, and were expert jumpers, particularly Valery Bykovsky and Valentina Tereskhova of Vostok 5 and 6 respectively. American astronauts — in the tradition of most aviators who quite rightly scorn the idea of actually jumping when they don't have to — were not required to make training jumps, but gained canopy handling experience through 'parascending'. One who put the training to good use was our Korean War 'caterpillar' Neil Armstrong. On 6

May 1968 he was practising simulated lunar landings in the Lunar Landing Research Vehicle at Ellington Air Force Base when the machine tilted out of control only 200 feet above the ground. He ejected as it slid to 100 feet, and the Weber zero-altitude zero-speed seat went through its magic sequence to deposit him gently under a fully opened canopy, a few yards away from the burning wreckage of the LLRV. Parachutes were not taken to the moon the following year: no air.

Those men of the Pararescue Teams who backed up the space-capsule 'splash-down' deserve a mention in this chapter on aerial life saving. Their primary role is to bring immediate aid to downed aviators, or anyone else, in distress in remote areas. To do that they are prepared to jump and to survive in any conditions — arctic, desert, jungle, mountain or ocean. They are distant cousins of the early 'smoke-jumpers' trained in Russia and in America during the late 1930s, and they must be amongst the toughest and most dedicated of our sky people.

To those of us sitting here reading about the 'cater-pillars', it may seem that the modern automated escape systems have taken some of the glamour from baling out: not the same as Harold Harris clambering from the cockpit of his disintegrating Leoning, or of Charles Lindbergh coolly dropping from his mail 'plane over the dense blanket of fog. The fact is, of course, that only in retrospect and from a safe distance is there any 'glamour' in escaping from a doomed aircraft, whatever the means of doing so might be. A life-or-death situation is rarely fun at the time. It is afterwards that our 'caterpillar' can look back on the experience with that laconic understatement and that fatalistic sense of humour that has been the hall-mark of professional aviators since man first took to the air. The aeroplanes and the escape systems may have changed dramatically, but the 'caterpillar' hasn't. When Squadron Leader Bob Iveson baled out over Goose Green during the Falklands War in 1982, he wrote to the Caterpillar Club:

'I am writing to you in the hope that I am eligible to join the Caterpillar Club. I had the extremely annoying experience of being shot down in a Harrier GR3 during the battle of Goose Green on the 27 May. To add insult to injury I had the misfortune to land on the wrong side of the lines and thus have to wait a couple of days before being picked up and returned to HMS *Hermes*. I hope this unfortunate experience makes me eligible to join your club.'[12.]

It most certainly did.

CHAPTER FOUR
The Paratroopers

Christmas Eve, 1944. In the forested hills of the Ardennes, a battle weary Sergeant of an American armoured division that was reeling back before the ferocity of a German counter-offensive, halted his tank-destroyer beside a bunch of troopers who were digging foxholes in the frozen ground.

Eight days earlier, in a desperate endeavour to stem the advance of the Western Allies towards the borders of Germany itself, Hitler had launched eight Panzer divisions against the Americans in what was to become known as the 'Battle of the Bulge'. The Germans had smashed through weak and surprised defences to create a dangerous breach in the Allied lines and to open the way for their armoured columns to pour back across the Belgian plain towards Antwerp. Amongst the reinforcements that the Americans had flung into that breach were the 101st and the 82nd Airborne Divisions, and it was amongst men of the 82nd, digging in on the northern flank of the 'Bulge', that the Sergeant in his tank-destroyer now found himself. One of the paratroopers looked up at him, and asked:

'Are you looking for a safe place?'

'Yeah,' said the tanker.

'Well, buddy, just pull your vehicle behind me. I'm the 82nd Airborne and this is as far as the bastards are going.'

Well, it so happens that it *was* as far as the 'bastards' went, but that is not the point of the story. Although he was putting it in a way that was essentially American, that soldier was expressing the creed of paratroopers of any nationality. He was representing the supreme confidence and boldness of men who are not only prepared but expect to fight against great odds: and win. Men who consider themselves — and are considered by most others — to be a little special.

Are they . . . ?

Outflanking manoeuvres are as old as battle itself, but apart from devious measures such as tunnels and

Trojan Horses, they were for many centuries limited to right or left. Going over the top was confined to legend. Bellerophon, mounted upon the winged horse Pegasus, was nigh invincible until Zeus himself brought about his downfall. The Valkyries were airborne. And Eastern mythology in particular abounds with flying warriors.

When man himself eventually took to the air in the balloons of the late eighteenth century, the reality of assault from the sky came a little closer. Amongst the first to realise this potential for aerial outflanking was Benjamin Franklin who, as an American diplomat in Paris, had witnessed the earliest ascents of hot-air and hydrogen balloons. On 16 January 1784, he wrote to a friend:

> ' . . . it appears to be a Discovery of great importance, and one which may possibly give a new Turn to human Affairs. Convincing sovereigns of the Follies of Wars may perhaps be one Effect of it since it will be impracticable for the most potent of them to guard his Domains. Five Thousand Balloons capable of raising two Men each, would not cost more than Five ships of the line: And where is the Prince who can afford to cover his Country with troops for its Defence, as that Ten Thousand then descending from the Clouds, might not in many Places do an infinite deal of Mischief, before a Force could be brought together to repel them?'

A few years later, fanciful prints depicted the invasion of England by Napoleonic forces ferried across the Channel by huge balloons, carrying troops, horses and artillery. Apart from serving as an observation platform, however, the balloon did not live up to these early military expectations. Its lifting capacity remained limited, and it stubbornly resisted all endeavours to influence the direction of its flight by the use of oars, paddles, sails, and similar devices.

Even when imaginative minds saw the parachute as a potential means of delivering troops from the air, it was the inadequacy of the balloon as a means of transport that discouraged serious consideration. In April 1889, in Berlin, the American aeronaut Charles Leroux jumped at 3,000 feet from a balloon to demonstrate the parachute to military observers. General Graff Von Schlieffen, Chief of the General Staff remarked, 'If only one could steer the thing, [meaning the balloon] parachutes could provide a new means of exploiting surprise in war, as it would be quite feasible for a few men to wipe out an enemy headquarters.'

To become a viable means of transporting men into battle, the parachute needed the support not only of men of vision like Von Schlieffen: it also needed the aeroplane. By the later stages of the First World War, both were available. The aeroplane was the Handley Page 0/400 bomber. The new man of vision was General Billy Mitchell.

We have already seen that Mitchell, as head of America's Air Service in Europe, was a staunch supporter of the parachute as an aircrew lifesaver, and in 1918 he also recommended and planned its use for the delivery of combat troops. He made his proposal to General John Pershing, commanding the American Expeditionary Force, in October 1918:

'I proposed to him that in the Spring of 1919, he should assign one of the infantry divisions permanently to the Air Service; that we should arm the men with a great number of machine guns and train them to go over the front in our large airplanes, which would carry ten or fifteen of these soldiers. We would equip each man with a parachute, so that when we desired to make a rear attack on the enemy, we could carry these men over the lines and drop them off in parachutes behind the German position. They could assemble at a pre-arranged strong point, fortify it, and we could supply them by aircraft with food and ammunition. Our low flying attack aviation would then cover every road in their vicinity, both day and night, so as to prevent the Germans falling on them before they could thoroughly organize their support. Then we could attack the Germans from their rear, aided by an attack from our army on the front, and support the whole manoeuvre with our great air force.'[1]

This was more than just a vision. Mitchell had one of his staff officers, Lewis Brereton — who will re-appear on the airborne scene — prepare detailed plans for just such an aerial assault by men from the US 1st Infantry Division, who would jump with Guardian Angel parachutes from the giant Handley Page bombers, to

take the key city of Metz. Although he may have underestimated the practical problems that such a scheme would pose, Billy Mitchell's concept contained most of the ingredients of what we now recognise as a successful airborne operation: as much firepower as could be carried; concentration in an assembly area; resupply; close air support; association and eventual link-up with a major land attack; and, above all, boldness!

General Pershing was not too keen, and the war was in any case over within a month. As in much of his thinking, Billy Mitchell was ahead of his time. So was the Frenchman Captain Evrard, who also advocated mass assault by parachute, and who was also unheard. But Captain Evrard was one of the few who *did* parachute behind enemy lines — as a spy on the Western Front. These clandestine drops represent the first recorded use of parachutes in an 'airborne' role. The Italians were particularly active in this field. Lieutenants Tandura, Nicolso and Barnaba, and several consignments of carrier pigeons, were successfully parachuted behind the Austrian lines on the Piave front in mid-1918. The system for delivering these agents was devised by British fliers seconded to the Italian Army, Lieutenant Colonel W. Barker VC, and Captain Wedgewood Benn. There were many practical difficulties to overcome. They had, for example, to decide on an ideal dropping height:

'It is clear,' said Wedgewood Benn, 'that we are between two opposing difficulties: if you go high you cannot drop the man where he will be safe; if you go low there is a risk that the parachute will not open and your agent will be wasted.'[2]

Then there was the question as to exactly how the agent was to be dropped. The ingenious solution gives an insight into attitudes toward premeditated parachuting at that time:

'The last and chief difficulty was how to persuade the agent to drop at the right moment. I cannot conceive of anyone having sufficient self control to throw himself from a moving aeroplane. The solution was considerably to relieve him of the embarrassment of choice. We arranged that the agent should sit in a cockpit on a trap-door hinged at the sides and opening in the middle. This floor was held in place by bolts controlled by a rope connected with the observer's seat. The result was that it was the observer who decided when the bolt was to be drawn and the agent, waiting presumably with some qualms, at the right moment found himself suddenly with nothing under him and thus launched into the future. The performance, in fact, was similar in its mechanics to that carried out by Mr. Billington in the course of his lugubrious duties.'

Mr. Billington was Britain's public hangman.

A trial drop of a dummy from a three-engined Caproni biplane wrecked the propeller of the central 'pusher' and nearly ended in disaster. A twin engined Savoia Pomilio (SP4) was therefore converted for dropping. A Guardian Angel parachute, equipped with a black canopy, was attached to an iron frame that could be lowered after take-off to a position below the undercarriage. Several successful descents were made by a fully uniformed dummy called 'George'. With little required of the agent other than exceptional fortitude, it was not thought necessary to train him in the art of parachuting.

Dropping would have to be under cover of darkness, so a system of navigation by fixed searchlights on the Italian side of the lines was devised. It was also decided to carry two hand-thrown bombs to camouflage the real purpose of the flight. All was ready:

> 'They bring out Tandura, who kisses his commanding officer; sheds tears; is attached by a long rope to the parachute which is slung beneath the machine; is sat on his trap door; is instructed to fold his arms, this to prevent him gripping the sides of the aeroplane should he lose his nerve, and all is ready. "How do you feel, Tandura?" I shout. "*Benissimo*, Signor Capitano." These farewells are drowned as the engines are started up and the machine begins to rumble across the field . . .'

Flying through threatening clouds, taking their direction from the vertical searchlight beams, they crossed the Piave. Wedgewood Benn lowered the parachute on its iron frame:

> 'Barker is to make a signal to me with his foot when he is ready. I sit down on the two bombs, with my hand on the thick ash handle which by means of a long wire controls the bolt under Tandura's seat. Barker slightly stalls the machine, the foot presses, I pull, and wait. No jerk, no apparent result. The bolts have stuck! I pull again. The wire slacks with a rush, the machine shivers and resumes its course. For good or ill, Tandura is gone.'

Lieutenant Alessandrio Tandura survived the experience, completed his mission, and subsequently received The Gold Medal For Valour from the King of Italy. He surely deserved it.

What happened to the airborne concepts of Billy Mitchell and Captain Evrard after the war? Nothing.

It is not unusual for bright ideas conceived in wartime to be put on a shelf when peace returns. The inevitable reduction in military budgets has much to do with it, but perhaps amongst the victors there is also

some smug satisfaction with the methods and the weaponry that gained that victory, and a reluctance to embrace new concepts. So it was that when, in 1928, a group of enterprising US Army officers dropped a small party of troops from Ford Trimotor aircraft as part of a military display at Randolph Field, word soon came from the War Department: 'Stop that parachute nonsense before somebody is hurt.'

Similarly, when another forward thinking Air Corps Captain named George Kenney captured an 'enemy' headquarters during 1932 manoeuvres at Fort Du Pont by airlanding an infantry detachment behind the 'lines', this was considered by more traditional military minds to be cheating. Kenney, as we shall see, was not to lose his airborne enthusiasm.

In Britain at this time some recognition was being given to the concept of air mobility. The post-war Royal Air Force had found itself fighting for survival in the face of financial stringency, government indifference, and the hostility of the Army and the Royal Navy who wanted their own aeroplanes back. Only the determination and personal impact of Trenchard as Chief of the Air Staff had kept the infant alive. One of the justifications that he developed for the continuing existence of an independent air force was its role in 'air control' of Britain's overseas territories, particularly the Middle East and India. This concept incorporated air attack on dissidents, and the ability to move troops rapidly to and within theatres of operation. The dropping of supplies either free or by parachute also featured on a small scale during overseas operations, but this application of air mobility made no great impression on the military mind, and the dropping of troops by parachute was not contemplated by the British.

The first nation to consider seriously the delivery of troops by parachute and to develop the capacity to do so was Italy. In the post-war years the Italians showed considerable dash and initiative in their development of both civil and military aviation, and in General Alessandrio Guidoni, former air attaché in Washington and London, they had a keen advocate of airborne delivery. They had the Caproni CA73 biplane bomber that could be used for dropping paratroopers, and they had the 'Salvatore' parachute. By 1927 the 'Salvatore' had proved its value as a manually operated lifesaver for aircrew, but the Italians realized that manual operation was not ideal for the delivery of paratroopers. Manual operation required altitude, and the higher they opened their parachutes, the more vulnerable in the air and the more dispersed on the ground the troops would be. The alternative was instant and automatic operation by static line, and although this system had been largely discarded as inadvisable for escape from a crippled machine, it could be used from aircraft in slow and level flight — as demonstrated by the Italian agents in 1918. Another advantage of automatic operation was

Russian paratroopers of 1935 climb from the fuselage and tumble from the wing of a Tupolev bomber before pulling the ripcords of their manually operated 'chutes. (Photo: Imperial War Museum)

that little would be required of the paratrooper other than the courage to leap from a perfectly functioning aeroplane.

The model B 'Salvatore' produced in 1927 could be adapted to either manual or static-line operation. Using it in its latter mode, trials were carried out at a parachute training centre at Tarquinia, and the theories were successfully put to the test in the first recorded 'mass' drop of paratroopers, when forty soldiers parachuted from their Caproni bombers at Cinisello, near Milan, on 6 November 1927. Techniques for dropping men and materials were further developed, but these pioneering efforts received a major setback when General Guidoni was killed on 28 April 1928. Jumping from 3,000 feet above Monte Celio with the manually operated version of the 'Salvatore', he fell back-down from the aircraft, yanked the release lever immediately, and became fatally entangled in the deploying canopy and lines. Despite this loss, by 1939 Italy would be able to field two battalions of paratroopers, trained at their schools at Tarquinia, and Castel Benito in Tripoli.

Meanwhile, Russia too had taken to the parachute. With military traditions swept away with the Czarists, and less constrained by a need to justify military

expenditure to an electorate, the Bolshevik regime was eager to embrace new ideas. Such as the tank. Such as the parachute. When Lyman Ford demonstrated the Irving 'chute by jumping it in Moscow in 1926, the Russians immediately ordered an initial consignment, carried out trials, and then began to manufacture copies of the manually operated assembly. Although its primary role was as a lifesaver for aircrew, Russia already saw more aggressive potential in the parachute.

In 1928, Russian officers were at Randolph Field to watch that demonstration drop of troops by the US Army Air Corps. They were more impressed than the US War Department, for they offered $1,000 a month and a commission in the Red Air Force to one of the instigators of that display, an officer called Claire Chenault. He declined, later to gain fame as the leader of the 'Flying Tigers' in China's fight against Japan.

By 1930 the Russians were able to stage their own demonstration. During Red Army manoeuvres, a lieutenant and eight men were parachuted behind enemy lines to capture a corps commander. A total of 500 military jumps were recorded that year. In 1931 the Test Airborne Landing Detachment was formed in the Leningrad Military District for the purpose of developing airborne techniques, and also in that year a small party of troops was successfully parachuted into action against dissident Basmach tribesmen in Central Asia.

If Russia needed a military 'visionary' to promote airborne forces, it had it in its Chief of Staff, Marshal Tuchachevski. He was actively supported by the People's Commissar for Defence, Marshal Voroshilov, who introduced and encouraged parachuting as 'a sport for the masses'. Civilian parachute clubs were formed under the direction of 'Osoviakhim' — the Voluntary Society For Assistance To The Air Force And Chemical Defence. Parachute training towers for controlled descents sprouted throughout the Soviet Union. Parachuting was valued and sponsored both for its direct military potential and as a means of developing those personal and national qualities deemed desirable by the Soviet leadership: courage, resourcefulness, and a sense of unity.

The result of these developments was seen by world-wide cinema audiences in 1935 in a newsreel that showed a battalion-sized mass drop into that year's Red Army manoeuvres at Kiev. The paratroopers were still using their manually operated back-packs, now augmented with chest-type reserve 'chutes. The film that shows them clambering from hatches in the fuselages of the giant four-engined Tupolev bombers, then tumbling off the wings like insects being swept off a barn roof, has become a classic. 'Locust Warriors', they were called.

The following year, foreign military observers were invited to attend in person the autumn manoeuvres of the Moscow Military District. On this occasion they watched a full brigade — some 1,500 men — drop from 2,500 feet, to seize river crossings. This they did with apparent success and no visible casualties, though Major General Wavell as Britain's senior representative reported that it required an hour-and-a-half to assemble the force after the drop. He thought it to be an interesting spectacle, but of doubtful tactical value. In fact the general British reaction was that this was a pretty stupid way to go to war:

'We doubt', said *The Aeroplane* of 6 November, 'whether such tactics could be practised in a civilized army. They are probably only possible in a country like Russia where the people can be driven like cattle and imbued with fanatical ideas'. Oh dear . . . !

Other observers were more receptive. The French had already followed the Russian example in 1935 when an Air Force mission had gained the Russian diploma of 'instructor parachutist', and had then returned to France to form a parachute school at Avignon-Pujant under the direction of Capitaine Geille, using manually operated 'chutes. Another training centre was established at Bakari in Algeria, and by 1939 France had two companies of Air Force 'Infantry of the Air'.

Poland was another to follow Russia's example when it set up a training centre for parachute instructors at Jablonna near Warsaw. The centre was expanded and moved to Bydgoszcz where more extensive training began in 1939. Some of those trained in Poland were to fight in World War Two with the 1st Polish Independent Parachute Brigade, as part of the Allied airborne forces. Roumania also formed a parachute training school in 1937, near Bucharest.

But Russia's star pupils were the Germans. After World War One, the victorious nations had placed severe limitations on German military redevelopment. As one way to circumvent this embargo, Germany made a treaty with Russia which enabled it to attach liaison officers to the Russian Army and Air Force, and eventually to establish a flying school at the Russian base of Lipetz, where German aircrew were trained to combat standard. Thus even before the world wide publicity given in 1935 and 1936 to Russian airborne developments, Germany had noted and learned from these military initiatives. At the same time, within Germany itself, aviation skills were being encouraged through the seemingly innocent sport of gliding, and a force of transport aircraft was being built within the State owned airline, Lufthansa.

wing cantilever monoplane with its distinctive covering of 'corrugated' aluminium was for its day an ideal airborne workhorse. It was rugged, reliable, had side-door access and exit, and could carry eighteen troops or 10,000 lb of stores to a radius of 350 miles. Above all, it was available in large numbers. 'Auntie Ju', it was to be affectionately called by the troops who flew in it.

A parachute too was available. It was the first of the RZ series, a product of admiration for the Italian 'Salvatore' combined with meticulous trials at the Luftwaffe testing station in Rehlin, where technical expertise was backed by the practical know-how of test jumpers such as the veteran Richard Khonke and the younger Willi Buss. From the 'Salvatore' came the single-point suspension system and an improved harness, and out of Rehlin came the twenty-eight-foot circular canopy. The performance of the RZ1, particulary in terms of stability, was to be improved in subsequent models, culminating in 1943 in the RZ36 with its very stable triangular canopy. Also from the 'Salvatore' came the static-line operating system, for the Germans too saw major disadvantages in manual operation for paratroopers. The RZ1 opened with sufficient rapidity and reliability from the Ju 52 to encourage a drop height of no more than 400 feet above the ground.

Thus equipped, Major Immans and his fifteen instructors at Stendal quickly devised basic parachuting techniques and a system of instruction. Jumping from the door of the Ju 52 involved a spreadeagled dive, not unlike the full-spread of the modern free-fall parachutist. Performed well, it provided a stable platform for smooth deployment of the 'chute from its back-pack. Performed poorly, it was an invitation to streaming rigging lines to grasp an ankle. Under the canopy, suspended from a single point between his shoulder blades in a slight forward-lean, the paratrooper had no means of controlling his 'chute. All he could do was try, by a form of swimming motion, to swivel himself round to face in the direction of drift. If successful he would take the landing impact on both feet and transfer it into a dive forward-roll. If unsuccessful, it hurt. Knee pads were standard issue. Initially, no major items of equipment or weapons other than pistols were carried on the parachutist, but were dropped separately in containers.

Trainees were all volunteers. There was no shortage. Many units volunteered *en masse*. There was an insistence upon high levels of physical fitness, and the training was tough and selective. Intensive ground training in aircraft drills, the dive-exit, and landing techniques preceded the six jumps that were necessary to gain the coveted insignia of the diving eagle that identified the *Fallschirmjager*: the 'Hunter from the Sky'.

After a year, the equipment, techniques and training methods were well established, and training began in

Left: The airborne image was created by the elite 'Fallschirmjager' when they fell upon a startled Europe in 1940. This dive exit from the JU-52 was made at an altitude that would not appeal to today's jumper. (Photo: Imperial War Museum)

Above: German paratrooper with sub-machine gun ready for action as he descends under the single-point suspension of the RZ parachute. (Photo: Imperial War Museum)

In 1933, as Prussian Minister of the Interior, Hermann Goering ordered the formation of a special police parachute unit, ostensibly to act against communist organizations within Germany. When in 1935 Hitler threw aside all pretence and began overt military development, this small body was formally constituted as part of the Luftwaffe, and given the grandiose title of the General Goering Air Regiment. On 20 January 1936, Goering issued an Order of the Day which called for the formation of a parachute battalion, with a parachute training school to be established at Stendal, in north-west Germany.

The tools to forge this airborne force were already available. By 1936 the tri-motored Junkers 52 had exchanged its Lufthansa livery for warpaint. This low-

earnest. But what was this embryo force of paratroopers to be used for? And who would control it? The Army, or the Air Force?

The Army had rather vague ideas of using an airborne battalion in a rapid reinforcement role for ordinary ground operations. The Luftwaffe had a more original concept: it saw the parachute force as an extension of the bomber, to attack and demolish targets whose anti-aircraft defences precluded the presence of the bomber itself. It was a role that anticipated that of subsequent 'Special Forces', and was successfully demonstrated in 1937 manoeuvres. The Army and the Luftwaffe could not agree, and the SS were trying to get in on the parachuting act as well. To mould these independent and early efforts into a powerful and coherent force, that essential 'man of vision' was needed. He appeared on the airborne scene in 1938. His name was Kurt Student. He was to become the true father of German airborne forces and the instigator of classical airborne doctrines.

Kurt Student had begun his military career at the tender age of eleven as a cadet at the Military School at Potsdam. As a combat pilot in World War One he had downed five of the enemy and had risen to the command of Jasta 9 — a Fokker squadron on the Western Front. After that war he had been involved in Germany's 'secret' aviation training through its flying school at Lipetz and through its own gliding centres — where he fractured his skull in a gliding accident in 1921. He had witnessed the Russians' early use of parachutes in 1931, and had attended the display of mass dropping in 1936. In that year he had also visited Stendal in his position as Luftwaffe Inspector General of Flying Schools. On 4 July 1938 he was summoned by Goering, who instructed him to expand the existing airborne force to divisional strength, and to have it ready for operations against Czechoslovakia in September. The division was ready in time, but Germany marched unopposed into the Sudetenland, and the paratroopers were not needed.

Meanwhile, in addition to expanding and welding together existing airborne units to create the 7th Airborne Division, Student turned his mind to the role of this force. He saw airborne assault as a natural and valuable addition to Germany's military philosophy of *blitzkrieg* — a concept born of expansionist ambitions and the aggressive tendencies of Germany at that time. It envisaged surprise strikes by armoured columns with concentrated air support to break through or to bypass the old fashioned linear defences that blocked its borders. Student saw airborne assault — with its reach, its element of surprise, and its potentially devastating effect on enemy morale — as a means of extending and supporting *blitzkrieg*. His paratroopers, to be delivered either by glider or parachute, could penetrate deep into enemy territory to capture airfields, secure bridges, and destroy strong-points to ease the advance of the

Panzers. Operations could be independent of main ground force actions, or an integral part of them. Surprise, deception, initiative, flexibility, and above all the quality of his paratroopers — these were his weapons.

Although the paratrooper was no longer to be a mere extension of the bomber arm, Student recommended strongly that all airborne forces should be under Luftwaffe command. It was a far-sighted recommendation, eventually to be accepted by Hitler in 1939. In the early years of the war the German leader was to be a strong personal supporter of Student and his paratroopers. He saw in them the embodiment of German militarism, and personally approved the 'Ten Commandments' issued to this new force. They are worth repeating, for airborne soldiers the world over have since then subscribed to similar, although usually less eloquent and sometimes even unspoken, creeds of offensive spirit, initiative, comradeship and excellence:

1. You are the chosen fighting men of the Wehrmacht. You will seek combat and train yourselves to endure all tests. To you the battle shall be fulfilment.
2. Cultivate true comradeship, for by the aid of your comrades you will conquer or die.
3. Beware of loose talk. Be incorruptible. Men act while women chatter. Chatter may bring you to the grave.
4. Be calm and thoughtful; strong and resolute. Valour and the offensive spirit will cause you to succeed in the attack.
5. The most precious thing when in contact with the enemy is ammunition. He who fires uselessly, merely to assure himself, is a man of straw. He is a weakling who merits not the title of *Fallschirmjager*.
6. Never surrender. To you death or victory must be a point of honour.
7. You can win only if your weapons are in good order. Ensure that you abide by this rule — first my weapons and then myself.
8. You must grasp the full intention of every operation, so that if your leader is killed you can fulfil it yourself.
9. Against an open foe fight with chivalry, but to a guerrilla extend no quarter.
10. Keep your eyes wide open. Tune yourself to top condition. Be as agile as a greyhound, as tough as leather, as hard as Krupps steel: and so you shall be the German Warrior incarnate.

Voluntary entry, the rigorous and selective training, and the demands of the 'Ten Commandments' provided the ingredients of elitism. And it was early recognised that the act of parachuting itself added to the mystique of the paratrooper. Major Brauer, soon to lead his troops into combat, commented on 'the almost super-human sensation of the parachute jump,' and added:

'It alone compresses into the space of seconds feelings of concentrated energy, tenseness and abandon: it alone demands a continual and unconditional readiness to risk one's life. There-fore the parachutist experiences the most exalted feelings of which human beings are capable, namely that of victory over one's self.'

This exhilaration, this cockiness, this supreme self-assurance — it can be a formidable advantage in battle.

Within Germany the force was given much publicity on newsreel and in print. The inclusion of well known sportsmen, such as Max Schmelling, the heavyweight boxer, and many from the 1932 and 1936 Olympic teams, was not just due to their physical aptitude, but also because of the prestige they would bring to the force. When they went on leave, the young paratroopers were allowed to parachute into fields near their homes, to impress the folks. Even before being committed to battle, the diving eagle badge of the *Fallschirmjäger* had become a symbol of military excellence. How would it stand up to the test of combat?

At the outbreak of World War Two in September 1939, Kurt Student's 4,000 paratroopers of the 7th Air Division and 12,000 glider troops of the 22nd Infantry Division stood at readiness on Silesian airfields for operations against Poland, but so devastatingly swift was the advance of the Panzers that there was no call for airborne assault. Student, called to the Reichs-chancellery in October, was assured by Hilter that the day of the paratrooper would come soon — as the spearhead of the Western offensive.

During the winter of 1940 the paratroopers, with typical thoroughness, practised dropping on to snow-covered ground in sub-zero temperatures. On 9 April, they did it for real, but only in small numbers. In Norway, in support of major seaborne landings, just one company of paratroopers dropped on to Sola airfield at Stavanger. Within ten minutes they had overcome resistance and had secured the airfield for a follow up by air-landed troops. A similar drop on to Fornebu airfield outside Oslo was frustrated by fog, and the air-landed troops went in alone, fortunately against only light resistance. In Denmark, the airfield at Aalborg was taken by just one platoon of para-troopers, and within two hours was serving as a forward base for German fighters in support of the invasion of Norway. The fourth target was the Vordingborg bridge connecting Falster and Zeeland. Two platoons dropped simultaneously from their Ju 52s at a height of 400 feet, one platoon at each end of the bridge. Without pausing to collect their weapons from the containers that had been dropped with them, the troops stormed the defences armed only with pistols. So stunned were the

Danish troops that they surrendered without firing a shot. Such was the shock effect of assault from the sky.

Subsequent reinforcement drops into Norway were over-ambitious and sorely treated by the now alert Norwegians, but those early *coups-de-main* spread ripples of alarm through Germany's adversaries that were out of all proportion to the actual scale of the operations. Amongst the defenders of the West there was much looking over shoulders. Where would these 'Hunters From The Sky' next appear? They were soon to find out.

On 10 May 1940 Hitler launched his *blitzkrieg* against the West. An Army Group was to strike through the Ardennes towards the Somme, and another was to pierce the frontier defences and occupy Holland and Belgium. To support the latter, Student was tasked with the capture of bridges across the great rivers of the Low Countries; the destruction of strong points; and the seizure of airfields around The Hague and Rotterdam. One of the objectives of the assault on The Hague was to capture the Dutch Royal Family and heads of government.

Student's plan was a brilliantly conceived combination of *coup-de-main* and holding operations that would strike deep into the very heart of military and political resistance, and would also lay a carpet of softened defences and intact bridges for the advancing Panzers.

The airborne assaults began shortly after five o'clock on the morning of the 10th. Some were preceded by aerial bombardment, others were launched from quiet skies to achieve utter and devastating surprise, such as the glider assault on Fort Eben Emael. This fortified concentration of artillery that dominated the low-lying border country at the junction of the River Maas and the Albert Canal was thought to be impregnable: not, however, to the mere seventy paratroopers who swooped silently out of the dawn in nine DFS 230 gliders. Landing directly on top of the huge strong point, they used specially prepared hollow charges to blast holes through the six-foot-thick reinforced concrete, and rapidly neutralized the fort and its 1,200 defenders at a cost of six German lives.

Further west the paratroopers were spilling from their Junkers 52s from heights as low as 300 feet above the ground to take the bridges at Moerdijk and Dordrecht. Glider-borne troops seized those at Velchrezelt and Vroenhofen. On the outskirts of Rotterdam itself, a force of 120 men were landed on the Niewe Mass in twelve old Heinkel HE59 seaplanes. They swarmed on to the bridge, where they were soon reinforced by a party of fifty paratroopers who had jumped into a Rotterdam sports stadium, then commandeered trams to take them, with bells clanging, to their objective. Outside the city, paratroopers took the airfield at Waalhaven, but further north the drops onto the three airfields around The Hague were fiercely resisted, and the follow up air-landing ran into intense fire. Some of the Ju 52s landed instead on the beaches or on the Rotterdam-The Hague autobahn. Losses of men and aircraft were heavy, and the attack on The Hague was abandoned, but those who had landed provided an important barrier between their colleagues holding the bridges to the south and the Dutch reserves trying to get at them from the north.

Fighting became fierce as the Dutch recovered from their initial shock, and the lightly armed paratroopers were hard pressed to hold their positions until the arrival of the 9th Panzer Division in the outskirts of Rotterdam on 14 May. That evening, German bombers dealt the final crippling blow to the city, and Holland surrendered to the invaders as darkness fell. Two weeks later, Belgium followed suit.

It was a German victory in which Student's *Fallschirmjager* had played a significant part. In addition to the purely physical blows that the force had dealt, the psychological impact on the enemy had been devastating. It was as much the temporary paralysis of the defenders as the speed of the attackers that prevented the demolition charges on the bridges from being detonated in those first few vital minutes. Further afield, Dutch and Belgian troops fighting to stem the advance of the Panzers across their frontiers were sorely demoralized by the knowledge that the enemy was not only in front of them, but also behind them. The confusion and disruption caused by the paratroopers struck at the heart of military and political willpower, and in a way that had never been known before, they brought the horror of the battlefield into the very midst of the civilian population.

In that battle the mystique and the reputation that have attended the paratrooper to this day were first established.

In Germany the victorious *Fallschirmjager* were feted as heroes. In the minds of Germany's foes, they loomed like giants on dark horizons. As the French laid down their arms and the remnants of the British Expeditionary Force struggled home across the beaches of Dunkirk, England braced itself for invasion — an invasion, it was believed, that would surely be spearheaded by the dreaded paratroopers and their Schmeisser sub-machine guns. Rumour greatly enlarged the numbers, the deviousness, and the very stature of the German paratrooper. Reports that Germans had jumped into Holland in a variety of disguises were not entirely unfounded, for small numbers of SS troops had indeed attacked targets on the frontier dressed in civilian clothes and Belgian uniforms, but it was not a common practice and the threat was greatly exaggerated. A booklet entitled *The German Parachute Corps* by P. E. Popham, on sale to the public at sixpence, warned that German parachutists were likely to appear dressed as:

Parson: with machine gun under cloak and grenades in trouser pockets. Revolver carried in shoulder holster.

Postman: with collapsible bicycles and grenades and machine gun in postman's bag.

Butcher Boy: with machine gun and grenades in meat basket covered with white cloth.

Policeman: with machine gun under cloak. Grenades carried in pockets and on strap round waist. In some cases, grenades of small size carried under a peaked cap.

Girls: with grenades and bombs on the inside of skirts and in the tops of stockings.

Popham also reported that the paratrooper would be wearing springs on his boots. In absorbing the shock of landing they would bounce the parachutist back into the air and probably throw him on to his face, at which point he would be at his most vulnerable. This was seen as being just as well, for many of those preparing to receive him in the southern counties were armed only with pikes and pitchforks. All very funny now, those imagined disguises and sprung boots, but in that summer of 1940 it was deadly serious. Nor were these fears entirely groundless, for Hitler's plan for the invasion of Britain, Operation Sealion, did include airborne assault. In the absence of Student, who was recovering from a head wound sustained in the closing hours of the battle for Rotterdam, there were differences of opinion over the role of the paratroopers in Sealion, but it was eventually decided that airborne landings would be made to the west of Folkestone in support of the main seaborne invasion. As the Royal Air Force clung desperately to the skies over England during that late summer; as the British Army drew breath and new equipment; as the obvious landing grounds for gliders and paratroopers were sown with mines, poles and old motor cars, Hitler's chance slipped away. Had he bounced straight across the Channel immediately after reaching it, the *Fallschirmjager* might have contributed to another German victory.

Amongst those who were much impressed by Germany's airborne force was Winston Churchill, who always was one to admire military enterprise and offensive spirit, even when exercised by an enemy. He was thinking of hitting back at the Germans even as they were throwing us out of France, and on 6 June he wrote to the Joint Chiefs of Staff:

'The passive resistance war in which we have acquitted ourselves so well must come to an end. I look to the Joint Chiefs of Staff to propose me measures for a vigorous, enterprising and ceaseless offensive against the whole German occupied coastline.'

The Prime Minister mentioned paratroopers as one of these possible measures, and a 'hastener' to the Joint

The face of the paratrooper, after the German 'coup-de-main' at Eben Emael. (Photo: Imperial War Museum)

Chiefs on 22 June was more specific: 'We ought to have a corps of at least 5,000 parachute troops . . .' he wrote.

This may have been a far-sighted directive, but at a time when British commanders were greatly preoccupied with measures to counter the onslaught of a powerful foe, including his own paratroopers, it was not well received. And in any case, the services knew nothing about airborne troops, for hadn't the British in 1936 dismissed them as 'uncivilised'? The Royal Air Force in particular was reluctant to devote any of its limited resources to such a venture. Co-operation with the Army, which this would surely entail, had never been a popular role, But Churchill had spoken . . .

It was decided to form a unit to be called The Central Landing Establishment, to comprise parachuting, gliding, and technical development capabilities. It was to be sited at Manchester's civil airport at Ringway, not because this was in any way a suitable location, but because it was removed from possible enemy interference, and above all because the RAF didn't want it for anything else.

So it was that within six weeks of Churchill's directive, there arrived at Ringway two rather bemused officers, Major John Rock of the Royal Engineers, and Squadron Leader Louis Strange, a distinguished pilot from World War One. Their orders were to establish a parachute training centre. They had one thing in common: neither of them knew the first thing about parachuting.

A stick of early British paratroopers emplane in a Whitley at Ringway, for a drop onto Tatton Park in 1941. The RAF Warrant Officer on the right is pioneer Parachute Jumping Instructor Bill Brereton. The shorter of the two RAF officers is Flight Lieutenant Fielden, who had been a Circus flier before the War.
(Photo: Imperial War Museum)

The only parachuting expertise immediately available to them was amongst the staff of RAF Henlow's parachute section, whence came Flight Sergeant Bill Brereton and eight airmen in response to a hasty call for volunteers. From the Army came Sergeant Major Mansi and five NCOs of the Army Physical Training Corps. Also from Henlow came a consignment of Irvin twenty-eight-foot manually operated back-packs, the only training 'chute available. Begrudgingly, the RAF provided four Whitley bombers, from which the rear gun turrets were removed to create a small platform for a despatcher and a single parachutist. A convenient dropping zone was located at nearby Tatton Park, and local defence commanders were requested not to shoot at the parachutists who would soon be making their appearance there. On 9 July, before the 'instructors' had made any parachute jumps themselves, their first pupils arrived, men of 'B' and 'C' companies of No 2 Commando. All were volunteers.

On 13 July 1940, the first live descents were made at Tatton Park. They were 'pull off' jumps, made from that platform where the Whitley's rear turret had been. Captain M. A. Lindsay was one of the first:

'We climbed into the aircraft and sat on the floor of the fuselage. The engines roared and we took off. I noticed how moist the palms of my hands were. I remembered a man I met years ago in some bar; he told me he had once been paid a pound apiece by the Chilean Government for testing thirty parachutes. Not enough, I thought to myself at that moment, not nearly enough.

'It seemed an age, but it cannot have been more than ten minutes when the instructor beckoned to me. The Germans have a chucker-out in their aircraft for the encouragement of nervous recruits. Flight Sergeant Brereton, six foot two inches, would have made a good *Absetzer*. I began to make my way down the fuselage towards him, screwing myself up to do so. I crawled on my hands and knees into the rear-gunner's turret, the back of which had been removed. I tried not to overbalance and fall out, nor to look at the landscape speeding across below me as I turned to face forward again.

'I now found myself on a small platform about a foot square, at the very back of the plane, hanging on like grim death to the bar. The two rudders were a few feet away on either side of me; behind me was nothing whatsoever. As soon as I raised myself to full height, I found that I was to all purposes outside the plane, the slipstream of air in my face almost blowing me off. I quickly huddled up, my head bent down and pressed into the capacious bosom of the Flight Sergeant. He held up his hand for me to watch . . .

'The little light at the side changed from yellow to red. I was undeniably frightened, though at the same time filled with a fearful joy. The light changed to green and down fell his hand. I put my right hand across to the D ring in front of my left side and pulled sharply. A pause of nearly a second and then a jerk on each shoulder. I was whisked off backwards and swung through nearly 180 degrees, beneath the canopy and up the other side. But I was quite oblivious to this. I had something akin to a blackout. At any rate, the first thing I was conscious of after the jerk on my shoulders was to find myself, perhaps four seconds later, sitting up in my harness and floating down to earth. The only sensation I registered was one of utter astonishment at finding myself so suddenly in this remarkable and ridiculous position.

'I looked up and saw the silken canopy billowing in the air currents — a thing of beauty as the sun shone on and through it. I reached down and eased the harness straps from the more vulnerable parts of my body. I looked down, reflecting that this was certainly the second greatest thrill in a man's life. Suddenly I realised that the ground was coming up very rapidly. Before I knew what had happened I was sprawling on the ground, having taken a bump but no hurt. As I got to my feet, a feeling of exhilaration began to fill me.'[3]

A descent by Sergeant Johnny Dawes was not so straightforward. As he positioned himself on the platform, Flight Sergeant Brereton gave him some last minute instructions.

'Watch my hand,' he said, 'and when you see it fall, pull the handle upward and outward.'

'You mean like this?' said the Sergeant.

'Not now, you bloody fool!'

Too late. Johnny Dawes had gone. A search party found him three hours later and six miles from Tatton Park, hanging helplessly from a tree.

The 'pull-off' was suitable for single familiarization descents, but not for putting groups of men onto the ground. To achieve more speedy and controlled delivery, the central 'dustbin' turret that projected below the fuselage of the Whitley was converted into a form of funnel, three feet deep and thirty inches across. It became known simply as 'the hole'. Five jumpers forward and five aft of 'the hole' would shuffle towards it on their backsides and drop from alternate sides, their parachutes being automatically operated by a line attaching their ripcord handles to a strong-point in the aircraft. It was an awkward, uncomfortable and at times painful means of departure. The pain came from a tendency to smash one's face against the side of 'the hole' if one made anything but a perfectly upright, perfectly rigid exit. 'The Whitley Kiss', it was called. Or 'Ringing The Bell'.

On 25 July, the 136th jump was made by Driver Evans, seconded to the Commando from the Royal Army Service Corps. The ripcord was yanked free by the static line, but Driver Evans, beneath a streaming silk canopy and a tangle of rigging lines, hurtled to his death. Training ceased while the matter was investigated. It was thought that the cause lay in the deployment sequence of the manually operated 'chute, which had not been designed for this sort of usage. When the pins were pulled, the canopy was released before the rigging lines, and in the turbulent airflow beneath the Whitley fuselage, there was a danger of them becoming entangled. Raymond Quilter and James Gregory, who had previously worked on static line systems, offered their help, and when jumping recommenced three weeks later it was with a redesigned parachute. It still incorporated the Irvin twenty-eight-foot canopy, but this was now stowed in a GQ back-pack from which the rigging lines were drawn and fully extended by the weight of the falling parachutist before the canopy was pulled into the airflow. The ripcord had been replaced by an integral static line. With subsequent minor modifications this parachute became the 'X-type' which was to give British paratroopers good service throughout the war and for almost twenty years beyond it. Although much improved, the Ringway parachute was not perfect. It did not easily forgive a bad exit, which could throw an ankle into the deploying rigging lines, or cause them to twist, and if excessive and high, those twists in the lines could delay or even prevent the opening of the canopy. There was no reserve 'chute.

Some welcome parachuting expertise was added

to the instructional staff when former professional jumpers Bruce Williams, then Harry Ward and Bill Hire joined them. The inventive Bruce Williams devised training apparatus to simulate as closely as possible the exit from the aircraft, the descent under the parachute, and the landing. A landing technique of rolling the impact over the less vulnerable parts of the body was introduced. A packing room was provided, so that 'chutes no longer had to be packed in the dining hall between meals. But despite these improvements, the Whitley remained ill-suited to the task. The 'hole' become no more popular, and the method of exit encouraged parachute malfunctions. Trooper Watts fell to his death in August; Corporal Carter in November. Little wonder that of the 342 volunteers who were the first men to be accepted for training, thirty were unable to screw up the courage to launch themselves through that dreadful, roaring hole. But those who did, those who overcame those early difficulties and their natural fear of them, drew immense pride, confidence, and camaraderie from having done so. They were exceptionally brave men, those first paratroopers.

The original Commando trainees had been reformed as No. 11 Special Air Service Battalion. In January 1941 they were paraded at Ringway, and volunteers for a forthcoming 'raid' were called for. The whole battalion took one pace forward. Fifty were selected, to form 'X Troop', under Major T. A. G. Pritchard. The target chosen by the Ministry Of Defence was an aqueduct in the remote hills of southern Italy — not an ambitious target, but the object of Operation Colossus was to alarm the enemy rather than wreak physical havoc, and coincidentally to give the British something to cheer about in that bleak winter of 1941. To 'X Troop' was added an Italian interpreter, Signor Picchi, a patriot and former London hotel worker. A mock-up of the target area was constructed at Tatton Park, and 'X Troop' trained eagerly throughout January. A final rehearsal was carried out in high winds which drove several of the parachutists into tall trees, from which they were rescued by the local fire brigade. On 10 February, six Whitleys led by Wing Commander Tait flew into the night from Malta to launch Britain's first airborne operation. Five of the aircraft found the target and dropped the parachutists accurately, but the sixth delivered its men and supplies in the next valley, a good accuracy percentage, but unfortunately the off-target drop included the demolition experts and most of the explosives. The main party at the aqueduct were able to damage but not to demolish the structure. They then struck into the hills, seeking to reach the coast and their rendezvous with a British submarine. None of them made it. All were captured. Brave Signor Picchi — a

British paratroopers drop onto Salisbury Plain from a formation of Whitleys in 1942. In the left centre of the picture, one of the 'chutes has 'candled': there was no reserve parachute.
(Photo: Airborne Forces Museum)

worthy successor to those countrymen of his who had pioneered clandestine jumping on the Piave front in 1918 — was summarily executed.

Operation Colossus was not a military success, but it demonstrated a capability to strike deep and with commendable accuracy into enemy territory, and certainly achieved its aim of alarming the Italians, who diverted more troops to home defence than they otherwise would have done. The men who carried out that raid deserved a better target. They were a brave band — and a merry one, for the survivors of 'X Troop' and the men who flew them still meet each February to celebrate their jump into the hostile darkness above the Tragino Aqueduct.

Back at Ringway, the training and the development of airborne techniques and equipment continued. So did the apathy and the outright opposition within the Ministry of Defence, which had not been impressed by Colossus. Then, on a grey and windy Saturday in April 1941, Winston Churchill visited Ringway. Bowler hatted and well wrapped against the weather, he reviewed the total might of Britain's airborne forces. On the ground were some 400 paratroopers on parade, and six single-seat gliders well suited for sport flying. In the air, he saw five ancient Whitleys drop forty-four troops in a mock attack on the airfield. He might well have wondered where his 'force of 5,000' were. But if he was not pleased by the scale of what he saw, he was impressed by the enthusiasm and dedication of the men that he met. On 27 May he again wrote on the subject to the Chiefs of Staff:

> 'I feel myself greatly to blame for allowing myself to be overborne by the resistances which were offered in respect of raising 5,000 para-troops. One can see how wrongly based these resistances were . . . A whole year has been lost, and I now invite the Chiefs of Staff to make proposals for trying, so far as is possible, to repair the misfortune.'

It was not just his visit to Ringway that prompted this terse note. Shortly after that grey Saturday, the Germans had again and with even more devastating effect demonstrated the capability of airborne assault — in Crete.

A week after Churchill had watched five converted bombers demonstrate Britain's airborne strength, the Germans, smashing their way down through Greece and the Balkans, launched 270 Ju 52s to seize the bridge over the Corinth Canal by paratroop and glider-borne assault. This was but the prelude to Operation Mercury — the invasion of Crete. There, against a defensive force of some 40,000 British, Australian, New Zealand and Greek troops, Kurt Student threw half that number of lightly armed airborne men. He had air supremacy and the support of 500 transport aircraft and seventy-two gliders. His plan involved

preliminary 'softening' by air attack; initial assault by parachute and glider; follow-up by airlanded troops; and reinforcement by seaborne landings. The aerial armada was launched from airfields in Greece on the morning of 20 May. Major Von Der Heydte, an aristocrat and classical scholar, and now leading the 1st Battalion of Student's 3rd Parachute Regiment in its assault on the northern coast between Malame and Canea, tells how it was:

> 'I got up and moved towards the open door. Our plane was poised steady in the air, almost as though motionless. Looking out, beyond the silver-grey wing with its black cross markings, I could see our target — still small, like a cliff rising out of the sea to meet us — the island of Crete.

> 'Slowly, infinitely slowly, the minutes passed. Again and again I glanced stealthily at my wrist watch. There is nothing so awful, so exhausting, as this waiting for the moment of a jump . . . A strange unrest had also gripped most of those who were flying with me. Each man attempted to overcome it in his own manner. Some told each other jokes which they had heard a thousand times before, others talked of their plans for after the war, and two or three stared silently ahead as if all that was happening around them was no concern of theirs . . . Scarcely able to bear it any longer, I stepped once again to the open door. We were just flying over the open beaches. The thin strip of surf, which looked from above like a glittering white ribbon, separated the blue waters from the yellow-green of the shore. The mountains reared up before us, and the planes approaching them looked like giant birds approaching their eyries in the rocks.

> 'We were still running inland as though to run against a dark mountainside. It seemed almost as though we could touch the steep slopes upon which trees and solitary buildings appeared like toys. Then our left wing dipped and we swung away from the mountain and the plane started to circle; but soon we straightened out again, and at that moment there came the pilot's order, "Prepare to jump!"

> 'Everyone rose and started to fasten his hook to the cable which ran down the centre of the fuselage. Next came the order, "Ready to jump!"

> 'In two strides I was at the door, my men pressing close behind me, and grasped the supports on either side of it. The slipstream clutched at my cheeks. Below me was the village of Alikianou. I could see people in the streets staring up at us, others running away and disappearing into door-ways. The shadows of our planes swept like ghostly hands over the sun-drenched white houses. Our plane slowed down. The moment had come.

' "Go!"

'I pushed with hands and feet, throwing my arms forward as if trying to clutch the black cross on the wing. And then the slipstream caught me, and I was swirling through space with the air roaring in my ears. A sudden jerk upon the webbing, a pressure on the chest which knocked the breath out of my lungs, and then — I looked upwards and saw, spread above me, the wide open, motley hood of my parachute . . . To the right and left of me parachutes were hanging in the air — an infinite number of them, it seemed. And then I glanced downwards and received a shock that almost made my heart stop. It seemed that I was drifting with increasing speed towards a reservoir which lay below me like the open mouth of a beast of prey . . . I tried to conceive some means of escape. I tried to pray . . . Then suddenly there came a rough jerk. The drifting, the falling has ceased. I was down to earth again — or, at least, I was connected with the earth. My parachute had been caught in a fig tree growing beside the reservoir. I unbuttoned the harness, dropped, and found myself on solid ground again, all alive. Nothing else could happen to me now, I reckoned. Anyone could come and I would fight him and show him how strong I was and how much I treasured life . . .'[4]

Von Der Heydte and his 1st Battalion were lucky, for their landings were initially unopposed. On other drop zones, the paratroopers fell directly amongst the defenders who, when they had recovered from their immediate shock at seeing the sky suddenly full of parachutes and gliders, fought back fiercely. Many paratroopers died before they reached the ground. Along the northern coast between Malame and Heraklion a confused and piecemeal battle raged. By nightfall of the first day the Germans seemed to be pinned down. None of the three targeted airfields had fallen to them, but during that night the Allies made the fatal mistake of withdrawing from Hill 107 that commanded Malame airfield. The paratroopers occupied it unopposed. The news was radioed to Athens where Student — this time wisely directing operations from afar — took the opportunity to concentrate his reinforcements at Malame. Despite heavy losses from artillery and mortar fire, a constant stream of Ju 52s air-landed troops and supplies to consolidate the German foothold on the island. The tide of battle slowly turned as the Germans threw back Allied counter-attacks, then launched their own offensive against a dispirited enemy. Even the destruction of their seaborne reinforcements by the Royal Navy could not stop the Germans now. On the same day that Winston Churchill once more urged the development of an airborne force on his Chiefs Of Staff, General Freyburg, commanding the Allied forces on Crete, began to evacuate his men from the lost island.

The failure of the German seaborne reinforcement merely emphasised the completeness of the airborne triumph. It was a victory that owed much to air superiority, good communications, effective use of reserve forces by Student, and the unity of command that he enjoyed. But it had been a close thing, and the quality of his paratroopers and their determination to maintain the offensive, often against odds, was a decisive factor. Perhaps it had something to do with that feeling of invincibility that Von Der Heydte had himself experienced on landing in Crete, and that he ascribed to the act of parachuting itself:

'Psychologists may ponder whence that sense of power and courage is derived once a parachutist has gained *terra firma* after a successful jump. It is a sensation almost of intoxication. He feels himself a match for any man and ready to take on anything that comes along . . .'

Operation Mercury was the first major battle to be won entirely by airborne forces. It was a feat never to be repeated, but this was not known at the time, and the *Fallschirmjager* had the aura of invincibility about them: at least, in the eyes of the dismayed Allies, they did.

In response to Churchill's hectoring, it was decided in September 1941 that a full Parachute Brigade of four battalions was to be formed, with a further battalion to be raised in India. Volunteers between the ages of twenty-two and thirty-two were called for from all existing units. Of the hundreds who came forward, only the fittest and the best were accepted for training. It was a creaming-off of quality troops that naturally met with some resentment from the rest of the Army, and which furthered the elitism of the paratrooper. Command of what was to become the 1st Parachute Brigade was vested in Lieutenant Colonel Richard Gale — to become affectionately but quite inappropriately known as 'Windy' Gale throughout airborne forces. To the overall command of all British Airborne Forces, Winston Churchill personally appointed Major General 'Boy' Browning. This elegant Guards officer, who had served with distinction in World War One and was married to the author Daphne Du Maurier, fought for his paratroopers in the corridors of power just as fiercely as they were to fight on the battlefield. Against much opposition, particularly from the Air Ministry, he was to expand the British airborne force to a strength of two divisions.

At Ringway, the proposed expansion demanded a corresponding increase in the training capability. Louis Strange did not remain to see it happen. His policy of doing things and then — if at all — seeking permission, had established a parachute school in the face of great difficulties but had not endeared him to higher authority. He was moved on to apply this talent for achieving the improbable to the formation from scratch of another unit — for training Hurricane pilots to be catapulted from merchant ships at sea! To Louis Strange must go the credit for laying the foundations of British military parachute training. Command of the parachute training unit passed to Wing Commander Maurice Newnham, and under his prompting, that training became the sole responsibility of the Royal Air Force, who put it into the hands of its Physical Fitness Branch. The Army instructors who had given such fine service during the first and formative year now withdrew to run the 'pre-para' training of prospective para-troopers, and the hard-core of RAF instructors were joined by the thirty-five Physical Training Instructors who survived a two-week course and Newnham's rigorous scrutiny.

Amongst the 'new boys' who came to Ringway in October 1941 was Squadron Leader John Callastius Kilkenny, known ever since as 'JCK'. He was charged with the development of a syllabus and methods of ground training that would prepare men for the parachuting phase of their course. JCK had no previous parachuting experience, but he had the professionalism of a trained teacher, the physical skills of an outstanding sportsman, an analytical mind, and a great deal of Yorkshire grit. Thus equipped, he refined the previous syllabus to produce a parachute training system which remains largely unchanged to this day. It was based on structured progression; frequent repetition of basic skills that had to become automatic if they were to be performed under the stress of actual parachuting; emphasis on safety; and a teaching approach that was one of personal example and polite but firm persuasion. He allocated ten men — one Whitley load — to one instructor, and the bond between the PJI and his section was to become one of the strengths of the training system.

JCK's ground training programme led naturally into the parachuting phase of the course, which now commenced with two jumps from a cage suspended beneath the belly of a captive barrage balloon. The balloon had made its appearance at Tatton Park in the previous April, to provide a reasonably safe but frightfully cold-blooded introduction to parachuting. Group Captain Maurice Newnham recalls his first descent:

'The monotonous wracking noise of the winch as it paid out the cable had suddenly stopped, causing a sharp fleeting sense of panic and now an uncanny quiet prevailed which was fraught with an almost unimaginable tenseness. And, as I sat and watched the great bulk of the balloon above me trim itself like a giant weathercock so that it flew head into the wind, I fervently hoped that

the emotions so taut within me did not reveal themselves to my companions.

'I had had no preparatory training, partly because I disliked physical jerks almost more than the prospect of a parachute jump and partly because Bill Hire — who gave me five minutes' verbal coaching and lent me his plimsolls — said that if I chose a calm day I should be all right.

'In deference, I suppose, to my position as newly appointed Commanding Officer of the School, the instructor in the balloon car had modified the staccato order "Go" which was normally required to despatch pupils on their earthward journey, to a quiet and friendly intimation that all reasonable precautions had been taken to ensure that my parachute would work. "Go when you're ready", he said, and I thought cynically and desperately that I should never be ready. . .

'To my eternal relief, mind had gained sufficient mastery over matter to make my reluctant and personally highly valued body voluntarily throw itself into space with what seemed to be a very inadequate means of support. Rock had told me that jumping from a balloon was exactly like committing suicide with a strong possibility — which you seriously doubted — that your attempt might fail. Evidently, in my case, the attempt hadn't failed, for here was no gentle floating down to earth but a horrid violent rush which a strange feeling in my stomach assured me was no ordinary matter. Suddenly I realised that someone was shouting at me. I opened my eyes and found myself rapidly approaching the ground with the parachute now wide open and apparently per-forming the function for which it was intended. I hit the ground with a bump which rattled every bone in my body.

'In a moment or two I looked up to see Bill Hire grinning broadly and asking me what I thought of it. "Words fail me", I replied . . .'[5]

On 1 November, with the Parachute Training School now established under RAF control, the new instructors and JCK's syllabus went to work. Parachuting remained a hazardous and frightening activity, but now the hazards were reduced by the more thorough prep-aration, and the fear was lessened by increasing knowledge and by the example and attitude of the new instructional staff. That 'hole' in the floor of the Whitley was still as uninviting as a coal-chute, but as they rattled back to Ringway in the trucks from Tatton Park, the trainees could now sing:

When first I came to PTS my CO he advised,
'Take lots and lots of underwear. You'll need it I surmise.'

The airborne image was fortified by the gallant action of the 'Red Devils' at Arnhem, some of whom are pictured here during the flight to the dropping zones. (Photo: Imperial War Museum) (page 119)

But I replied 'By gad Sir, whatever may befall,
I'll always keep my trousers clean when jumping
through the hole.'

I went into the hangar, instructor by my side,
And on Kilkenny's circus had many a glorious
ride.
'On these ingenious gadgets,' he said, 'soon you'll
learn to fall
And keep your feet together when jumping
through the hole.'

One morning very early, damp and cold and dark,
They took me in a five-ton truck to a place called
Tatton Park.
In keeping with the weather I announced to one
and all
'I take a dim and misty view of jumping through
the hole.'

They fitted me with parachute and helmet for my
head.
The Sergeant looked with expert eyes, 'They fit
you fine,' he said.

'I'll introduce you now to Bessie — that is what
we call
The balloon from which you soon will be jumping
through the hole.
'Okay, up to six hundred, four to drop!' said he.
'Four to drop! Good God!' I cried, 'And one of
them is me!'
Then clinging very grimly to the handles in the
floor
I cursed the day I'd volunteered for jumping
through the hole.

The Sergeant told a story, but I couldn't see the
joke.
In fact I didn't think he was a very funny bloke,
But when he shouted 'Action Stations!', when he
shouted 'GO!',
I simply couldn't stop myself from jumping
through the hole.
I hit my pack, I rang the bell, I twisted twenty
times
Got both my feet entangled in the rigging lines,
But floating upside down to earth I didn't mind at
all,
For I had kept my trousers clean when jumping
through the hole.

On 27 February 1942, Major John Frost and 120 men of C Company of the 2nd Parachute Battalion 'jumped through the hole' in a daring night drop onto the French coast at Bruneval, near Le Havre. The aim was to gain access to, examine, and obtain key parts of one of a chain of new German radar installations. The German garrison was totally surprised and overwhelmed; Flight Sergeant Cox, the radar expert specially trained for the operation, was able to examine and dismantle the equipment; and the force was evacuated from the nearby beach by a Naval flotilla. It was a classic *coup-de-main*: a victory not just for the men of C Company, but also for the small but growing band of those with faith in the airborne concept.

The performance of the German paratroopers in Crete also had significant influence on the development of what was to become the largest airborne force of World War Two — that of the USA.

During the 1930s the Americans had shared Britain's indifference towards the airborne concept. In 1939, however, as the USA began at last to modernize and expand its armed forces, the US Army undertook an appraisal of 'air infantry', which concluded that certain tasks could be undertaken by infantrymen landed by aircraft or parachute, and which recommended practical trials. No action was taken until prompted by the outbreak of war in Europe and in particular by the report that the Russians had dropped small parties of paratroopers near Petsamo in their invasion of Finland. The air infantry project was taken off the shelf and put into the hands of Major William Lee. All new-born paratroop forces need a 'father' to guide them through their growing pains, and to persuade others that they should be allowed to grow at all. Germany had Kurt Student. Britain had 'Boy' Browning. The USA had 'Bill' Lee.

In early 1940 his first task was to find a parachute that would 'allow an armed infantryman to debark from an aeroplane at altitudes ranging between 300 and 500 feet'. There wasn't one. Manual operation was ruled out by the low altitude requirement, and there was no static-line operated 'chute readily available. Air Corps technicians at Wright Field took another look at the 'chute that Charlie Broadwick had offered to the Army in 1914, and at Leslie Irvin's 1918 design for a statichute. The outcome was the T-4 parachute. It was a static-line operated back-pack with a twenty-eight-foot canopy. Unlike the British 'X' type, the canopy deployed before the rigging lines, which gave a fierce opening jolt. However, the American paratrooper was to have the comfort of a manually operated reserve 'chute on his chest.

In June 1940, Bill Lee called for volunteers from the 29th Infantry Battalion to form a Parachute Test Platoon. He stressed the high risks that would be involved, and underlined them by insisting that all volunteers be unmarried. There is something in man's nature that responds to such challenge. Two hundred volunteered: forty-eight were accepted, led by Lieutenant William T. Ryder. To train them in the basic techniques of parachuting, Bill Lee brought in experienced Air Corps jumper Warrant Officer 'Tug' Wilson, and three other rigger/parachutists from Wright Field. An eight-week programme of physical training, parachute packing, preparatory ground training, flying experience and actual jumping was devised. It included a visit to Highstown, New Jersey, to train on and evaluate the 'parachute towers' of the Safe Parachute Company. Copied from the Russian towers in the 1930s, one tower provided controlled descents, the other hoisted the parachutist under an opened canopy to 100 feet, then released him for a 'free' descent. Similar towers were later to feature at Fort Benning's training school. The team made fifteen tower jumps each, then went back to Lawson Field for the real thing.

No 'hole' for the United States troopers. They had the relative comfort of a C-33, with real seats and a side door for exit. Lieutenant Ryder was the first to jump:

'About five mintues from the field "Tug" called me to the door. I stood up, hooked up, checked equipment, and, on "Tug's" order took the prescribed position in the door. I felt the prop blast rushing past, tugging at my coveralls and flattening my helmet against my cheek. Looking ahead I saw the red ground panels and felt the adrenalin rise as I awaited "Tug's" shouted "Go" and the whack on the behind that were the exit commands.

'When they came I leapt out, felt the prop blast full at my rear, and began my count. Before I completed two thousand I felt that violent but welcome opening shock; glanced up and saw my opened 'chute. It's difficult to do justice to the elation one feels the first time one looks up into a fully deployed canopy and down towards the silent and seemingly unmoving earth beneath one's feet.'[6]

The man who should have jumped next never did feel that 'elation'. The previous evening he had won the draw for the honour of becoming the first enlisted man to jump. Others had tried to buy the Number One ticket from him. Bids rose to $50. He turned them all down. The honour was to be his. But standing in that open doorway, the slipstream tugging at the flesh on his face as he looked at the moving earth 1,500 feet below, he froze. He couldn't do it. 'Refusal' to jump sometimes comes from the subconscious. Mind wants to go. Pride wants to go. But the body itself says 'Don't be bloody stupid!' and refuses to move. It doesn't happen often, but it happened to Number One, so the first enlisted infantryman to become a military parachutist in the USA was the man behind him, Private 'Red' King.

US Airborne troops of the 503rd Parachute Infantry Regiment drop onto Neomfoor Island during a series of imaginative and successful operations in the Pacific in 1944. (page 123)

The following day a new jump rule appeared, and is still in force: when standing in the door, look straight ahead at the horizon, and never look down. Another refinement to technique came when Private Adams was knocked unconscious in the slipstream by a connector-link that cracked him on the head as the rigging lines deployed. New lesson: tuck your chin in and keep your head down when you jump. Trial and error — that is the way that most parachuting techniques are learned and polished.

On 29 August the platoon made a demonstration jump and mock attack on Lawson Field. It was a 'mass' drop from three aircraft, and right on target — except for Private Leo Brown who, as the lightest man in the platoon, was drifted off the airfield to land unhurt on a hangar roof. South American military observers were reported to be much impressed by a degree of dropping accuracy that could actually land an attacker on top of a building. The Parachute Test Platoon had done its job of evaluating parachuting techniques, equipment, and training methods, and the entire platoon was re-assigned to form the nucleus of the USA's first airborne unit — the 501st Parachute Infantry Unit.

In 1941, with the training of three more battalions envisaged, an independent parachute training school was established at Fort Benning. Above its entrance were and still are the words:

> 'Though these portals pass the toughest para-troopers in the world.'

Well, there would be some who would disagree with that. But certainly not at Fort Benning, for toughness of body and spirit was at the heart of the American parachute training system. The hard physical demands of that training; the punitive discipline; the constant haranguing by the instructors; the chanting and the drilled, shouted responses — they were all designed to that end. And the push-ups — always the push-ups! 'Gimme twenty!' began with the Test Platoon and still echoes around Fort Benning today. It wouldn't have gone down well at Ringway. It wouldn't have suited the *Fallschirmjager*. But it worked for the Americans, for parachute training systems reflect national characteristics, and the end product is the same, however it is achieved: tough men, embued with that essential belief that there are none better.

As in Britain, the development of a United States airborne force received a major boost from the success of Student's paratroopers in Crete. The training of new battalions was hastened, and when the USA itself eventually went to war after the Japanese attack on Pearl Harbor on 7 December 1941, the airborne capability grew to two Divisions within a year — the 82nd and the 101st. There remained some uncertainty in Washington over the role of these Divisions. Many still saw them as no more than mobile infantry, whilst those with more imagination and a knowledge of German usage and British development — such as Bill Lee — envisaged more specific tasks ahead. Unfortunately, it was with the role of airborne forces still unidentified and little understood by more senior commanders that the British and American para-troopers were committed to the first of their joint operations.

The Allied invasion of North Africa in late 1942 aimed to block the German retreat from the British 8th Army offensive in the Western Desert. It was predominantly a seaborne invasion, supported by airborne forces. The targets assigned to the para-troopers were poorly selected and unworthy of the effort, and the planning by staffs with no experience of airborne operations was woefully inadequate. With great optimism and little sense, the Americans launched their first assault from airfields in England, with the result that little more than half of the battalion arrived for the attack on the airfield at Tafaraoui. It didn't matter, for US ground forces were already there. The 3rd Battalion of the British 1st Parachute Brigade also dropped unopposed onto the airfield at Bone, but the rock-hard ground took a heavy toll. One officer remained unconscious for several days, stirring occasionally to mutter, 'I'll have a little more of the turbot, waiter.' The 1st and 2nd Battalions, transported to Algeria by sea, subsequently dropped at Souk el Arba and Oudna, but again both operations were poorly conceived and planned, with vague and quite unworthy objectives. Through no fault of the paratroopers themselves, airborne operations contributed little to the battle in North Africa. But the paratroopers made their mark as superb fighting men. Used for five months in a pure infantry role, men of the 1st Parachute Brigade had conferred upon them by an impressed enemy the title of *Die Roten Teufeln* — 'The Red Devils' — either from their red berets or from the red dust of the Tamera Valley where they fought with such distinction against great odds.

The men of the 1st Parachute Brigade were not in fact the first British troops to jump into action in the North African campaign. The previous year, a young officer of the Scots Guards called David Stirling had conceived and formed a small unit for the purpose of carrying out deep penetration raids on enemy targets along the North African coast: it was the birth of the Special Air Service. 'Acquiring' fifty 'X-type' parachutes which were passing through Alexandria on their way to India, Stirling and his small band of adventurers undertook their own parachute training. The first descents were made near Mersah Matruh from an old Valentia biplane, with the static lines tied to its seats. When training began in earnest at Kabrit it was still without the benefit of any parachuting expertise, and in the first day of jumping two men fell to their deaths when their static lines became unclipped from the strong point within the Bombay aircraft now being used. The equipment was modified, and when training recommenced, Stirling was the first to jump. Then on 16 November 1941 he led his men on their first operational drop. In the Tobruk area, sixty-six men jumped at night onto rocky ground in a sandstorm and a 45 mph gale. Only twenty-two of them reached the rendezvous with the Long Range Desert Group. Stirling chose to go overland for his subsequent and highly successful raids in North Africa, but the parachute was later to transport a much expanded Special Air Service on its clandestine missions into Europe.

When the Axis forces had been driven from North Africa, the Allies turned their attention to the invasion of Sicily. At least they got the airborne concept right this time. Larger airborne formations were to be used in direct support of two main amphibious landings. The British 1st Airborne Division was to seize and hold key bridges ahead of the advance of the 8th Army, and the 82nd Airborne Division was to block enemy counter attacks on the US beach-head. The idea was sound: it was in the planning and the actual delivery of the troops that it all went badly wrong. There were differences of opinion and some friction within the joint planning staffs, and a failure to take advice on airborne tactics from those best qualified to give it. The crews of the USAAF Troop Carrier Command which was to lift both Divisions into battle were poorly prepared. The outcome bordered on disaster.

Of the 3,400 American paratroopers who flew from Tunisia in 226 Dakotas on the night of 9 July 1942, only some 200 were dropped on target. The remainder were scattered throughout southern Sicily, as far as sixty miles from their drop zones. At the same time, Britain's 1st Airlanding Brigade in 144 Waco and Horsa gliders was also falling victim to poor navigation by the USAAF crews, compounded by a fierce barrage of anti-aircraft fire from our own ships. Seventy-five gliders were released far out at sea, drowning 600 men. The remainder were dispersed along the south-east coast of the island, few where they should have been. The following night, an attempt to reinforce the Americans with a further 2,000 paratroopers again came under intense fire from 'friendly' guns, and dropping was once more widely scattered. On 13 July, the British 1st Parachute Brigade joined the battle, and suffered the same treatment. Of their 116 aircraft, twenty-nine failed to drop at all, and only thirty-nine dropped their men on or within half a mile of the drop zones. In one of these, Colonel Alistair Pearson, commanding the 1st Battalion, took his pistol to the pilot to persuade him to head through the flak towards the target.

Winner of four DSOs, Alistair Pearson was one of the greatest airborne warriors of World War Two, and amongst the chaos of the Sicily landings it was quality such as his that averted total disaster. In the American sector the men of the 82nd gathered into small groups and fought fiercely where they had landed, against an enemy who was even more bemused than they. To the east of them, the British glider troops who reached their target took the Ponte Grande Bridge but were too few in numbers to hold it against Italian counter attack. A similarly depleted 1st Parachute Brigade took the Primasole Bridge, lost it, then retook it in some of the fiercest fighting of the Sicily operation — fiercest because it was paratrooper against paratrooper, 'Red Devil' against *Fallschirmjager*. As the British paratroopers were being strewn over south eastern Sicily, men of the 1st German Parachute Division were being dropped to reinforce Catania. In the darkness of one drop area, a British paratrooper came across another shadowy figure who asked '*Wohin sei mein Schmeisser?*' then faded away into the night. Perhaps they met again later in the epic battle for the Primasole Bridge.

Although in Sicily the fighting quality of the paratroopers made up to some extent for the enormous deficiencies in planning and dropping, those major shortcomings threw the whole future of airborne forces into question, particularly in Washington. General Eisenhower ordered a full enquiry. General Joseph M. Swing who presided over the enquiry concluded that airborne forces did have a part to play, provided that they were given realistic tasks, adequate support, and proper training.

Since 1941, the balloon has provided a cheap but not always popular method of introducing British airborne trainees to parachuting. These 1959 RAF pupils approach the 'cage' with some dread before being hoisted to 800 feet for their first descent at RAF Abingdon.

The next major 'task' took these considerations into account. It was the Allied invasion of Europe — Operation Overlord. By early 1944 Britain had raised another Airborne Division, and the US had two stationed in England, the 82nd and the 101st. There still remained differences of opinion as to what to do with this force. The American airborne enthusiasts favoured a deep penetration by four Divisions to establish an airhead between Paris and the invasion beaches of Normandy. At the other extreme, Eisenhower's air commander, Air Chief Marshal Leigh-Mallory, forecast eighty per cent casualties and advised against any large-scale airborne operations at all. Eisenhower took the middle road and agreed to airborne landings in strength to protect the flanks of the seaborne assault. General 'Windy' Gale's 6th Airborne Division was to seize vital bridges and destroy selected strongpoints on the British left flank, whilst the American 82nd and 101st created a defensive block on the American right. Paratroopers and Glider borne forces would land at night, guided to the drop zones by pre-landed Pathfinder groups, and in advance of the main dawn assault across the beaches. The paratroopers emplaned on the late evening of 5th June 1944. A trooper of the 82nd wrote:

> 'We all pushed and tugged each other into the "ship" and settled down with the least amount of discomfort possible under the circumstances. Butterflies held a rally in my stomach as I heard the whine of the starter winding up; a few throaty coughs as the engine caught and finally roared into a full crescendo. We idled down the taxi strip, tested the engines, and started down the runway for a one-way ride.'[7.]

The Americans were brought to their feet and ordered to hook up as they crossed the French coast and the flak began to search for them. It was a long wait. A reporter who flew with the 101st wrote a heart-touching account of how those tough paratroopers knelt together in prayer on the run-in to the drop zones. They weren't praying. They were kneeling on the floor to rest their heavy equipment containers on the seats. Another trooper told how it really was:

> 'The plane rose and fell under the impact of bursting anti-aircraft shells. Sometimes it felt as though a giant hand had slapped the ship sideways. I was standing near the open door of the plane and could see the tracers, flak bursts and what appeared to be rockets screaming up through the black night. A quick ticking sound as a string of machine gun bullets walked a fast line of holes across our left wing. Large pieces of flak chunked through the ship every once in a while, but there seemed to be constant pinging of smaller pieces . . .

> 'We had our static lines hooked to the anchor cable and were hanging onto them for support in the bouncing ship. Suddenly the green light flashed on.

> ' "Let's go!" screamed Lieutenant Muir at the top of his voice, and he gave the big bundle a shove. Lieutenant Muir followed it out; Carter did a quick left turn and followed him into the prop blast . . . I could see their static lines snap tight against the edge of the door and vibrate there with the force of the outside wind pulling on them . . . Everything seemed to be happening in slow motion, but I knew it was really happening in just fractions of seconds as I made my right turn into the door and leaped into dark space.

> 'Doubled up and grasping my reserve 'chute, I could feel the rush of air, hear the crackling of the canopy as it unfurled, followed by the sizzling suspension lines, then the connector links whistling past the back of my helmet. Instinctively the muscles of my body tensed for the opening shock, which nearly unjointed me when the canopy blasted open. I pulled the risers apart to check the canopy, and saw tracers passing through it; at the same moment I hit the ground and came in backwards so hard that I was momentarily stunned . . .

> 'More planes went over, but they were flying so low, fast, and scattered that it was impossible to orient myself with their direction. I would have to play this one by instinct. In fact all the troopers would have to do it this way. We were so widely scattered that all the months of practised assemblies in the dark were shot in the ass . . .'[8.]

They were shot in the ass all right. The two American Divisions had been spread over an area some twenty miles wide. Gathering into small groups, they fought isolated and unplanned minor battles that sowed immense confusion and alarm amongst the foe. By dawn, most were well on their way to achieving their assigned objectives, despite the poor dropping.

And what of the British on the left flank? The 6th Airborne Division had been dropped by their more experienced RAF crews at least close to, if not always on, their drop zones. Achieving total surprise, glider-borne troops seized vital bridges over the Caen Canal and the River Orne and held them until reinforced by paratroopers and eventually by the main ground forces advancing from the beaches. Paratroopers destroyed other bridges over the River Dives, then fought a fine holding and harrassing action against heavy German forces trying to reach the beach-head. At Merville, the 9th Battalion carried out a classic *coup-de-main* by glider and parachute to silence the heavy guns that covered the eastern invasion beaches. The 750 men of the battalion were well scattered. Only 150 of them

The fighting qualities of the paratrooper were effectively demonstrated by the 1st Airborne Division in the battle of Arnhem. (Photo: No.1 P.T.S.)

could be mustered for the final assault on the strongly defended position. Of those, only sixty-five survived. But the Merville Battery was taken.

'What you get by stealth and guts you must hold with skill and determination', 'Windy' Gale had told his commanders at their final briefing before the battle. That was exactly what his paratroopers — and their American colleagues of the 82nd and 101st — did in Normandy.

Then came Arnhem.

The epic struggle for the Bridge at Arnhem is perhaps the best known of all airborne battles. Even though it ended with the defeat and virtual destruction of Britain's 1st Airborne Division, it has attracted greater renown to the paratrooper than has many a successful action, purely through the heroic nature of his fight against great odds.

Arnhem was one part of Operation Market Garden. Just as Kurt Student in 1941 had laid an 'airborne carpet' across the Low Countries for the advance of the German Panzers, so in 1944 General Montgomery planned to lay his own 'carpet' across the great

waterways of Holland. It would stretch almost seventy miles, to Arnhem, and along it would roll the British 2nd Army, to gain a foothold beyond the Lower Rhine, then wheel to the east to strike into the heart of Germany. Market Garden was a bold plan, and some of it went right. The airborne assault took place in daylight on 17 September 1944. The US 101st Airborne Division was well dropped at the southern end of the 'carpet', and successfully took the crossing points over major canals in the Eindhoven area. Further north the 82nd Airborne were also well delivered near Nijmegen. They took two major crossings, but only after some delay and through an unplanned and heroic amphibious assault were they able to capture the main bridge over the River Waal. At Arnhem itself, against unexpectedly stiff resistance, one battalion of the British 1st Airborne Division fought its way to the Bridge and held the northern end of it for nearly four days before being overwhelmed. The rest of the Division, unable to fight through to the Bridge, were squeezed tighter and tighter into a defensive perimeter on the northern bank of the Lower Rhine at Oosterbeek until, after eight days of unceasing combat, the survivors were forced to retreat across the River. Of the 10,095 who had landed at Arnhem, only 3,000 came back over the Rhine. What went wrong?

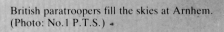

British paratroopers fill the skies at Arnhem.
(Photo: No.1 P.T.S.)

THE SKY PEOPLE

The mistakes began at the top. There was at that time a belief amongst the Allies that the German army was on its knees: it was an ill-founded supposition. Even those who feared that optimism was taking them 'a bridge too far' swallowed their doubts through sheer eagerness to commit the airborne forces to battle. Sixteen times since the Normandy landings had the 1st Airborne Division been brought to readiness for airborne operations that never materialized; patience was wearing out, and taking caution with it. Yet again, the planning suffered from division of responsibilities and differences of opinion amongst commanders. 'Boy' Browning, as commander of the airborne aspect of Market Garden, didn't get on with his immediate American superior, the Lewis Brereton who as a young staff officer had 'planned' Billy Mitchell's airborne vision in 1918, and who now commanded all Allied airborne forces in Europe. The Americans, after their painful experiences of dropping in darkness, insisted that there would be no night dropping. This factor, compounded by poor air planning, limited the already inadequate airlift to one delivery per day, and the landing of the whole 1st Division would in fact be spread over three days. It also meant that the RAF was not prepared to fly into the daylight flak barrage that could be expected close to the Arnhem Bridge, so dropping zones were chosen seven miles to the west of the town. Surprise and rapid concentration of forces at the target — two of the most important ingredients for airborne success — were thus eliminated even before battle was joined. Also lost, largely because of the haste with which such a complex operation was mounted, were a reliable communications plan; a workable system for close air support; and an adequate intelligence scenario. The latter greatly underestimated the likely strength of German opposition, and failed in particular to acknowledge the presence at Arnhem of heavily armed Panzer units.

The men of the 1st Airborne Division were therefore pitched into battle with the odds already stacked against them. Bad weather was to add to their problems by delaying resupply drops and the reinforcement by General Sosabowski's 1st Polish Parachute Brigade. Yet the British paras did what had been asked of them. Their orders were to hold the Arnhem Bridge for two days: they held it for three and a half. Only the 750 men of John Frost's 2nd Parachute Battalion reached the Bridge. Against constant assault and vastly superior fire-power, they held the northern end well beyond the time when the tanks of the British 2nd Army were expected to rumble into view from the south. For a further five days the bulk of the Division held a potential bridgehead at Oosterbeek before the survivors were forced back across the River. There they at last met the long overdue vanguard of the British 2nd Army. Against German forces whose strength and determination had been so fatally underestimated, it

had taken the ground forces seven days — not the promised two — to reach the Lower Rhine.

It was not the paratroopers who failed at Arnhem. Failure lay with the planners, and with the British 2nd Army.

Fortunately, the lessons were learned, and the same mistakes were not made when, on 24 March 1945, some 21,700 airborne troops of the British 6th and the American 17th Airborne Divisions were carried over the Rhine near Wessel in 1,696 transport aircraft and 1,348 gliders, to provide cover for the amphibious crossing of the River. Both Divisions went in simultaneously in one 'lift'; well concentrated in time and space; right on top of their targets; and with no lack of close air support. They achieved their objectives, and linked up with the main ground forces within twenty-four hours. It was a success, but a costly one, particularly in numbers of aircraft lost to intensive ground fire. There were some who wondered if such effort and expenditure of men and materials were justified. Had the 'airborne sledgehammer' become almost too large? Too unwieldy? Too expensive? Too vulnerable? There was no opportunity to pursue the argument, for the crossing of the Rhine was the last full scale airborne assault of the war. Germany surrendered six weeks later.

At the other end of the airborne scale to the mass drops of the European theatre had been the worldwide use of the parachute for the clandestine delivery of agents and special forces. Surely those men and women who jumped, often alone, into alien darkness and to an uncertain reception, were amongst the bravest of our sky people? For them, the act of parachuting was but part of a hazardous and frightening venture. George Noble was the first agent of Special Operations Europe to be dropped into France, ' . . . with a rather inefficient transmitter in the Dordogne on May 5 1941.'[9]

Of the 480 members of SOE who followed him into France alone, 210 died either in captivity, by summary execution, or in combat. Larger in scale were the drops of 'special force' parties, parachuted into occupied territories to relay information; for sabotage; and to co-operate with local Resistance groups. Europe during the months after 'D Day' became the prime target for the Special Air Service, much expanded since its formation in northern Africa. In April 1945 alone, 700 men of the French SAS and Chasseurs Parachutistes dropped in fifty small parties to harrass the enemy in north east Holland.

Also in contrast to the 'airborne sledgehammer' as developed and wielded by the Allies in Europe had been the use of paratroopers in the Pacific theatre, where their characteristic audacity and flexibility had been applied to good effect.

122

Japan began parachute training in 1940, aided by Germany, who had 100 jump instructors in the country by 1941. The major Japanese airborne operations took place in early 1942, when Naval 'Special Landing Units' captured airfields in the Celebes and in Dutch Timor, and Army paratroopers took the airfield and oil refinery at Palembang in Sumatra, although greatly out-numbered. Then, as Japan was forced onto the defensive, the airborne initiative in the Pacific passed to the Americans.

Commanding the US 5th Air Force in the south-west Pacific was Major-General George Kenney, who as a junior officer in 1932 had 'cheated' in those Fort Du Pont manoeuvres by airlanding troops behind the lines. Now, in 1942, he put his ideas on air mobility into splendid use by airlifting troops into hastily prepared strips along the northern coast of New Guinea in a series of brilliant outflanking movements. He used paratroops too, and used them with great flair. When the 503rd Parachute Infantry Regiment prepared to take the airfield at Nadzab in the Markham Valley, they were joined by thirty-four Australian gunners and their twenty-five-pound guns. Neither gunners nor guns had been dropped before. The men made one practice jump, and within twenty-four hours a system for parachuting the dismantled guns to earth was devised. The drop and the operation were completely successful.

The next jump by the 503rd — without their Australian friends — was ten months later, onto another airfield at Neomfoor. It was a rough drop zone, and through a wrong altimeter-setting some of the C-47s released the men only 200 feet above the ground. As many American paratroopers have had cause to say, 'Hell of a way to earn your jump pay!' So was the drop onto Corregidor Island, surely one of the most spectacular parachute assaults of all time. Guarding the mouth of Manila Bay in the Philippines, Corregidor was an American-built fortress rather like Gibraltar, with a low-lying tail and a rocky head rising 500 feet from the sea and known as Topside. The obvious place to land paratroops was on the tail. So with admirable audacity the Americans decided to put them down on Topside. It offered as drop zones a parade ground 325 yards by 250, and an overgrown golf course slightly longer but even more narrow, both pocked with craters, bordered by buildings and steep cliffs, swept by strong winds, and manned by an enemy prepared to fight to the death. A sporting drop zone if ever there was one — yet it worked.

At dawn on 16 February 1945, two columns of C-47s ran in over Topside, one aircraft at a time, each dropping six men, then circling to rejoin the column for another pass, and then a third. The first sticks were blown into the buildings and over the cliffs by winds above 20 mph. Colonel Jones, commanding the drop from another C-47 circling above the scene, ordered a change in drop run and a reduction of drop height to 500 feet. It took just over an hour to drop 1,000 men onto Corregidor. Twenty-five per cent of that first lift were injured, but the Japanese had completely discounted the possibility of such an attack, and were taken by total surprise. Before they could respond effectively, their communications centre had been destroyed and their commanding officer was dead. The initial assault was followed by amphibious landings and by the drop of a further 1,000 paratroopers that afternoon. It took another nine days to clear the caves and tunnels of Corregidor of some 5,000 Japanese. 'Clearing' meant killing, for only fifty allowed themselves to be taken prisoner.

A week later, a company of paratroopers of General Joseph Swing's 11th Airborne Division carried out a raid that ranks with Eban Emael as one of the classic *coup-de-main* operations. It also served a unique purpose. As the US forces began to gain the upper hand in the Philippines, there was fear that the Japanese were about to execute some 2,000 civilian captives, mostly Americans, in the Los Banos prison camp, situated in jungle terrain twenty-five miles behind Japanese lines and two miles from the coast. It was decided to launch an airborne assault, assisted by local guerrilla forces, and to evacuate the captives by a fleet of amphibious tractors. Total surprise was essential to overcome the guards; speed was essential to avoid counter attack by the large Japanese forces positioned within a few hours' march; boldness of an unusual degree was essential to even contemplate the idea.

Elements of the 11th Airborne had already been parachuted into action on Tagaytay Ridge on Luzon early in February. On 21 February, a company of some 125 paratroopers commanded by Lieutenant John Ringler were pulled out of the battle. Thirty-six hours later, they were on their way to Los Banos in nine C-47s.

'We in B Company had mixed emotions about the operation', said trooper Jim Holzen, one of the jumpers. 'We were very proud that we had been selected. However, rumours were rampant. This was to be a "suicide jump!" Or "few of us would return . . ." But for no amount of money would you have bought a seat on the plane from a Company B trooper.'[10]

The C-47s flew in just above sea level in three Vs of three, then climbed to 400 feet as they ran onto the target. Ringler was the first out. As his 'chute cracked open, the small force of some sixty Filipino guerrilla fighters and thirty men of an airborne reconnaissance platoon stormed the perimeter fence and guard posts. The attack had been timed for 0700 hours, for it was known that at that time most of the guards would be doing PT, their clothes in their billets and their weapons stacked in the armoury. The Japanese were stunned by the sudden onslaught from the air and from the surrounding jungle. Within minutes they were either dead or scurrying for the hills. The equally surprised but far more joyous internees were hustled onto the 'amtracs' which crashed into the camp right behind the assault, and the total force withdrew before any opposition could be mounted. All 2,122 inmates of the Los Banos camp, including a three-day-old baby, were rescued. Not a single member of the raiding party was lost.

At Corregidor and Los Banos, audacity paid off because it was backed by meticulous planning, and above all because that planning was entrusted to the junior commanders who would actually carry out the operations.

Elsewhere in the Far East, an Indian Parachute Brigade had been formed by late 1943, trained at Chaklala by Parachute Jumping Instructors from Ringway. Its only large scale parachute assault was on 1 May 1945, when Indian and Gurkha paratroopers dropped at Elephant Point at the mouth of Rangoon River, to destroy Japanese gun positions. Although paratroopers took no part in General Orde Wingate's deep penetrations of Japanese-occupied Burma, his Chindit columns depended almost entirely on air support and resupply by glider, airlanding, and parachute. It was at that time a unique operation, and one that presaged modern concepts of air mobility.

While the Allies had been forging and using their airborne weapons, what had the Germans been doing? And what of the great pioneers themselves — the Russians?

Kurt Student's *Fallschirmjager* had paid dearly for their victory in Crete. One out of every four paratroopers had died, and the carcasses of 172 JU 52s, as well as seventy gliders, were strewn along the northern coast of the island. Two months later, whilst pinning medals for valour onto some of those who had fought there, Hitler announced to Student that 'Crete has shown that the day of the paratrooper is over.' He reasoned that the surprise factor was gone, but undoubtedly he was influenced by the heavy losses and by the diversion of his attention and effort to the battle with Russia now looming on his eastern front. How ironic that whilst the outcome of the battle for Crete persuaded the Allies to expand their airborne forces, it persuaded Hitler to call a halt to any more large scale parachute operations! He even turned down Student's brilliant plan for an airborne seizure of Malta in 1942. Yet he did not disband the *Fallschirmjager*. Indeed, their numbers increased, for Hitler had recognised the fighting qualities of this elite corps, and for the remainder of World War Two, as infantrymen, they would be flung into battle wherever it was hardest. On the eastern front; in North Africa; in Sicily; at Monte Cassino; in the heroic defence of Brest — the distinctive helmet and battle-smock of the German paratrooper would be much in evidence. Nor was the development of equipment and techniques halted. Better parachutes;

night-dropping techniques; methods of carrying weapons; use of dive-gliders; use of paratroopers in a 'counter-landing' role — all were introduced, but rarely used.

And the Russians? What had become of the 'Locust Warriors' who we last saw tumbling in Brigade strength from their giant monoplane bombers in 1936? They in fact contributed little to the Russian war effort. Small groups were dropped with little effect in the 1939 invasion of Finland. Against the German advance into Russia, units were parachuted behind the lines to act in a partisan role or to reinforce beleagured formations, but they had no significant influence on the course of battle. And as the tide turned and the Germans were swept back, the one major airborne offensive launched by the Russians failed dismally. Three Parachute Brigades — some 5,000 men — were dropped on the western side of the River Dneiper to hamper the retreating Germans. The operation was poorly mounted and the drops were widely dispersed. Groups of paratroopers gathered in defensive pockets. They fought bravely but without imagination, and were systematically wiped out by the Germans.

Why were the 'Locust Warriors' so relatively ineffective, particularly after such a head-start? Above all, they lacked a 'father' and the operational doctrine that he might have given them, for Marshal Mikhail Tuchachevski and other military visionaries had died in the Stalinist purges that followed shortly after those 1936 manoeuvres. They lacked leadership; they lacked a doctrine; they lacked a force of transport aircraft; and for much of their war with Germany they lacked the air superiority that is a pre-requisite of large-scale airborne assault. Also, the Russian soldiers themselves, although undoubtedly brave, lacked those qualities which in battle could overcome the problems presented by a poor plan or a widely scattered drop, or the 'inevitable chaos' of an airborne assault. They lacked initiative, and they lacked that degree of elitism without which a paratrooper is not fully armed. In a totalitarian society which encouraged a belief that all were equal and nobody should be better than anyone else, the paratrooper was an anachronism. He *has* to be better. And he has to believe it.

Although in the eyes of most nations the paratrooper emerged from World War Two as a particularly formidable warrior, he was not universally popular. Airborne forces were still young. There were some who thought them precocious, and who resented the aura of elitism that had grown up around them. And there were still differences of opinion as to how the paratrooper should be employed, if at all. The full process of trial and error had not run its full course, and the questions prompted by Arnhem and the Rhine Crossing had not been answered. And hadn't the atom bomb made all this a bit academic anyway? It was in this

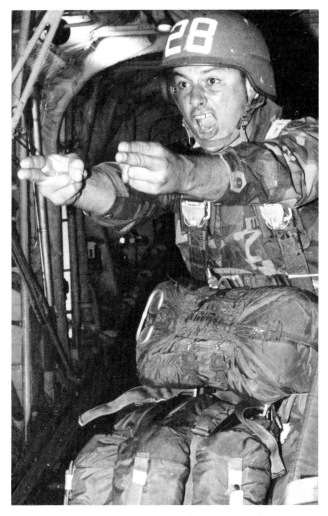

Above: HRH The Prince of Wales was appointed Colonel-in-Chief, the Parachute Regiment, in June 1977. In April 1978, he qualified as a military parachutist at No. 1 Parachute Training School, RAF Brize Norton.

Right: 'Geronimo' is the jump-cry of the United States Airborne Soldier . . .

atmosphere of uncertainty that airborne forces faced the post-war years.

In Britain, as part of the overall run-down in military strength, airborne forces were more than halved with the disbandment of 1st Airborne Division and the Special Air Service Brigade. The surviving 6th Airborne Division was assigned to the newly formed Imperial Strategic Reserve as an air-mobile peace-keeping force, but in fact spent the rest of its days bogged down in counter-terrorist action in Palestine. Even had there arisen a need for it to become 'air mobile', the available RAF airlift could have delivered only one battalion. In 1949 the force was reduced to one regular brigade — named the 16th to perpetuate the 1 and the 6 of the

disbanded Airborne Divisions — and the 44th Parachute Brigade (Volunteer) of the Territorial Army. The Parachute Training School moved from Ringway to RAF Upper Heyford, thence to RAF Abingdon in 1950.

The United States Army progressively reduced its airborne strength from five to two Divisions. Although the new Fairchild C.119 — the 'flying boxcar' — was designed specifically with the parachuting of men and materials in mind, its range was too short and its numbers too few to support even this reduced force. This became apparent when Communist North Korea rolled across the 38th Parallel in 1950, and the USA, as the major power within the United Nations, hastened to reinforce the reeling South Koreans. 'I know of no single thing that General MacArthur needs more now than an airborne division and the ability on the part of all his other forces to operate in an airlanding role,' said General James Gavin. It is significant that this distinguished paratrooper who had led the 82nd into Sicily, Normandy and Nijmegan did not confine the need for air mobility to the airborne division.

Two large-scale airborne assaults were launched by the Americans during the Korean War. Both were successful, but not significant. Nevertheless, the war gave a considerable boost to US airborne capability. The need for an aircraft that combined ruggedness with reach had been recognised, and the first C-130 Hercules took to the air in 1954. The T-7 parachute was replaced by the T-10, which offered more stability, slower rate of descent, and more assured opening at the higher drop speeds of the new breed of aircraft. And in Korea, the helicopter appeared on the battleground.

Just as the stagnation of US airborne forces had become apparent in Korea, a similar lack of progress was painfully obvious when, in 1956, British para-troopers jumped into action for the first time since 1945, for in the assault on Suez they used almost the same equipment, techniques and weapons with which they had crossed the Rhine eleven years before. They did so in a threadbare force of eighteen Valetta and fourteen Hastings aircraft which were still confined in their 'heavy drop' role to whatever could be slung beneath the fuselage. The only major addition to the British paratrooper's kit since 1945 had been a reserve parachute, and now, at Suez, he was leaving it behind in favour of more ammunition.

Paratroopers of three nations took part in this politically disastrous endeavour to wrest the Suez Canal from Egypt after President Nasser had seized control of the waterway. On 29 October, 395 Israeli troops dropped from their C-47s to capture the Mitla Pass ahead of the main force of Colonel Sharon's 202nd Parachute Brigade advancing across the Sinai desert. The first Israeli parachute unit had been formed in 1948 by Yoel Palgi, the sole survivor of a group of Jewish volunteers who had parachuted into Yugoslavia on clandestine missions during World War Two. He began with one aircraft, and bought 4,000 surplus British parachutes that were on their way to a shirt factory. In 1949, command passed to Yehuda Harari, who added discipline and sound training to raw enthusiasm, to lay the foundations for one of the most efficient and respected parachute formations of all time.

The British airborne force of Lieutenant Colonel Paul Crook's 3rd Parachute Battalion jumped onto Gamil Airfield early on 5 November, with orders to take the airfield then advance on Port Said to support the main seaborne landing. Sandy Kavanagh, the young Regimental Medical Officer of 3 Para says of it:

'After a long trundle round the perimeter track the Valetta turned to face down the runway. The pilot warmed his engines carefully and opened the throttles wide. We sagged back in our seats as the speed built up. After a very long run we were airborne, and turned away south for Egypt.

'Each man was wrapped in the cocoon of his own thoughts. Many of the Toms slept, Noel Hodgson, who was to command 'D' Company, marvelled as he stared at the snoring figures. Chin straps loosened and helmets perched on the backs of their heads. The wonderful capacity of the British Tom for sleep. There you are, he thought, the finest soldiers in the world and you don't even know it.

'The dark sky faded gradually as we flew south. It would soon be daylight. Alternately I dozed and read *The Lonely Road* by Neville Shute, surely the gloomiest book he ever wrote. Then my neighbour nudged me and pointed out of the window. It was dawn and below us on the grey sea the fleet steamed for Port Said. We were beating the gunboats to it.

' "Prepare for action!" The shouted instruction brought us all to our feet as the despatchers lifted off the door. The webbing strops were run along the cable and we hooked our static lines to them. A last look as we tightened the parachute harness, slotting the lugs of each strap into the release boxes on our chests. "Stick stand up." And we hitched on the ponderous weapon containers, hooking them on to the parachute harness, fastening the suspension cords to our waist-bands, tightening the leg straps. We were ready.

'All of us were feeling the same thing. The apprehension of an impending jump. For it is always the same. Knowledge may dispel fear, the uncontrollable ignorant fear which renders people useless. No amount of knowledge or experience can remove that hollow-gutted awareness of what is coming. Adrenalin and the "fight or flight reaction" is how the physiologists dismiss it. But I doubt whether the professor who coined the phrase had parachute soldiers in mind.

'Surreptitiously my right hand fingered the release-box of the parachute harness. Let that come undone at six hundred feet and . . . Don't be a fool. You've already checked it three times and so has the despatcher. How much longer can they expect us to stand here like this? At six hundred feet, straight and level, the Valetta flew into the eye of the rising sun. Our ears strained for the pregnant revving of engines which precedes the green light. The red light shone for ages, and we began to wilt under our loads. Stay alert. Anyone slow to move when the time came might not live to regret it. One out of the twenty of us could expect to get hit anyway.

'The green light flashed. Sergeant Crompton and the next two men had jumped before I realized it. Left-right, left-right, I hustled after the Corporal towards the doorway. The long flight from Cyprus was over. Left-right, left-right, left-right. The left foot is in the lead all the time if you are to jump out of the port door of an aircraft; the right shuffles along behind it. Most of the stick had gone. Most of our twenty seconds over the dropping zone had gone too. Hurry to catch up. Left-right. Drop the static line. Left. Hand round the edge of the door. Right! Into the fanning warmth of the slipstream, and falling away, spiralling, into the mother-of-pearl Egyptian dawn.

'Down, twisting down obliquely, down the kaleidoscope of shapes and colours which surround you before the parachute opens. Turquoise sky, buff sand, slate sea and black smoke in a great pall towering out of the control tower buildings. The streaming, opening parachutes of the men ahead of me slanted across, below and behind against the sand. The white streaks of harness over their shoulders and the floss of the rigging lines were light streaks against the darker distance. Twisting. Damn. Never get out of twists at 600 feet. The kaleidoscope whirled clockwise for one revolution and, with the sag of deceleration, whirled back again as the parachute opened. Relief. Without the reserve parachute I had felt more than ever a hostage to fortune on jumping. "Look up!" Yes it's all there: wonderful thing. "Look down!" How like the reconnaissance photographs, but in Technicolour, with fierce orange flames feeding that huge pillar of oily smoke. "Look around!" No one near me and no risk of entanglement with another parachutist. Rat-tat-tat from below and firing in all directions. Look down again. Little luminous glow-worms whizzing all over the view. Dully, I never realized they were tracer bullets directed upwards from the ground.

' "Lower equipment!" The old Abingdon parrot-cries came back. Those hours spent on "synthetic" in the big hangar were worthwhile after all. "Feet and knees together." Thump, crumble, crunch, forward to a light landing on damp sand.'[11.]

3 Para had landed. Even though under fire, the troops discarded their helmets and pulled on their red berets before setting about the defenders. At the same time, south of Port Said, 487 French paras were being dropped alongside the Canal in a manner that served to highlight the deficiencies of British methods and equipment. Less heavily laden and some with weapons already firing before they landed, the French parachuted from the twin doors of their Nord Atlas transports from ony 350 feet onto a drop zone 500 yards by 200, controlled from another aircraft circling overhead as an airborne command post. The very speed and ferocity of their assault overcame stiff opposition. Both parachute forces achieved their objectives, and the seaborne

French 'paras' drop at Suez from the Nord Atlas aircraft in 1957. (Photo: S.I.R.P.A./E.C.P.A. France)

landings were also successful, but all to no avail, for diplomatic pressures against the 'gunboat policy' of the British and French forced a cease-fire and subsequent withdrawal before a military solution could be achieved.

The techniques and attitudes displayed at Suez by the French derived from almost ten years of airborne operations in Indo-China, and a freedom from pre-occupation with large-scale airborne warfare. Their airborne experience in World War Two had been confined to Special Air Service operations, which bred techniques and an attitude of mind well suited to the unconventional demands of jungle warfare against the Viet Minh. During the nine years that France struggled to hold its colony against communist insurgence, paratroopers were in the forefront of the fighting, and carried out 156 parachute operations, mostly at company strength. Based on that hard core of ex-SAS men and augmented by former *Fallschirmjager* who had joined the Foreign Legion parachute units after 1945, 'Les Paras' gained a reputation for toughness and proud independence that was eventually demonstrated to a worldwide audience at Dien Bien Phu. As at Arnhem, it was magnificence in defeat that appealed to the crowd — defeat that was not of the paratroopers' own making, but which was in this case a result of a disastrously conceived plan and political ineptitude. The aim was to establish an airhead that would threaten the Viet Minh supply routes. Taken by a brigade drop on 20 November 1953 and initially reinforced by land, Dien Bien Phu was a badly chosen battleground and the enemy, as at Arnhem, had been grossly under-estimated. Slowly, vastly superior numbers of Viet Minh closed in. Heavy artillery was hauled through the jungles to pound the airstrip until it became unusable. The battle became a siege, and the siege became a catastrophe. The only way in was by parachute, and to reinforce the dwindling garrison, more and more paratroopers leapt to what was now certain captivity or death, not as a coherent military act, but as a statement of courage and commitment. It ended on 7 May. Seven parachute battalions died or were taken captive at Dien Bien Phu.

Amongst the closely-knit paratroopers who survived Indo-China, this experience bred a cynical discontent with French political leadership, which was hardened during the subsequent and bitter fight against Algerian insurgents, and by the military frustration at Suez. By the 1960s the elitism of 'Les Paras' had become so pronounced that it set them apart from the rest of the French Army. Their fierce independence, when coupled with what they saw as a further act of political betrayal, prompted the 1961 revolt of the 'Para Colonels' under General Massu when they led their men in direct rebellion against De Gaulle's declaration of Algerian independence. The revolt was crushed. So were many of the airborne units and individuals who had been at the forefront of the rebellion.

It was as though, in France, the paratrooper might have become too big for his jump boots. Yet on the worldwide stage, the image of the paratrooper was if anything heightened by this declaration of individuality. Every emergent nation in the 1960s had to have its airborne soldiers. They may not have had aeroplanes to jump from, but they had the big boots and the distinctive beret and the camouflaged smock with the winged badges on it. They often formed the 'Presidential Bodyguard', and were prominent in well publicized parades. But what were they to do in battle? What were any paratroopers to be used for in the 60s and 70s?

Certainly the day of the mass assault against a prepared enemy was over. The development of air

To infiltrate normal methods of detection, this small group of 'Special Force' paratroopers follow their stabilised equipment-bundle in free fall from high altitude.

defences had far outstripped the ability of a large transport force to evade them. The first warning shots had quite literally been fired on the far banks of the Rhine. And for 'tactical' operations, the helicopter was largely replacing the parachute. It had the distinct advantage of not only taking troops in, but of bringing them out as well. It had made its debut in Korea; had supported the British counter-insurgency operations in Malaya; had brought in the first wave of seaborne landings at Suez; had carried the French paras into combat in Algeria more often than had their parachutes; and was about to dominate air mobility in Vietnam.

Were the days of the paratrooper numbered?

In the darkness of early morning on 24 November 1964, 300 Belgian paratroopers climbed quietly into seven USAF Hercules aircraft on the airfield at Kamini in the Congo. Seven hundred miles due north, at Stanleyville, 1,300 white hostages were threatened with massacre at the hands of African insurgents, the dreaded 'Simba'.

The paratroopers belonged to an airborne force that had its origins in the Special Air Service Brigade of World War Two. Many of those now emplaning at Kamina had taken part in the small-scale operations that had been mounted to restore order during the troubled transition of the Congo to independence in 1960. Now, the country was torn by bloody civil war, and the hostages at Stanleyville were beyond the reach of the ground forces advancing slowly from the south. Time was running out.

One by one, the laden transports lifted their noses into the air and headed north. Off their starboard wings, the skies began to lighten, and at 0500 hours, the first parachutes blossomed above the airfield two miles west of Stanleyville. Within two minutes, all 320 men were on the ground. A small force of defenders,

Having opened their 'chutes, they will continue to follow the equipment container under their highly manouverable ram-air canopies — being tested here by RAF test jumper Sergeant Dave Piercey, still wearing oxygen mask, and with his personal equipment ready to be lowered before landing.

stunned by this awesome arrival from the skies, was quickly overcome, and thirty minutes after the first parachute opened, a further formation of Hercules landed on the secured airfield to disgorge another 250 paratroopers, in jeeps. This force raced into the town, brushing aside sporadic resistance by the surprised 'Simba'. Sixty of the hostages already lay dead in Lumumba Square and on the Rive Gauche. The remaining 1,200 would undoubtedly have joined them had the rescue attempt been launched with anything less than total surprise and devastating swiftness. Two days later, 240 paratroopers jumped in similar fashion onto the airfield at Paulis to recover a further 300 prisoners, and again prevent wholesale massacre.

On 18 May 1972, bomb disposal expert Captain Williams arrived in great haste and secrecy at RAF Abingdon's Parachute Training School, where he received thirty minutes of intensive instruction in water-descent procedures. He had previously made a few sport jumps, but had no experience of military parachuting. He was whisked to RAF Lyneham where he was joined by two hastily summoned Royal Marines parachutists and another from 22 SAS Regiment. They took off at 1535 in a Hercules, which turned west, and headed out over the Atlantic. During the following hours, Flight Sergeant Terry Allen, the Parachute Jumping Instructor charged with supervising an operation for which there was no standard procedure, lashed the team's equipment into grossly over-weight loads, devised the dropping system, and briefed the parachutists. In the fading light of late evening, flying under a 500-foot cloud base, they were over their target: below them in the grey Atlantic lay the giant

liner, the QE2. It had been reported, some ten hours earlier, that a bomb had been planted on the ship.

A cutter was launched, and took up position ahead of the liner. The aircraft ran in towards it, flying just below the overcast. At the last moment it climbed steeply into the cloud, levelled at 800 feet, and despatched the two heavily laden Marines into the murk. Captain Williams — with a little help from the Flight Sergeant — followed on the next run, with his SAS escort. The drop to the QE2 was a novel and completely successful response to an unforeseen event. No other method could have delivered that hastily assembled team to its Atlantic rendezvous so swiftly and effectively. A similar technique was used in the Falklands War in 1982. With no airlanding facility available to Britain's long range aircraft, the quickest means of delivering specialist personnel — including groups of Special Air Service — to the combat zone was to parachute them into the sea to be picked up by waiting vessels for transfer by helicopter or landing craft to their eventual destination.

In 1983, the democractically elected government of Grenada, one of the Leeward Isles, was overthrown by dissidents favourable to Cuba. The USA decided to intervene. With the approval and nominal support of several Caribbean States, it invaded the island on 24 October. The combined amphibious and airborne assault was spearheaded by two separate forces of US Rangers who parachuted from 500 feet onto Pearls Airfield in the north and at Point Salinis in the south to secure landing strips for the main airlanding of the 82nd Airborne Division.

These airborne operations — Stanleyville, the QE2, The Falklands and Grenada — although different in scale and purpose, had one thing in common: they were all rapid and long-distance reactions to largely unforeseen contingencies. This ability to support or to strike from afar has been the basic role of the paratrooper during the past three decades.

It is a role that has not often required him actually to jump, but the potential to do so has been applied on several occasions. Three thousand US and British paratroopers prepared to jump into Lebanon and Jordan in 1958 in response to military threats against those two countries, but were able to airland instead. Similarly, the arrival of British paratroopers in Kuwait in 1961 could have been by parachute had the threat of an Iraqi invasion not retreated. The 101st Airborne Division stood by to spearhead an invasion of Cuba during the 1962 missile crisis: they were part of an American statement of intent that caused Russia to withdraw from the venture. In 1965, when the USA sought to counter a deteriorating situation in the Dominican Republic, 1,750 paratroopers of 82nd Airborne took off from Fort Bragg to jump onto San Isidro airfield. Only at the last moment was it found possible to airland the troops rather than drop them —

much to their disgust, for when a paratrooper has prepared himself physically and mentally to leap from 800 feet into battle, to walk down off a ramp is a great anti-climax. The Soviet invasion of Czechoslovakia in 1968 was led by airlanded paratroopers, as was their massive arrival in Afghanistan in 1979.

This ability to strike quickly and from long range, by airlanding if possible, but by parachute if necessary, features in numerous national contingency plans for reinforcement of major trouble-spots or actual combat areas; for protection of overseas interests; for rescue and evacuation of overseas nationals.

The fact that the paratrooper has not been called upon more frequently to fulfil this role favours his continuing existence, for as the nuclear weapon has deterred major conflict, so a potent airborne force deters aggression on a less spectacular scale.

On the battlefield, where the importance of air mobility for ground forces is now accepted, the parachute has been largely replaced by the helicopter as a tactical vehicle. America launched only one major assault by parachute during the war in Vietnam, whilst the helicopter was in constant use as both a delivery and retrieval vehicle. Not all armies, however, enjoy such massive helicopter support, nor may circumstances always favour its use. The parachute can still feature as a tactical response — again to the unforeseen: as a method of meeting that old United States cavalry dictum of 'getting there fustest with the mostest'.

The more far-sighted military powers accept the philosophy that the principle value of the paratrooper is this ability to respond rapidly and effectively to the unexpected, and do not confine him to specific tasks. Britain, with its insistence on defined and financially measurable 'operational requirements', has been reluctant to subscribe to this concept of the unforeseen. Of the three regular Parachute Battalions, only two are maintained 'in role' and on permanent standby for 'Out-of-Area' operations as the spearhead of 5 Airborne Brigade. But although the numbers of 'Red Devils' has been permitted to decline, the quality remains supreme.

If further justification for the continuing existence of the paratrooper is needed, it is surely provided by his pure fighting ability — a product of volunteerism, selection, training, and that formidable belief in himself and his unit. As with Student's *Fallschirmjager*, and ever since, he has appeared wherever the battle has been hardest, fighting as an elite infantryman. US paratroopers formed the core of the heliborne 'Air Cavalry' in Vietnam. The British 'Red Devils', and their cousins of the Special Air Service, have fought with distinction in the Arabian peninsula in 1965; in the jungles of Borneo in 1966; in the streets and lanes of Northern Ireland; and in the liberation of the Falkland Islands in 1982.

Today's paratrooper is a better equipped young man than his predecessor, more adequately supported with firepower, vehicles and communications. His parachute tends to be bigger, safer, and more stable in flight, and might even be steerable. His aircraft gives him greater range and can deliver him in larger concentrations. Although technical endeavours have and still are being made to drop him from altitudes as low as 300 feet, the basic delivery system remains a low-level approach beneath an enemy radar screen, then a 'pop-up' to whatever drop height the situation requires. But what's new about 300 feet? That was the drop height for the *Fallschirmjager* over Holland in 1941.

At the other extreme, however, he now has the equipment and ability to drop in small groups from extremely high altitude — as high as 40,000 feet. He can either free fall from there to lower altitudes, or open his high-performance ram-air canopy at altitude and fly himself to a distant destination, possibly on the other side of a hostile border. Delivery from high altitude offers Special Forces just one more possible means of reaching a target, undetected.

New equipment, new roles, new techniques . . . But little else has changed. The training remains much the same. It's still 'feet-and-knees-together!' echoing through the hangar at Brize Norton where the RAF now continues its tradition of training Britain's paratroopers. It's still 'Gimme twenty!' ringing round the training areas of Fort Benning and Fort Bragg. Above all it is still the dry mouth and the fear in the belly as young men the world over prepare to take that first step into space, that first step towards the coveted badge of the paratrooper. That great airborne warrior, John Frost, recalling his first jump at Ringway's Tatton Park in late 1941, described 'the learner parachutist's smile, which has no joy or humour in it. One merely uncovers one's teeth for a second or two then hides them again lest they should start chattering.'[12.] That hasn't changed. Overcoming that fear still provides great personal benefit. Parachuting also remains a significant source of *esprit de corps* — and is a great leveller. 'You'll 'ave to do better than that Sir!' chided my instructor when I was having problems keeping my feet and knees together during my own basic training many years ago. 'Officers 'it the ground just as 'ard as 'umans.' Indeed they do.

Elitism? Few would now question the need for it, nor the existence of it, nor the fact that the paratrooper is a prime example of it. Even the Russians, in their reformed and vast airborne force recognised that their paratroopers were poorly armed without it, and duly insisted upon above-average individual standards, and incorporated a higher percentage of Party members within its ranks than exist in other formations. Although perhaps to a lesser extent than it once did, the act of parachuting still contributes to that elitism — to that belief in his own and his unit's superiority that is the ultimate quality of the paratrooper.

Yes, he always was, and still is, a little special.

CHAPTER FIVE
The Skydivers

In the Parisian barber shop in 1951, Raymond Young — American writer, actor and former soldier who had spent most of his life in France — browsed through a woman's magazine. In it, he found an article telling of a new sport being practised by French women and men: for the sheer thrill of it, they were hurling themselves out of aeroplanes. Intrigued, he joined the Neuilly Aero Club and began to take lessons in parachuting at La Ferte Gauche airfield, fifty miles from Paris. He worked his way through carefully monitored progressions until he was competent enough to free fall for a full minute from 13,000 feet.

Hoping to continue his parachuting when he visited America in 1953, he was received with shaking heads and suspicious looks when he sought permission to jump at airports in the New England States. The airport managers could not accept that anyone in their right mind would want to jump out of a good aeroplane just for the fun of it. Professional show-jumpers appearing at county fairs and major air meetings they could just about understand, but a *fun* jumper? Oh no! The guy must have something loose.

Raymond Young looked further afield, and at Benedict airport in Pennsylvania found at least a sympathetic ear. He made his first jump there in August 1953, from 4,400 feet, and a further twenty during the following weekends. He attracted considerable local publicity and growing numbers of spectators — many of them surprised that they weren't expected to pay to watch the 'crazy Frenchman' falling from the sky. In the April 1954 issue of *Flying Magazine*, he wrote an article entitled 'The Free Fall French', and in it he condensed the sensations and act of falling freely through the air into one beautifully descriptive term: 'Skydiving.'

Although Raymond Young coined the term to describe the free fall element of a jump, and although this is still its main application, 'Skydiving' has come to embrace the whole field of parachuting for fun: for sport. In sporting terms, parachuting has developed in two separate but merging streams — competition and adventure. It began long before Raymond Young gave it a name . . .

A taste for adventure and excitement must be present to some extent in anyone who takes a premeditated leap into space, so in this broad sense there is a touch of the sportsman in most of our sky people. But we shall be more restrictive and look for our skydivers amongst those who have parachuted *primarily* for sport, either entirely or on specific occasions. We need the caveat 'on specific occasions' so that we might include those parachutists who were the first to compete against each other, for they were in fact show-jumpers in the old tradition, rather than sportsmen in the modern. It was to add more of that all-important novelty to exhibition jumping that the organizers of air shows in the United States added 'spot landing' contests to their programmes in the 1920s. They would invite a handful of professional jumpers to compete for a cash prize which would go to the one who landed closest to a 'spot', or be divided amongst those who could land within a marked 'pay-off circle'. The winners would pocket the cash; the losers would mark it down to experience; the crowd would have their novelty; and the promoters would have five or six jumpers for the price of one or two.

It was not easy money. There was no such thing as a wind limit. It was either jump, or no-pay-and-don't-come-back. No 'pit' of sand or gravel to soften the landings. No steerable 'chutes: the only way to direct them was to haul on the liftwebs and 'slip' the canopy towards the target. This was worth only a few feet in a descent of several hundred, although partial collapse of the canopy by pulling in a handful or two of rigging lines could reduce an overshoot by a useful margin.

Probably the most capable of the professional 'spot jumpers' on the American circuit was Joe Crane. Joe was an acknowledged master of his parachute, not just a passenger. On most descents he could persuade his canopy to set him down for a graceful stand-up landing, and in competition he was rarely out of the pay-off circle. In 1926 Joe suggested a parachute accuracy competition to the organizers of the National Air Races, America's most prestigious aviation meeting. It was accepted and a 'spot landing' contest became a regular feature at this annual event. At a time when a landing anywhere on the airfield was considered good accuracy, the 'spot' was rarely troubled. At the 1928 National Air Races in Los Angeles, George Wheeling won the $380 first prize with an average of sixty-six feet nine-and-a-half inches for three jumps. The following year at Cleveland, Joe Crane won the event. This time it was worth $700, a trophy, and a merchandise voucher, and the jumpers were edging a little closer to that 'spot'. By 1932, forty-six jumpers entered the competition.

By that time, Joe Crane was established as Chief Parachutist at Roosevelt Field on Long Island, New York, which was one of the major centres for flying and parachuting on the east coast. He had taken the post in 1930 when the previous 'chief', Buddy Bushmeyer, had been killed. Joe — who as a wild, young barnstormer had risked his neck with the rest of them — now began to campaign vigorously and successfully for safer parachuting; improved organization of parachuting competitions; and a better deal for professional jumpers. In 1932 he impressed The National Aeronautics Association (NAA) by his splendid organization and supervision of a parachuting programme during a two-day air meet at Roosevelt Field. It wasn't easy. Parachutists by their very nature are individualists. Organizing them and persuading them to follow a common code has always been difficult, but Joe Crane managed it at Roosevelt Field, and when later in the year the forty-six jumpers who had entered the parachuting event at the National Air Races successfully banded together with the pilots to demand the return of entry fees, the time was ripe for solidarity. Joe called together at Roosevelt Field as many of the professional jumpers that he could muster, and together they formed the National Parachute Jumpers Association (NPJA), with Joe as secretary. He achieved further respectability when the NAA asked him to preside over

a new department called 'The Board of Parachute Experts'. In this dual capacity as virtual leader of America's pro jumpers and as adviser to the governing aviation authority, Joe Crane was instrumental in advancing the safety and status of parachuting in America during the 1930s. The regulations that he initiated were not always popular with his fellow jumpers. The introduction of NAA sporting licences in 1933, the wind limit of 20 mph at official events, and the rules that governed the conduct of competition were seen by some of the old-time show-jumpers as a threat to their independence and individuality. On the other hand, when Joe led a boycott of the 1937 Cleveland Air Races until the prize money was increased, they loved him for it.

This experience was unique to America. Although there were a few impromptu competitions for landing accuracy amongst individual show-jumpers in Europe, there was little attempt to organize events, and none to form any association of parachutists.

In Russia, however, sport parachuting was being developed on a large scale, but in a different form and for different reasons. In America the motivation had been commercial: in Russia it was political.

We have seen how the parachute was adopted by Russia in the late 1920s for military purposes — as a life-saver for aircrew, and as a means of transporting troops into battle. We have seen also how this military usage was backed by the formation of civilian parachute clubs. A pamphlet issued by the People's Commissariat of Public Health stated:

'The importance of parachute jumping is enormous. Jumps from an aeroplane develop courage, resourcefulness, train will-power and the ability not to lose one's head in an emergency and to make decisions in case of complications.'

The pamphlet went on to quote People's Commissar of Defence, Comrade Voroshilov:

'At the present time parachuting in the USSR has become a sport for the masses. In many towns there are parachute jumping towers. In factories, works and attached to aviation clubs there exist parachute jumping groups where young people learn this interesting job. This type of sport is of considerable importance for defence . . . I must tell you, Comrades, that this parachute business, one of the most complicated and delicate technical arts, is perfected not only as a sport and training in fortitude, but also as an important branch of our fighting strength.'

Russia claimed that in 1935, from 115 training centres, 10,600 parachutists had jumped from aircraft, and a further 30,000 had made descents from 730

One of the first of the sky people to discover the techniques of skydiving was the American professional jumper Spud Manning, pictured here with Leslie Irvin before making a high altitude jump at Los Angeles in 1932.

parachute towers throughout the country. These towers hoisted parachutists to some 150 feet under an opened canopy, then released them for either a cable-controlled or a free descent. Copies of these towers appeared at American fairgrounds in the late 1930s. Their purpose, however, was not to develop fortitude and community spirit amongst young Americans, but to separate them from their dollars.

Although contests in accuracy were sponsored, it was the act of parachuting itself rather than competition that was nurtured in Russia. In addition to its military significance, the scheme was also an early recognition of the character-building value of adventurous pursuits in general, and of parachuting in particular.

So it was that the 1920s and '30s saw the quite separate development of the two streams of sport parachuting that would eventually converge in modern sky-diving. Whilst Joe Crane and his fellow show-jumpers were pointing the way towards competitive parachuting, Russia was establishing it as an adventure sport.

Both of these initiatives were swallowed by World War Two.

Russia was the first to pick up the threads after the war. The State-run parachuting centres were gradually brought back to life. Jumps from captive balloons were added to the tower-descents for novices, and at the other end of the scale 'centres of excellence' for instructors were established at Tushino aerodrome outside Moscow, and at Saratov on the Volga. Other 'Eastern-Bloc' nations followed the Russian example. Although the primary purpose remained that of 'character development' through adventurous activity, the foundations were being laid in the Communist countries for standards that would dominate sport parachuting during the first decade of formal competition.

The only challenge for that early dominance would come from France, also through a State-aided training system. In 1949 the French Government, as part of an overall scheme to encourage participation in aviation, opened ten parachute training centres. Again, the initial objective was to give young people opportunity to meet the challenge of the skies, in a particularly exciting and cost-effective way. To provide the expertise needed at these 'schools', French aviation authorities turned to the professional jumpers of the time — men such as Pierre Lard, Michel Prik and one-armed Sam Chasak. To become a responsible teacher of others, Sam had to curb some of his natural instincts. He was one of that band of jumpers who rarely reached for a ripcord until the ground was staring them in the face. The story is told that at a meeting at Montpellier in 1957, an official threatened to withdraw the licence of 'Le Grand Chasak' if he persisted in opening below 300 metres. *Trois cent metres! Mais c'est la stratosphere!'* exploded an indignant Chasak. The bringing together of professional experience and youthful enthusiasm at those French 'schools' was to have an important influence on the development of skydiving, and not just in France.

It was at these State-aided parachuting centres that the Russians and the French — the latter taking their lead from Leo Valentin — began independently to formulate their techniques for controlled free fall. It was rediscovery of those basic principles that Corporal East had just begun to understand before he died in 1927; that Spud Manning had mastered in the early 1930s; and that no doubt other jumpers of those forgotten years had discovered either by deliberate trial or pure accident.

The first of those principles was that if the body presented a symmetrical and convex surface to the airflow, it would achieve a position of balance or 'stability' as it fell. Preferably that position should be face down, with arms and legs spread, for that attitude provided both a comforting view of the approaching earth and a good launching platform for a back-mounted parachute.

The second principle was that a controlled deviation from that symmetrical attitude — such as the bending of one lower leg, or the dipping of a shoulder, or a reaching forward with both arms, or even an angling of the palms of the hands — would initiate movement. Lateral turns, somersaults, barrel-rolls, and changes of basic position were all possible through this controlled loss of stability and the re-distribution of the air pressure acting against the body surface.

The third principle was that by reducing the area of body surface presented to the airflow — as in a head-down dive — vertical speed could be increased.

The fourth principle — to be appreciated and applied a little later than the others — was that by inclining the body surface at an angle to the vertical airflow, an element of horizontal 'thrust' could be added to the inevitable downwards fall.

Free fallers could achieve stability; full control of body attitude; limited control of vertical speed; limited control of horizontal direction. Man, in the mid-1950s, was beginning to fly. At least, French, Russian and Eastern European man was beginning to fly — elsewhere he was still spinning and tumbling earthwards with little idea of what it was all about.

No State generosity was extended to the jumpers of Britain and America. Indeed, in the USA several backward steps were taken by Federal authorities during the years immediately following World War Two. We have earlier seen how ex-paratroopers, bitten by the jumping bug, turned to show-jumping at that time, and how in America their enthusiasm tended to exceed their skill. Several young men died while trying to free fall with inadequate equipment and insufficient knowledge. The Civil Aeronautics Administration reacted by issuing regulations banning free fall demonstrations at air shows. In 1947 the Authority also re-issued its parachuting rules, and perhaps in the interests of economy, merely deleted most of them. They had been good regulations, formulated largely by Joe Crane in the 1930s, and it was Joe who once more interceded in his quiet but persuasive manner to restore the situation on behalf of America's parachutists.

In 1947, under the guidance of Joe Crane, his National Parachute Jumpers Association (NPJA) was expanded to include riggers and to become the NPJR, and was also affiliated with the National Aeronautical Association. Joe became an influential representative of that body on the newly formed International Parachute Committee of the Fédération Aéronautique

Dumbo Willans, the 'father of British sport parachuting'.
(Photo: Sue (Burges) Phillips)

Internationale (FAI) which controlled worldwide sporting aviation. Although organized sport parachuting had not yet come to America, it was Joe Crane in the late 1940s and early '50s who laid the administrative foundations for the day when it would. In 1948 he became the first recipient of the 'Leo Stevens Award' presented for the year's most valuable contribution to parachuting in the USA.

In England, as we have also seen, it was a handful of former paratroopers and RAF Parachute Jumping Instructors who brought show-jumping back to the aviation meetings, and did so in pursuit of adventure rather than profit, thereby bringing the 'sporting' touch to British parachuting. The Apex Group would have been an even greater influence on British parachuting had they followed up the idea of Ollie Owens to form a civilian parachuting school, but it was left to another show-jumper to extend the opportunity for aerial adventure to others. He was called Dumbo Willans.

Dumbo operated from Denham Flying Club, and it was inevitable that someone would ask him to teach them to jump. That 'someone', in 1948, was a girl — Phyl Weir. Dumbo tried to dissuade her, but she was insistent, so he taught her how to exit from the Auster, how to operate the main 'chute after a count of three seconds, how to use the reserve if necessary, and how to land. Then he took her up and dropped her over Denham. Phyl Weir went on to make another fifty or so jumps, some at air displays and others at the French training schools. Dumbo also taught Jimmy Basnett,

then former Spitfire pilot Bill Sykes, and in 1956 they together formed the British Parachute Club, the first school for civilian jumpers in Britain, operating initially at Denham, later at Fairoaks in Surrey. It was not a commercial enterprise. Instruction was free, and pupils paid only for the hire of the aircraft and for any minor repairs to equipment.

One of Dumbo's earliest pupils at Fairoaks was another girl — Sue Burges. Sue's youthful ambition was to become a pilot. She began with gliding, at Lasham, and it was whilst on a gliding holiday in Yugoslavia that she saw parachuting for the first time. She instantly asked to have a go, but wasn't allowed, and when she returned to England was directed to Dumbo and duly made her first jump — a 3-second free fall from 1,500 feet. Having started parachuting through curiosity, she found that not only was it fun, but that she could also earn money as a show-jumper to finance her pilot training. In fact, she became so taken with leaping from aeroplanes that her ambition to fly them was momentarily put aside, and her earnings from the shows were ploughed back into more jumps and new equipment. She was in great demand as a show-jumper, and for the film industry she put on a blonde wig and stood in for Virginia McKenna in the parachuting sequences of *Carve Her Name With Pride*.

Sue Burges became one of Britain's foremost competitive jumpers of the late 1950s. In July 1958, in a one-jump spot-landing competition at Coventry billed as the National Championships, she jumped in rain and strong wind to land forty-two feet from the target and beat the other five competitors, all men. That took her to Czechoslovakia for the 1958 World Championships, where she was Britain's top scorer in the competition as well as the first woman to represent Britain at that level. In early 1959 she qualified as an instructor and started her own club at Stapleford Tawney, called 'The Stapleford Swallows', later to become 'The Ripcord Club'. She explained to the Ministry of Transport and Aviation:

> 'The main idea behind all this was to co-ordinate all the delay-droppers spread over the country, some of whom have been abroad and learned a lot of useful information on the sport, and to meet to practise long delays. Here, without any fear of control zones, we can do formation descents, learn how to use smoke trails, and generally improve the art and exchange ideas.'[1]

Sadly, Sue Burges was not able to see these ideas come to fruition. In May of that year, she set out to beat her own record of forty-five seconds for a delayed drop by a British woman. With Mike Reilly in another Tiger Moth, she set out for 11,000 feet. The two dropped and Sue established her new record with a free fall of fifty-five seconds, but during that long climb to altitude the wind had changed, and the parachutists were swept towards Epping Forest. Sue steered away from power lines and a quarry, but caught her feet in the top of a tree, and crashed to the ground. The fall broke her back. She was put together with two metal plates in her spine, learnt to walk again, but was told that another parachute descent could cripple her. But she could still fly. She qualified as an aerobatic pilot, married her instructor Peter Phillips, and has remained active in aviation ever since.

When Sue Phillips looks back on the adventures of Sue Burges at a time when British parachutists were struggling for stability and status, it is the wonder and the sheer fun of it that she recalls — jumping with perforated tins of Vim strapped to her wrists to create a smoke trail; just missing the Gents at a display at Lasham 'with a chap rushing out of the hessian square trying to button himself up, and falling over'; having to wear total cover-up frocks at the office on Mondays to hide the bruises on her collar bones collected from the weekend's canopy-first openings "in case I got any funny looks"; standing in the slipstream on the wing of a Tiger Moth at some thousands of feet when the pilot handed her a scrap of paper on which was written in green chalk 'Will you marry me'. 'I just had time to grin and shout "NO" before bunny-hopping backwards and disappearing,' said Sue.[2.]

By the time that Dumbo Willans had founded the British Parachute Club, parachuting had been established as an international competitive sport, and he himself had been an influential figure in its early development.

In August 1951, Yugoslavia staged what became known as the first World Parachute Championship, even though the event was not organized by the FAI, and even though Russia and Czechoslovakia were not represented. Parachutists from France, Switzerland, Italy, Britain and Yugoslavia competed against each other in a series of three 'spot landing' jumps: a four-second delayed drop from 500 metres; a thirty-three-second drop from 3,000 metres; and a combined water-landing and swimming-race after a drop from 300 metres. There were no points for free fall 'style', no steerable 'chutes, and the closest to the ground target was an Italian with thirty-five metres. Representing Britain were Dumbo Willans and Chuck Thompson. Although most of his thirty-three-second drop was spent in a vicious spin, after the first two events Dumbo had a comfortable points lead over the rest of the field. All he had to do for the third jump was land close enough to the marker in Lake Bled to reach it within five minutes, and he would become the world's first parachute champion. He splashed down only a few feet away from the line of buoys that marked the target. His canopy settled gently over his head, but he still had plenty of time to free himself from it and swim the few strokes that would take him to the gold medal. Alas, an over-zealous boat crew whose job was to retrieve the

parachutes hooked onto Dumbo's canopy before he was clear, and dragged it — and him — away from the target and the world championship. Pierre Lard of France took first place. Dumbo was fourth.

Dumbo was subsequently appointed to the International Parachute Committee of the FAI as Britain's representative, and in fact chaired the Committee for one year. It was fitting that when he retired from active parachuting in 1960 he should be presented with the Royal Aero Club's Silver Medal, and be dubbed 'the father of British sport parachuting'.

In 1954 the FAI sponsored a second World Championship, at St Yan in France. Competition was primarily for accuracy, with one jump devoted to 'style', which in 1954 meant being able to hold a stable position on a given heading for fifteen seconds. Eight nations were represented — the USA by a single jumper, Sergeant Fred Mason who paid his way from his base in Germany, and Great Britain by a team of hastily trained RAF Parachute Jumping Instructors and one civilian, Arthur Harrison. This team was sponsored by the 'GQ' parachute company, and equipped by the firm with the first blank-gore parachutes to appear in international competition.

The blank-gore parachute embodied a simple but at the time quite revolutionary aerodynamic principle. Some of the air trapped inside a plain canopy needs to escape. Some does so through the material itself, dependent upon porosity, and some through the apex vent if there is one. If it has nowhere else to go it slips out under the periphery, often setting up that oscillation that had distressed André Garnerin and many another sky person since. What the blank-gore parachute did was to control and utilize that flow of air by directing it through a 'hole' in the canopy created by the removal of one of its 28 segments or 'gores'. The effect of air escaping through this aperture was to impart thrust in the opposite direction — of about 3 mph. A pull on the bottom corner of the aperture, via a line and toggle, would angle the direction of the escaping air and cause the canopy to rotate. Drive plus rotation equalled steerability! It was an innovation that caught the Russians and French by surprise. The Russians had a square canopy with a trailing edge vent, but it was still steered by hauling on liftwebs. They had nothing like this. There was talk of the British team being banned from the competition, but when it became obvious that even with this secret weapon the British jumpers were not going to be in the chase for medals, the objections were dropped. Instead, the Russians carefully noted the measurements and specifications of the British 'chute whilst their own jumpers hauled on their liftwebs to dominate the competition. The Czechs were runners up, the French third.

Sure enough, when Russia staged the next Championships at Tushino, in 1956, their team was jumping with an improved version of the blank-gore 'chute.

They hadn't fully mastered it, and in the variable winds that blew during much of the accuracy competition, couldn't match the well drilled liftweb technique of the Czechs, who took all the team and individual gold medals. The French, also with plain canopies, were even more frustrated. They suffered one of the few penalties of State sponsorship by being obliged to use the State parachute, which was not a particularly responsive beast.

The Russian parachute at Tushino not only had a blank gore; it also had a 'sleeve'. The opening shock imparted to the body by the canopy-first openings of the standard parachute — and sometimes concentrated where it hurts the most — had been one of the major drawbacks to the excitements and delights of falling free. Now the Russians and other Eastern Bloc teams had stowed their canopies in long sleeves, which allowed the rigging lines to deploy first, and so spread and smoothed that fierce deceleration. They may have taken the idea from Germany, where a light canvas sleeve had been used to reduce the opening shock of the parachute developed for the earliest ejection seats and tested by Willi Buss at Rehlin. At Tushino, the Russians added further to their physical comfort by wearing sponge-rubber cushions on their backsides to accommodate those feet-forward landings that took them valuable centimetres closer to the target.

The Americans had sought an alternative method of reducing 'opening shocks' by placing rubber bands round the mouth of the canopy and the upper rigging lines. It was a hopeful rather than scientific measure, and when Lew Sanborn's canopy 'candled' and he had to take to his reserve at a dangerously low height, his remark on landing was 'too many rubber bands!'

In those Moscow championships, ten nations were represented; women competed for the first time in their own events; the Czech Kaplan made a landing only forty-seven centimetres from the target centre; the style event required four 360-degree flat turns in alternate directions; and the Americans fielded a full team. There were no British jumpers. They couldn't afford the fare to Moscow.

Czechoslovakia hosted the 4th World Championships in 1958. Variations of the blank-gore were now in general use, although not yet by the French. The Russians had mastered it, and took all team and individual accuracy titles. Competitors were creeping closer to that fifteen-centimetre disc in the centre of the target cross, and the style event now required six of those 360-degree turns. The American team, smart in uniform black jump-suits and crew-cuts, won no medals but were placed sixth out of the fourteen teams competing. The British team of Mike Reilly, Jake McLoughlin, Denis Lee and Sue Burges (Burgessova, she was called in the programme) came eleventh. They had paid their own expenses and provided their own 'chutes.

The 1960 Championships, at Sofia's Moussatchevo airfield in Bulgaria, provided a turning point in international competition. All except the Hungarian team used blank-gore parachutes, but no longer were they merely standard canopies with a missing gore. They were designed for the job. The Russians had a double-blank which they handled with workmanlike skill; the French had an inverted triangular cut that was skittish on the turn and gave rise to many a Gallic expletive just above the ground; the Bulgarians had a single bowed aperture that gave their 'chute an almost solemn stability; and the Americans unveiled their 'TU' configuration that was powerful in all respects — drive, turn, and rate of descent. The optimum in steerable round canopies had not yet been reached, but the ideas in canopy design expressed at Moussatchevo were prolific. The main surprises, however, were in the results.

Until Sofia, the victors' rostrum had been dominated by Russia and Czechoslovakia, with an occasional French or Yugoslav jumper allowed to join them on one of the lower steps. But in 1960, when the medals were presented for the men's style event, there on the very top of the rostrum with a gold round his neck stood a young American — Jim Arender. Later, in second place for the men's overall World Championship stood Dick Fortenberry, and he was unlucky not to be wearing gold. During the team-accuracy event, in which the USA came fourth, he had already become the first competitor in a World Championship to slam his foot onto the disc for a dead-centre landing. He then took sixth place in the style competition, and in the individual accuracy event was leading the combined scores after his third jump. But the rapidly descending 'TU' had slammed him into the target 'pit' and dislocated his elbow, and he was unable to make his fourth attempt. To beat him, the Russian Akiev and Kaplan of Czechoslovakia had to land within a metre of dead centre on their final jump. Akiev swung wide. Just Kaplan to go. He landed two metres out. American jubilation was cut short when it was announced that the Czechs had demanded and been granted a re-jump for their man on the grounds that a change in wind had drifted smoke from the flare across the target as Kaplan was making his final approach. So Kaplan jumped again. This time he made an immaculate stand-up landing three centimetres from the disc. Dick Fortenberry, in his brown sling, was the first to congratulate him.

A gold, a silver, and fourth in the team accuracy event — where had the Americans come from?

The skills and equipment that the Americans brought to Sofia were not the product of State-aided training schools, but derived in traditional American style from individual initiative combined with a nose for commercial opportunity — in the shape of Jacques Istel. A graduate of Princeton and former lieutenant in the Marine Corps, Jacques Istel had met Joe Crane in 1950 and under his guidance had made his first parachute descent, primarily as a private pilot wishing to familarize himself with the parachute. In 1955 he went to Vienna to represent Joe at a meeting of the International Parachute Committee. There, from the French and Eastern European delegates he heard for the first time of 'stable free fall' and 'style manoeuvres'. Before returning to America, he went to France where, at Chalon-sur-Saone, Sam Chasak taught him the rudiments of controlled free fall. It opened a new world of parachuting possibilities to the American. He took his enthusiasm and knowledge back to the USA where, working with Joe Crane, he selected and led the team that represented America in Moscow in 1956. Istel jumped himself, and in Bratislava two years later he led the Americans a little higher up the scoreboard. It was not as a competitor, however, that Jacques Istel made his impact: it was his influence on others that brought American parachuting out of the doldrums.

When he returned from the 1956 World Championships, Jacques Istel enlisted the support of American parachute manufacturers to fund a nationwide lecture and demonstration tour. Clubs and groups began to appear in his wake. It was a development that was aided by the availability of surplus US Air Force twenty-eight-foot back-packs that could be bought cheaply and adapted readily for sky diving, with an increasing number of them now being packed into the 'sleeve' that Istel had introduced from Europe. Colleges in particular were receptive to his enthusiasm. The first inter-collegiate meet took place in 1957, and would lead to the formation of the National College Parachute League in 1961. He also gave talks and demonstrations to State aviation officials and later to Federal authorities, and effectively turned the tide of anti-parachuting sentiment that had long prevailed at those levels.

Only on the West Coast did Istel receive a cool reception, for his quasi-military manner and his talk of 'associations' for parachutists did not go down well with jumpers who still retained much of the devil-may-care independence of the Californian stuntman, and who at the time amused themselves by jumping from the oil-rigs near Taft by deploying their 'chutes into any wind above 10 mph in a form of 'pull off'. One of the most influential of them was Lyle Cameron. When he first met Istel at Orange County Airport, and the former Marine asked about 'sleeves', the Californian replied 'Yeah, I got a sleeve, one on each arm. Why?' Although he would never entirely lose his 'Californian' attitude towards jumping, Lyle Cameron would make an important contribution to the development of the sport by opening Elsinore to parachuting and through his editorship of *Skydiving* magazine.

While Jacques Istel spread the parachuting gospel in a practical sense, Joe Crane was still actively preparing the administrative structure for the sport. In 1957 his NPJR became the Parachute Club of America (PCA).

Sue Burges and Mike Reilly carried on where Dumbo Willans left off in the 1950s. (Photo: Sue (Burges) Phillips)

Istel's motives were not entirely altruistic. He sensed commercial potential in parachuting. In 1958 he and Lew Sanborn founded Parachutes Incorporated, and the following year opened the first fully commercial parachute centre — in the New England woods at Orange, Massachusetts. 'We sell gravity' was the trading motto of the Centre. It became a Mecca not only for practising parachutists, but for complete novices too, for the one-jump course that Istel introduced to America was a novel attraction to the adventurous. It was run with conveyor-belt efficiency. Pupils would book in at the administration office, then proceed with a diminishing fist-full of tickets through the equipment room, the lecture room, the ground-training area, the fitting area, and into the aeroplane, from which they would be launched from 2,500 feet with a static-line to open their 'chute, a friendly voice over the loud hailer to guide them down to the soft sand of the drop zone, and someone to dust them off, shake their hand, and present them with their first jump diploma. They might never jump again, but that diploma would evermore testify to a spirit of adventure and the acceptance of a great challenge. It was a recognition by Istel of a concept long followed by the Russians: that testing oneself against the inherent fear of leaping into space, and overcoming that fear, is good for the soul. At $30 a head, it was quite good for Jacques Istel too, some cynical observers might have remarked. And why not? Jacques Istel put more into the sport than he ever took out.

Orange catered also for those who wanted to progress beyond that first jump, and for the already experienced skydiver. At weekends, the latter would be invited to 'drop in' to Istel's Inn at Orange, which was set on the wooded slope above the airfield with a small clearing amongst the birch and pine to serve as drop zone for those impromptu accuracy competitions — the prize for which was a steak dinner at the Inn.

Sue Burges and Mike Reilly at the 1958 World Parachute Championships at Bratislava, with the American team led by Jacques Istel, on
their right. The jump-plane in the background is an Antenov-2.
(Photo: Sue (Burges) Phillips)

Despite his initial unpopularity amongst the West
Coast jumpers, Istel was able to open another centre at
Hemet in California. Symbolically, he took over the
parachuting operation there from Cliff Winters, a
stuntman in the old tradition whose particular brand of
dicing with death was to launch himself from an
aeroplane trussed in a straight-jacket.

Although his impact on civilian parachuting was
extensive, of more immediate influence on American
sport jumping was Istel's association with the US
Army. Until 1958, military authority had strictly
forbidden free-fall parachuting, but in that year Istel
lobbied the Army to such good effect that he was
contracted to train a select group of volunteers in free
fall techniques. The seven men that he trained became
the cadre of instructors for the US Army, which,
in Army Regulation 95-19, authorized personnel to
participate in free fall parachuting. It was a major
breakthrough. Military clubs sprang up almost over-
night. In 1959 the Strategic Army Corps team was
formed at Fort Bragg, to provide the basis for the Army
Parachute Team that would be established in 1961 and
become the world-renowned 'Golden Knights'. Army
jumpers swept the US Team try-outs in 1960, and went
to Sofia to announce the arrival of American parachutists amongst the best in the world. It was a position
that would be confirmed in 1962 at Orange when Jim
Arender and Muriel Simbro became overall World
Champions. In 1964 the titles would go to two more
Americans — Dick Fortenberry, at last, and Tee
Taylor. By that time, the USA would also hold fifty-
five of the parachuting records recognised by the FAI,
which in 1961 had all been in Russian and Eastern Bloc
hands. Apart from two four-man accuracy records
taken by Jacques Istel, Lew Sanborn, Nate Pond and
Bill Jolly in 1961, they would all fall to the US Army
Team.

Military involvement in sport parachuting was not confined to the USA. The British Team in Orange in 1962 was drawn entirely from the Army: in fact, it was drawn entirely from 22 Special Air Service Regiment. When Dumbo Willans had withdrawn from the scene, his place at the centre of British sport parachuting had been taken by Mike Reilly, a former soldier and member of Dumbo's British Parachute Club. Others who had caught the parachuting bug from Dumbo had established clubs and groups at Thruxton, Kidlington, Stapleford, and Plymouth. It was Mike Reilly — with his own Nottingham-based group — who pulled these loose threads together in 1959 to form a Parachute Committee of the Royal Aero Club, which in early 1961 was formerly recognised as the British Parachute Association (BPA) with a membership of seventy and Mike as Chairman. By that time, military interest was already established. In 1959, the potential of free fall parachuting for Special Forces had been recognised, and four RAF Parachute Jumping Instructors had been sent to the French Army training centre at Pau to be weaned from their static lines. Their new-found knowledge was added to that already gained through the initiative of other RAF Instructors such as Geordie Charlton, Norman Hoffman, Jake McLoughlin and Mike McCardle who, with civilian Dennis Lee, were the most advanced group of free fallers in the country at the time. This new expertise was applied to the training of the Special Air Service in 1960, and had almost immediate overspill into sport parachuting. Indeed, it was frustration with the restrictions of the military training system that led the Commander of 22 SAS, Colonel Dare Wilson, to involve his jumpers in intensive sport jumping, in France, America, and at their Hereford base. The result was a clean sweep of the British National Championships at Goodwood in 1962, and a complete team of SAS jumpers, led by Dare Wilson himself, for the World Championships at Orange.

Military involvement in skydiving was influenced by factors other than the vision of such as Jacques Istel. Firstly, there was a recognition by the military in the late 1950s that free falling from altitude offered a potentially clandestine method of delivering Special Force units. Secondly, show-jumping and eminence in the sport were seen to have good public-relations and recruiting value. Thirdly, skydiving was recognised as the type of adventurous activity that provides a means of keeping the fighting mind in trim: a challenging alternative to combat. The US Army would eventually have taken to the skies in this fashion without the prompting of Jacques Istel, but he certainly hastened and guided the process.

Sue Burges leaves the wing of the Tiger Moth.

In England in early 1962, Mike Reilly was drowned when he parachuted into the English Channel from a Flying Fortress during the filming of *The War Lover*. Dare Wilson took his place as Chairman of the BPA, and was to fill the post for four years. His autocracy gained him few immediate friends amongst the civilian membership, but he brought to the Association a level of discipline and administrative skill when it was most needed, and which saw the toddling sport safely onto its feet in Britain. Other military formations had quickly established their own clubs and display teams during the early 1960s, and for much of that decade and with a few notable exceptions, military jumpers dominated British sport parachuting at the higher levels. In 1968, Geordie Charlton, Doug Peacock, and Ken Mapplebeck of the RAF, with Brian David of the Army, brought back bronze team medals from the 9th World Championships — the best performance yet by British jumpers. Coach for that team and a major influence on its success was Mick Turner, who like many other British jumpers of the '60s had honed his skills at the French parachute centres. A talented competitor himself, this former soldier with the Royal Engineers brought to coaching the same discipline and strength of character that Dare Wilson had brought to the administration of the sport.

During the 1970s, the increase in international training centres, and cheaper air fares to bring the best of them within reach, would enable the dedicated civilian jumpers to compete on equal terms with the military parachutists, whose influence on the sport would wane, but never disappear.

The accuracy events in those 1968 Championships were decided within centimetres of the 'disc'. In the four rounds of the individual event for men, 117 'dead centres' were scored, despite the notoriously variable winds of Graz. Jaroslov Kalous of Czechoslovakia and Col King of Australia had four each, and it required a jump-off before the Czech took the gold medal.

This great advance in accuracy standards since Dick Fortenberry had scored that first 'DC' at Sofia in 1960 owed much to skill, but more to canopy design. Improvements to sport parachuting equipment had received little initial support from the major parachute companies in the USA and in Britain. For them, parachuting was primarily concerned with delivering aviators to safety and paratroopers to war. It was a serious matter. It wasn't meant to be fun. And surely there wasn't going to be much profit in developing complex equipment for a handful of sport jumpers — was there? At the urging of Jacques Istel, Pioneer Parachutes had reluctantly begun to manufacture sport parachuting equipment in 1959, and in the same year Steve Snyder had set the scene for the future by establishing a small company, Steve Snyder Enterprises, for the development and production of equipment specifically for skydiving. Mostly, however, it was an era of do-it-yourself modification to surplus military canopies intended for aircrew survival or airborne delivery. In 1960, Loy Brydon, a member of the US Army and National teams, patented the 'TU' blank gore canopy, to be marketed as the 'Conquistador' and widely copied by skydivers with a plain twenty-eight-foot canopy, a pair of scissors, and a sewing machine.

The 'TU' cut was about as far as one could go in converting a basic round canopy into a steerable 'chute, but in 1961 Pierre Lemoigne filed a patent for a parachute that would be built around the 'holes', rather than have the holes built into the canopy. He called it a 'Para-Sail', and although it was originally designed to be towed aloft like a kite and would give birth to the associated sport of parascending, it revolutionized competition in parachuting accuracy. Although it still relied on the basic blank-gore principle of diverted airflow, the partial inversion of an ultra-low porosity canopy and the elliptical shaping of the front skirt greatly increased that flow, then directed it through driving apertures and steering slots to provide a quick and stable turning capability and a forward drive of 13 mph at a descent rate of thirteen feet per second. What was particularly important was the degree of control that could be exercised over that speed. The toggles served not just as a steering wheel, but as brakes and accelerator as well. A competitor could now drive towards the target on a down-wind approach with toggles at shoulder level on 'half brakes', thus holding a reserve of forward speed to be gently turned loose if he was dropping short, or reduced still further by depressing the toggles if he was overshooting. Pioneer Parachutes developed the canopy into the 'Para Commander', but remained reluctant to market it until persuaded to do so in 1964 by the appearance of Loy Brydon's 'Crossbow' rig, with a similar canopy. Within a year, derivatives of Pierre Lemoigne's design would appear throughout the parachuting world.

Loy Brydon's 'Crossbow' introduced another revolutionary concept: the removal of the reserve parachute from its traditional location on the chest to a position in separate stowage above the main pack. It was called a 'piggyback system'. Although not all skydivers immediately favoured (or could afford) the 'clean front' style, the 'piggyback' would eventually become the system favoured by free fallers beyond the pupil stage, particularly when used to accommodate the next revolution in canopy design, for even as the 'Para Commander' was making its first appearance in competition in 1964, Domina Jalbert in Florida was filing a patent for a parachute that would eventually make the 'PC' look almost old-fashioned — we'll come back to it later.

Accuracy competition was becoming a succession of 'dead-centres'. In the 1972 World Championships, Kumbar of Czechoslovakia led the men's individual event with nine consecutive 'DCs', then in the tenth and final round missed the disc by over a metre to drop to tenth place. The style event of turns-and-loops was being decided by hundredths of a second and the sometimes-contested eyesight of the judges. It was not exactly boring stuff, but world championship standards in style and accuracy required a lonely application to specific skills that were seen by some to be restrictive. For them, a new form of competition was taking shape in the skies. It was called 'relative work'.

We have seen how, in the mid-1950s, the French and the Russians re-discovered and began to teach the rest of the world the principles of controlled free fall. This new-found ability to stabilize the body in flight, and then to exercise some degree of control over the speed and direction of fall, inevitably led skydivers to manoeuvre their bodies in relation to each other. The early goal of this 'relative' free fall was for two jumpers to guide themselves to a mid-air meeting whilst hurtling earthwards at approximately 120 mph. To mark that achievement and possibly to prove it to dubious earthlings, they carried a baton to pass from one to the other. The Frenchmen Chalom and Potron recorded the first such 'baton pass' in 1956. In 1958, Lyle Cameron and James Pearson of the 'Seattle Skydivers' passed a baton in Vancouver, followed a month later by Steve Snyder and Charlie Hillard at Fort Bragg. In Britain, the author and Johnny Thirtle made the first all-British baton pass in early 1961. I can't speak for the others, but ours was more of an ill-controlled collision than an encounter of the smooth kind. Soon, everyone was doing it. There were triple, then quadruple passes. When the girls got in on the act, the mid-air kiss sensibly replaced the baton. Passing through a hula-hoop held by a fellow skydiver had its day, and now there was often a free-falling photographer hovering alongside like a great bird with a camera on its head, to record and popularise this new game of relative work, or 'RW'. It was a game that appealed in particular to the Californian jumpers — they had the blue skies for it too — and they were the first to throw their batons and hula hoops away and become 'star' makers.

In 1964, six of them tumbled from two aircraft into the sky above Arvin and flew their bodies into a six-man 'star' — actually a linked circle, all facing inwards. The following year it was eight, at Taft. Both 'stars' were filmed by Bob Buquor, and when he drowned off the Malibu shore whilst filming for Hollywood in 1966, his major contribution to the sport was recognised by the foundation of the Bob Buquor Star Crest awards for accomplishments in free fall relative work, initially presented to anyone who participated in an eight-man link.

In July 1967 at Taft, a group calling themselves 'The Arvin Good Guys' created the first ten-man star, and three weeks later 'The Group' achieved a similar formation at Elsinore. There was some friendly argument over a jug or two at The Rumbleseat Tavern — an establishment at Hermosa Beach much favoured by thirsty skydivers — as to which was the better team. Which of them could put together a ten-man star in the shortest time? There was only one way to find out — Garth Taggart drew up some draft rules, and with another group called 'The Old River Rats' the teams met at Taft that November. 'Arvin Good Guys' won with two ten-man stars in forty-five and sixty seconds. Relative work competition was born.

In 1969, five ten-man teams took part in a 'Star Meet' at Zephyrhills, Florida, and at Elsinore the ladies joined the act with an eight-girl formation. Elsinore was also the scene for the first twenty-man formation in 1970, and in Yugoslavia that year, Jerry Bird's 'All Stars' demonstrated formation relative work to the best parachutists in the world, gathered for the 10th World Championships. At last, in 1973, RW had its own FAI recognised World Championships, held at Fort Bragg in the USA and attended by teams from seven nations. The USA won both the ten-man and the four-man events, with fastest times of 17.3 and 5.6 seconds respectively.

As the creation of speed-stars became almost routine, imaginative skydivers extended the range of formations that could be put together, using four-man patterns as the basis. A new vocabulary was born: 'Diamond', 'Snowflake', 'Caterpillar', 'Donut', 'Murphy' — with one man facing the wrong way — and many other four-man links that could be doubled or combined or added to almost *ad infinitum*. Even that wasn't enough. If you formed your pattern within the first few seconds of a dive from 1,200 feet, what were you going to do with all the rest of that sky? Why, you were going to break, and form a different pattern. And then perhaps another — and still time for another before splitting and opening your 'chutes. 'Sequential Relative Work', it was called, and by 1976, in four-man and eight-man teams, it formed the basis for RW competition.

This advance from baton passing, through star making and formation flying to sequential relative work, required a refinement of techniques that changed the concept of skydiving. It involved the gradual realization that a controlled body does not *fall*: it *flies*. With the torso as fuselage, arms as wings, legs as rudder and tailplane, it flies — as does a descending aeroplane — by the manner in which it presents these various control surfaces to the airflow. At terminal velocity of some 120 mph that airflow is thick, and full of convertible energy. The skydiver does not have to know everything about angles of attack and relative airflow and Newton's law of action and reaction, but he does need to think *flying* rather than *falling*, and to have a feel for that airflow, and a knowledge of the basic positions and body movements that will make the best use of it. He must refine those techniques for increasing and decreasing his vertical speed, for however fast the exit from the aircraft of a large group, the last one out has got a lot of catching up to do. A vertical dive or a 'no-lift' dive will take him down, fast, but he will have some lateral distance to cover as well. He can do it by converting vertical speed into a 'swoop', or he can combine increased vertical and horizontal speeds in a delta or a track or a max-track approach towards the pattern of bodies forming beneath and before him. He needs to know how to flare out and slow that approach too, or he could become unpopular with those he is about to join. And when he has 'docked', he must know how to 'fly' a formation with others. The ability to pivot smoothly in a lateral plane, and to slide backwards or sideways by adjusting those inclined surfaces is particularly important in sequential relative work. And what if he misjudges his approach and drops below the group? How does he get back up to them? How can he reduce his relative speed? He does it by assuming a reverse arch position — the whole body arched as though balancing on finger-tips and toes, thus compressing the airflow against a concave flying surface to obtain increased 'lift'. 'Wait a minute!' you will say, 'That is against the whole principle of stable free fall, the exact opposite of Valentin's concept of presenting a convex surface to the airflow.' Absolutely! If our man in reverse arch doesn't have sufficient feel for the air to get a perfect balance upon it, he will most certainly finish up on his back. The difference is that Valentin — with the greatest respect — was falling: this man is flying. Flying, as the Wright brothers found out, is a matter of controlled rather than inherent stability.

As the physical techniques of skydiving became more precise and productive through the development of relative work, so did mental attitudes change. *Alone in the Sky* was the title that Mike Reilly chose for the book he wrote in 1961. Had he lived a little longer, into the era of relative work, he need not have remained alone up there. Although that loneliness had an attraction of its own, and can still be experienced by the modern skydiver should he seek it, relative work offered companionship in the sky. Indeed, that was the essence of it. Joining together in free fall became an almost symbolic act of close and friendly relationship. The group became the sum of all the individuals within it and more important than any one of them. 'As the ego is trimmed down, flying abilities improve respectively', said B. J. Worth, one of the greatest relative performers and teachers. In RW competition, teamwork was the most important factor: the ability to relate to each other on the ground as well as in the air. When Jerry Bird selected the jumpers for his 'Columbine Turkey Farm' team that won the US ten-man nationals and then the first World Championship in 1973, he chose them primarily as people, secondly as parachutists.

Jerry Bird was perhaps the most creative influence on relative work during its formative years. He was a skilled performer, an outstanding 'producer' of large formations, and above all an imaginative and inspiring leader of others. Roger Hull was another great innovator and teacher, and amongst his disciples is Dave Howerski who has been a major influence on British relative work. Americans Skratch Garrison and Pat Works, gave relative work a voice, and articulated its philosophy of freedom and fellowship and perfect flight. 'Cloud Jump', Pat Works called this one:

'The ride up is always a pain in the ass. If you fly at the back of the bus, the windows in the Beech are too high to see out of. Conversation and the guys clowning at the door pass the time.

'On jump run you sit as long as you can so you don't have to stand crouched in the thin air.

'When you do stand, ready for the sprint, you put your head in that state of aggressive, relaxed, total concentration that you've found really lets you get it on.

'Cut. Ready? 54321! Go! go go go go . . .

'Head low, down the hall, sharp right and out, you arch to dive and your left side stalls briefly in the subterminal air.

'Into the dive. Far out! A valley of clouds! The base disappears into the fluffy side of a cumulus mountain and the swarm follows.

'You dive, swoop, brake and set up your approach in sinewy movements.

'While grey-white masses roar up around your ears. Wet air. Your vision flashes in and out like a strobe light. The adrenalin rush bobbles your approach and slows your entry. Drop you ass for a wrist entry — and you're in.

'Shake and break. Check out the star as the white world waterfalls up around you with an eerie, silent roar. Awed and exhilarated, you split as the star explodes like a Fourth of July rocket.

'Sit up, pull, and the world starts.'[3.]

It can be dangerous, relative work. The very aim of bringing bodies together during free fall presents a possibility of violent mid-air collision. Then there is the danger of pre-occupation: of becoming so absorbed with the wonder and excitement of flight with others that the ground and the slow creep of the altimeter are forgotten. Finally there is the hazard of a large number of canopies being opened in close proximity. Constant awareness of these potential dangers; specific procedures and techniques to counter them; and progressive training in RW skills have kept the accident rate to a commendably low level. A few have died. Two who almost did were French star Monique Gallimard and cameraman Doyle Fields, whose complete absorption in their filming took them down to 400 feet above Leutkirch before they became aware of the imminence of death and grabbed for their ripcords.

Another, who was saved only by the quick thinking and RW skills of his instructor, was Gharib Amor

The ram-air 'square' canopy has introduced the era of
Canopy Relative Work and the Canopy Stack, demonstrated
here by the Royal Marine team. (Photo: Mandy Dickinson)

Suleman of the Omani National Parachute Team. It was in 1984. The team was undergoing RW training at Hazm drop zone, monitored by British instructor Chris Lyall. Gharib was second man out of the aircraft at 9,000 feet. His immediate task was to catch and link up with the first man, flying stable below him. Gharib set off after him in a max-track position. His aim was good, his braking non-existent. He smashed into the spread-eagled body with a force that broke his jaw, fractured his thigh, and sent him spinning away on his back, totally unconscious. The base man had taken the impact on his pack and his backside, and was still flying. Chris Lyall, hovering close, saw it happen. They were at 7,000 feet — about thirty seconds from the ground, which is all the life that would have remained to Gharib had Chris not swept back his arms to dive in pursuit of the helplessly rotating body, caught him, turned him onto his side, and pulled the unconscious man's reserve parachute before opening his own. Gharib was still unconscious when he landed. Chris Lyall's skill and disregard for his own safety were recognised by the award of the Royal Aero Club Gold Medal, and the Sultan of Oman's Gallantry Medal.

The Omani National Parachute Team? Yes indeed! Dubai had one too. They were military teams, and capable of competing with the best at international level. And so they should, with all those blue skies to train in, and good financial backing, and British instructors of the calibre of Doug Peacock and Pete Sherman to coach them. The fact was that during the 1970s, competition had become truly international, no longer dominated by the Russians, the Czechs, and the Americans. The French were back amongst the medals, and the Germans, both East and West, and the British and the Australians and the Canadians — and the Chinese too were making an appearance that would lead to World Championship medals for them in 1984.

Relative work, particularly in its competitive forms, has influenced and also been influenced by the development of parachuting equipment. One very visible effect was on skydiving dress. During the mid-1970s, in an endeavour to increase drag and flying surface for relative work, jump-suits became so baggy that it was almost a return to 'bat-wing' days. The fashion has swung back to generally slimmer custom-built suits, highly colourful. More significant has been the inter-action between parachute and parachutist. We need to go back to 1964, the year that Domina Jalbert filed that revolutionary patent . . .

His invention was a para-foil — an inflatable fabric wing. It comprised two rectangular sheets of ripstop nylon, connected by airfoil shaped ribs to make a layer of open-ended cells which would fill with air when the canopy was opened to create a stiffened surface with true aerodynamic qualities and a forward speed of some 25 mph. It bore little relationship to what had

gone before. It was not just an improvement to existing parachute technology: it was a major departure from it. It was winged flight. It was, for the parachutist of the time, awesome.

The design was not immediately converted into a parachute. Prototype para-foils were tested in 1966, but did not appear on the market until 1970 when Steve Snyder's Para-Flite company produced the 'Para-Plane', which was followed a few months later by Pioneer's 'Volplane'. Not many rushed to buy them. The concept was difficult to accept. It was a bold parachutist who would switch from a well proven round canopy to something that resembled a fast-flying mattress. Also, the deployment of the early models was usually painful and sometimes non-existent, and the canopy was unstable in turbulent air.

As improvements were made — particularly through the introduction of a 'slider' reefing system to regulate and soften deployment — the new parachute became more acceptable, and amongst the first to adopt it were the relative workers. Their pre-occupation with what happened *before* their canopies opened often left them hanging in the skies far from their ideal 'opening point'. The drive of the ram-air 'chute helped them back to their drop zones, and also enhanced safety by allowing them to scatter from those increasingly large formations without being tempted to seek a common opening point.

As they accepted the 'square' — as it was commonly but inaccurately called — the relative workers then began to exert their own influence on the design. For those fast flowing exits through the door of their aircraft, they wanted a slim 'piggyback' rig that would enable them to snuggle up even a few inches closer to the person in front of them. They also wanted to carry as little weight as possible. Lightweight became ultra-lightweight, so that today's RW rig comprises 'square' main and reserve canopies in a tandem pack only five inches deep and twelve pounds in weight — compared with the forty pounds of bulky 'Para Commander' and reserve with which RW competition began.

The accuracy jumpers were initially reluctant to buckle themselves into a ram-air parachute, partly because of the instability of the early models in gusty conditions, and also because it required a drastic change in technique. Although the principle of turning, braking and accelerating by smooth use of toggle controls was the same as for the 'PC', the final approach to the target with a 25-mph flying machine could no longer be made with additional wind behind it. The 'square' had to be landed like an aeroplane, with a down-wind leg, a smooth turn onto a pre-determined set-up point, and a final approach into wind. Within striking distance of the 'disc', full depression of the toggles could bring the canopy to the edge of stalling point and stop it almost dead in the air. The gradual change to the ram-air for accuracy

'The British Skydivers Club' of Norman Hoffman, Mike McCardle, Dennis Lee, Geordie Charlton, and Jake McLoughlin emplane in a Rapide at Thruxton for a jump from 14,000 feet in 1959. (Photo: Norman Hoffman) (page 140)

competition gathered pace in 1974 with the production by Para-Flite of the first of its 'Strato' series, the 'Strato Star' and then the even more effective 'Strato Cloud'. As with the early blank-gore 'chutes, the ram-air concept was quickly adopted and produced by other countries, including the Eastern bloc. By the 1978 World Championships there wasn't a round canopy in sight.

The outstanding flier of a ram-air parachute at that Championship was a British girl. In 1972, as a sports-mad Physical Training Instructor of the WRAC, Jackie Smith used to watch the Parachute Regiment's display team, the Red Devils, jumping into the sports fields alongside Queen's Avenue in Aldershot. It inspired her to take a four-jump course at the Army Parachute Centre at Netheravon. The bug bit her hard. There were more weekend jumps, then a continuation course,

until after only twenty-two descents there was victory in the novices' event at the Army Championships. She was encouraged by Peter Schoffield, leading the Red Devils at that time, and when he heard that she had begun to make display jumps with another Army team led by Alec Black, he asked if she would like to join the 'Freds', parachuting's own nickname for the Red Devils. Would she! It wasn't easy, though. The Queen Bee of the WRAC had to be persuaded. 'How could you expect one of my girls to parachute in over a crowd — everyone would be able to see up her skirts,' complained one letter to the Depot of the Parachute Regiment. Jackie was eventually allowed to join, and after more training, she made her first appearance with the team. It was at Swansea. Her main parachute malfunctioned.

'As if that wasn't enough, my reserve inverted, then blew thirteen panels. Luckily I landed in the harbour. It was good news for the team though. The story was on all the local news and papers, and the next day thousands turned up just to see if I'd do it again. I didn't.'[4.]

Great Britain's 1978 World Championship team, at Zagreb. Left to right: Paddy Byrne, David Tylcot, Bob Hiatt, Dicky Bird, Scotty Milne, Dougie Young, John Meacock, Bob King, and kneeling — Sandy Milne and Jackie Smith with her gold medal.

Jackie spent five years with the Red Devils, and during that time followed the example of an impressive number of 'Freds' who have appeared in the British national team. By 1976 she found that the fun was going out of the constant round of exhibition jumping and competition training. She left the Army, sold her car, and headed for Pope Valley in America with the British RW team, 'Symbiosis', formed by Willi Grut the previous year. The fun came back, and in 1977 she was one of the 'Symbiosis' team that won the British eight-man RW title and then represented Britain in the World RW Championships in Australia.

In 1978 she was back to what had become known as 'the classics' — accuracy and style. The World Championships that year were at Zagreb, Yugoslavia. Individual accuracy events were to be decided over ten rounds, every jump to count. Jackie, flying a five-cell 'Strato-Star', began to stamp out the 'dead centres' — two on her first day of jumping, five more on the next, and another two on the third. Nine jumps, nine 'DCs'. One more to go. Nobody had ever scored ten consecutive 'DCs' in a World Championship. Could Jackie Smith?

'One of the first things I ever learned about competition was not to compete with the scoreboard but just to carry out each jump to the best of my ability. Because of this I was oblivious of the fact that Cheryl Stearns (USA) was in second

place with a total of 0.02 centimetres, followed by a Russian lady with 0.03. One more jump to go and that would be it. Scoring 0.00 is one thing, but scoring 0.00 under such pressure is a different kettle of fish. Between the ninth and tenth round there was a three-day gap due to bad weather and those three days were the longest, rainiest, windiest days I have ever had to sit through. I think I lost about ten pounds in weight due to loss of appetite. I also needed to be alone as conversation was not something I could concentrate on.

'The fourth day broke with glorious sunshine and light winds. We drove from the hostel to the drop zone and on arriving at the competition site the officials announced the commencement of the men's style. Phew! I could sit and watch the conditions for a while and maybe relax in the sunshine. This feeling was short lived when another announcement was made to the effect that the Ladies Accuracy Round Ten would commence instead. My heart started pounding so hard I could hardly hear anything. I sat by the pit to observe the wind drift indicator then retreated to the British Team tent to avoid the much appreciated but at the time unwanted messages of "good luck."

'The announcement of my name and number meant I had ten minutes to get ready and out to the emplaning area. This was it — the acid test. I emplaned with nine other competitors and the An-2 climbed slowly to jump altitude. The aircraft did four circuits dropping one competitor over the opening point on each occasion. The fifth girl to go was standing in the door giving corrections to the pilot. We were on jump run again. As she exited the aircraft, the co-pilot walked swiftly to the rear of the 'plane and closed the door. He was making motions to the effect that no one else would jump and we should circuit. He couldn't speak English so we didn't know what the problem was. I looked out of the window. The canopies of the ladies who had already jumped were scattered everywhere and not one parachute had landed in the pit. My mind was working ten to the dozen asking all kind of questions. Had the winds increased? Were there lots of thermals?'

Jackie wasn't to know until later that a Turkish girl had landed heavily in the pit, and as she was stretchered off with a suspected broken back, the other competitors had been waved off. The scatter of canopies on the ground was nothing to do with the wind. But Jackie didn't know that:

'We flew around for twenty minutes then the co-pilot re-opened the door and made gestures

The 'square' parachute brought even greater consistency to accuracy competition — particularly in the hands of jumpers like Jackie Smith, Britain's most successful sport parachutist, seen here stepping out of the sky for another 'dead centre'. She scored ten of them in succession to win the gold medal in the 1978 World Championships. (Photo: Dave Waterman)

indicating we should recommence the competition. I was next! The aircraft was on jump run and after one minor correction, I took a massive deep breath all the way to my feet, then made my exit. I watched the aircraft fly away and then my parachute deploy. For the first time in my life I spoke to it and said, "Please, please, lets make this last one a good one". I flew on the upwind side and observed the wind-sock, swinging and swaying in the breeze. Not knowing what the conditions were like, I set up on my final approach too close to the pit and had to do some real radical corrections. My canopy was nearly on the point of stalling but I kept it under control. Descending on the last twenty feet I could feel my left foot start twitching, then I saw the disc and hit hard with my right heel. The next point of contact was my backside and I just sat there in total suspension awaiting the read-out to register my result. After what seemed an eternity, 0.00 lit up and I just laid back in the pea gravel, not believing my eyes.'[5.]

Jackie Smith was Britain's first World Parachute Champion and the first jumper to score ten consecutive dead-centres in World competition. She had spent £2,000 on equipment and training to help her towards that gold medal. Now, and not for the first time, Britain had a champion who was the best in the world in her

Accelerated Free Fall training enabled Richard Branson to familiarise himself with free fall sensations and techniques before his balloon crossing of the Atlantic in 1987. Over Netheravon, his instructors were Shaky Sheridan and Nick Harrison. (Photo: Leo Dickinson) (page 154)

chosen sport, and who was also stony broke and out of work. That has been the story of too many British sport parachutists — lack of funds and lack of good training weather. To pay for winter training at Zephyrhills one year, Jackie Smith worked a summer season at an amusement park in Cincinatti . . .

> 'Firestone Tyres had a DC-3 there for us to use, and the idea was for us to jump into the park every night. It was a really tight DZ as well — between two roads, an open zoo with lions and tigers, and then the funfair itself. And if you didn't jump, you didn't get paid. Still, it can be pretty cheap living in America in the summer. You can pile a dollar salad so high that you need a sherpa to reach the top of it . . .'[4].

She was back on the World scene in 1979. In France for the World RW Championships, she jumped as a member of the Symbiosis eight-man team that came fifth, and gained a silver medal as alternate for the four-man team that won a commendable second place. Jackie Smith — now Jackie Young, married to former British champion and Red Devil, Dougie Young — deserves her place amongst the greatest of sporting sky people.

Fliers of ram-air canopies were quick to appreciate that one of the inherent dangers of descent under a traditional round canopy had been removed — the danger of collapse if someone happened to fly immediately below you and thus steal the air on which your nylon umbrella relied for its lift. In fact, they found that the highly maneouverable ram-air canopy, feeding on lateral airflow, could be deliberately positioned directly below another, with another below that — and another joining on — each parachutist with his feet hooked into the canopy or the lift-webs of the man below. Canopy Relative Work (CRW) it was called. Its development followed a similar pattern to that of free fall relative work. First there were bigger 'stacks' of canopies. Then faster stacks. Then 'rotations', with parachutists changing positions within the stack. Then different formations. Then sequential formations. Stacked canopies became a feature of display jumping, and CRW entered international competition with the first World Cup in CRW held at Zephyrhills, where British teams won both the four-man and eight-man events. Also, like free fall relative work, it encouraged new skills, and demanded changes of attitude, particularly amongst those brought up on round canopies and taught to keep as far away from each other as possible. The danger of canopy collapse is still there, but is minimized by safety regulations specific to CRW and by progressive training in the required techniques. It tends to be a specialist event, and prominent amongst those specialists has been the British Royal Marines Free Fall Team, co-holders in 1987 of a world record

The classic 'French Cross' stable position was taught to the rest of the western parachuting world in the French state-aided parachute training centres during the 1950s. (page 134)

thirty-man stack and holders of the night record of twenty-two.

In 1986, the FAI gave official recognition to World Championship CRW, and also gave its blessing to Para-Ski. The combination of parachuting and ski-ing was by no means a new sport. It began in the 1960s with races between the Alpine rescue teams who used parachuting to reach accident sites before the helicopter was sufficiently advanced to take its place. The races took the form of a parachute descent onto the top of a ski-run, then on with the skis, and away! The first international event was in Austria in 1965, and the first World Cup competition in 1973. The accuracy and ski-ing events became separated — the accuracy still taking place on to a snow slope of not less than twenty degrees, and the ski-ing in the form of a giant slalom. Understandably, those countries that have mountains with snow on them dominate the sport, but Britain and Holland and Belgium were there at the first World Para-Ski Championships held in 1987 at Sarajevo, Yugoslavia, perhaps taking it a little less seriously than the Swiss and the Austrians and the Yugoslavians:

> 'On the giant slalom run the British foursome of Les Carrol, Alan Dumbell, Kevin Hardwick and Andy Law were all grouped together in the thirties, some fifteen seconds behind the condom clad leaders. All the good teams wore racing ski suits, the Brits took their jackets off. A masseur pumelled the thighs of the French team seconds before they left the starting gate; our chaps jumped up and down to keep warm . . .

> 'The accuracy event also proved difficult to British competitors used to pits approved by the flat earth society. The minimum slope for pits in Paraski is twenty degrees, this plays havoc with the inexperienced competitor's perception of the target.'[6].

In reviewing the competitive aspects of parachuting, we have been looking at the peak of a very large pyramid. In Britain alone, the seventy members of BPA when founded by Mike Reilly in 1961 have grown to over 5,000, of whom only a handful feature in major competition. What do the rest of our skydivers do? The answer is quite simple: they have fun.

Not every jumper aspires to the 'perfect flight' of Johnathan Livingstone Seagull as created by flying mystic (and skydiver) Richard Bach, and much admired, emulated and quoted by the modern gurus of the sport such as Pat Works. Most, however, can identify with Pat Work's own *Godfrog*:

Oh come with me and   we'll go up there
Where the wind blows cold and there ain't much air
Where the clouds are ice and the blood runs thin . . .
But don't worry, toad, we're comin' down again.
Like a frog, a screamin' Godfrog!

When the airplane gets so high she won't go no more
With a laugh and a holler it's out the door,
Down amongst them clouds to play
Like that ol' eagle who does nothin' else all day.

Then back on the ground when the Whuffos ask 'how come?'
And you don't really know, and feel sorta dumb . . .
Well, you may wonder, but I know why —
You're a screamin' Godfrog and you love the sky.[7.]

Where does the fun come from? It comes partly from that early Russian concept that the challenge of a parachute descent and overcoming the attendant fear promote good feelings. The feeling may be one of extreme relief and a resolve never to do it again, but it will be touched with pride and a sense of achievement, and grandchildren will eventually be told of it. For those who do 'do it again' — and again — there is continuing satisfaction, lessening fear, sheer physical exhilaration, and the fellowship of the sky and the club-house. You don't have to wear a gold medal round your neck to enjoy all that.

The popularity and acceptance of the challenge is expressed in the numbers who take a 'first jump course', as pioneered by Jacques Istel at Orange, and now offered by parachute centres throughout the world. The philosophy of 'fun' finds more advanced expression in the immense popularity of parachuting 'boogies — international gatherings organized at major centres to provide large-capacity airlift, preferably with a C-130 Hercules, to fill the skies with constant showers of relative workers and gaily coloured canopies, and to back up the jumping with social and other fun events.

They began in America in the early '70s, and as cheaper air travel brought them within reach of larger international audiences, the 'boogies' spread throughout the parachuting world, naturally finding most favour where the skies are bluest, and reaching as far as China by 1987. They are, at their own level, an extension of those great 'friendship jumps' that have followed major international events since the 1950s, when the sharp edge of contest is forgotten, parachutes are exchanged, and politics left on the ground as competitors of all nations join together in the skies.

For those who may no longer have the stamina for 'boogies', there is fun enough in the meetings of the POPS — the Parachutists Over Phorty Society. The 'Rocking Chair Follies' held at Elsinore in 1972 must have been one of the first POPS meets. It centred on a 'hit-and-rock' competition, which called for a landing as close as possible to a centrally placed rocker, a forty-year-old dash, and one rock to lift the front legs of the chair from the ground. Imagination has run riot with POPS events ever since. In Britain, one of the most loved and remarkable POP was the late Archie McFarlane. Born in 1898, Archie lied about his age to join the Royal Naval Division and fight on the Somme in World War One, and lied about his age again to make his first parachute descent in 1973. He made another twenty jumps at Thruxton and Tilstock, travelling to the clubs on his motor-bike, and once driving it home to Bristol after having a dislocated shoulder put back following a hard landing. When he wasn't jumping, he was usually in the club-house bar, downing a pint or two and beating everyone at cribbage. He made his last descent at the age of eighty-nine, harnessed to instructor John Boxall in a 'tandem jump' at Shobdon. For his dedication to parachuting he received the Royal Aero Club Certificate of Merit from HRH The Duke of York, which he enjoyed almost as much as his interview with Anne Diamond on Breakfast TV. He died a few months later whilst trekking in the Cambrian mountains. Archie McFarlane knew all about fun.

Fun, yes — fun in the club jumping, fun at the 'boogies', fun at the POPS meets. Gravity, however, has a poor sense of humour. Behind the fun, danger lurks. Skydivers still get hurt. A few still die — as do mountaineers and white-water canoeists and drivers of racing machines and participants in any other adventurous sport. An element of risk is a necessary ingredient of adventure, and some would say of life itself.

'The acceptance of the risk of death is the acceptance of life; and love of danger is love of life,' wrote aviation's philosopher, Antoine De Saint Exupery.[8.]

Charles Shea-Simonds, Vice-President of the Royal Aero Club and a skydiver whose participation in and administration of the sport have been outstanding, puts it another way: 'Risk sharpens things up, makes you more aware. You have an increased perception of things. You know how green the bloody grass is.'

Above: Over the Belgian coast, a group of international skydivers build a 124-man 'star'. (Photo: Leo Dickinson) (page 158)

Right: Norman Kent films the building of a 99-man 'star' over Vancouver, while he himself is filmed by camerman Leo Dickinson. (Photo: Leo Dickinson) (page 143)

Although the danger is there, it has diminished. Parachuting is safer today than it was yesterday. Sound administration of the sport has laid the guidelines, and within them, improvements in equipment and training have reduced the hazards.

In most of the parachuting nations, the sport's own governing body designs and applies the safety regulations and operating procedures on behalf of the ruling aviation body. Thus in Britain the BPA administers sport parachuting on behalf of the Civil Aviation Authority. In the USA, the United States Parachute Association inherited a similar role from Joe Crane's PCA in 1967. They do it well, but not without difficulty. The difficulty often comes from within, for as Joé Crane himself discovered in the 1930s, parachutists are an adventurous and articulate bunch, not easily governed. In the 1970s, for example, that spirit of adventure found new expression in what became known as BASE jumping: parachuting from Building, Antenna, Span, Earth. In fact from anything that was high enough. Well — it wasn't exactly new. The 'tower jumpers' of the Middle Ages had tried it, and so — with more success — had Orde Lees from London's Tower Bridge, and Rod Law from the Statue of Liberty, and the Californian jumpers from the Taft oil rigs, and many others. A well publicized jump in 1970 by Don Boyle from the Royal Gorge Bridge 1,000 feet above the Arkansas River revived the habit, and the subsequent search for high places led thrill seekers to the eventual Mecca for fixed-object jumpers — the sheer face of a mountain called El Capitan, in California's Yosemite

National Park. Jumping 'El Cap' was sensational, spectacular, and highly photogenic. The Park authorities tried to accommodate the craze, but were overwhelmed by skydiving enthusiasm, and El Cap was put out of bounds to hikers with parachutes instead of rucksacks on their back. Still they came. They came also to the deadly face of Norway's Trollvegen, which claimed the life of Carl Boenish, amongst others. They came to high buildings and bridges and gorges. They came against the advice of parachuting's governing bodies, and sometimes against the law. Defiance of regulations became, for a minority, almost as important as defiance of gravity. 'Who owns the mountain?' they would say. 'Who owns the air? Who owns US?' Sadly, BASE jumping attracted an irresponsible and sensation-seeking fringe, as well as the ideological, and parachuting's governing bodies were quite right to disown the BASE jumpers in order to protect the sport as a whole and to maintain the 'safe' image that is now essential to its social acceptance.

The image — and the reality — of safer parachuting owe much to improvements in equipment since the sport came of age in the 1950s. The introduction of static-line operated 'chutes was the first major advance. Then came steerable 'chutes to help jumpers avoid those trees and power-cables and other things unfair to parachutists. The introduction of automatic opening devices, canopy release systems, and custom-built reserves lessened the dangers further, and the ram-air canopy in main and reserve packs gave the jumper greater command over the wind. Radical changes in canopy performance and operating systems have required periods of physical and mental adjustment and have introduced temporary hazards of their own. However, the eventual outcome of accumulated improvements is seen in today's range of advanced sport parachutes adaptable to specific purposes, and parachutes for trainees that are undoubtedly more reliable and forgiving than their predecessors.

Ultimate safety lies in training — not just the teaching of the necessary physical skills, but in the teaching also of that sense of self-discipline and awareness that is the greatest insurance against parachuting disaster. It is best taught by example — the example of instructors such as John Meacock, who pioneered the commercial parachute centre in England just as Jacques Istel had done in America.

John Meacock trained as a Territoral Army paratrooper in 1961 and began sport jumping at Thruxton two years later. He was Chief Instructor at Thruxton during 1966 and 1967, on a part-time basis, and in 1971 gave up a promising career in printing to open Britain's first full-time parachute centre, at Peterborough. From 1968 until 1976 he was the most consistent of Britain's growing band of world-class sport jumpers: seven times national style champion; twice accuracy champion; four times overall champion; and a member of the British team in 1972 and 1974 World Championships. From 1968 he served on the BPA Council for eleven consecutive years, the last three as chairman, and became one of the Association's two vice-presidents. These are but the most significant of the achievements that won John Meacock the Royal Aero Club Silver Medal in 1980. He hasn't finished yet, and his son Stuart is now amongst the foremost cameramen in the sky.

The Peterborough Parachute Centre at Sibson airfield represented a major shift in Britain from the self-supporting parachute clubs of the 1960s — which were primarily gatherings of enthusiasts, providing instruction for a few — to a commercial centre that offered a full range of parachuting services and training courses at all levels. Other centres have followed, but Peterborough remains the prime example of the safety standards that can be achieved through well administered and professionally supervised training. In the sixteen years up to 1988, 198,587 descents had been made at the Centre, at a cost of 222 injuries and one fatality, in 1976. During that time 28,200 people were introduced to parachuting, either on basic or one-jump courses. In 1987, 16,300 jumps were made, with only ten injuries.

Not all centres are as good as Peterborough. The emphasis on the more lucrative one-jump-courses adopted by some commercial operators is not always balanced by equal incentive and opportunity to continue the sport. Some of the centres have lost the spirit of the traditional and more informal 'parachute club'. There are signs that the trend may be reversing. In Great Britain, the commercial market has reached saturation point, and has in fact declined in recent years. This may lead to a corresponding reduction in commercial centres and some return to the smaller and perhaps more specialist 'club', which many would see as no bad thing.

The basic training of the skydiver is still primarily a matter of progression from ground training to static-line descents to free fall jumps of steadily increasing duration, all in accordance with an official 'category' system that requires a defined level of skill to be demonstrated at each stage before the next is attempted. The BPA requires the completion of eight categories and an instructor's recommendation for a 'C' Certificate before our skydiver is considered fit to go 'solo'. Two further categories take him through more advanced individual manoeuvres and into relative work. With a Category Ten in his log-book, the skies are wide open to him.

For those who can afford it, there are now short cuts to the exhilaration of prolonged body flight: Accelerated Free Fall Training (AFF) and Tandem Jumping.

The 'Paracommander' and its various derivatives brought new meaning to parachuting accuracy during the 1960s, as demonstrated here by British jumper Mick Geelan who aimed for the swimming pool of the Appolonia Hotel in Limassol for this exhibition jump in Cyprus. It was superseded in the 1970s by the 'square'.

The Tandem Jump also allows the relatively untrained to become Sky People for a day. Molly Sedgwick, daughter of Dolly Shepherd the Edwardian 'Parachute Queen', drops from 12,000 feet above Peterborough with instructor Dave Morris, in 1987.
(Photo: Stuart Meacock)

AFF takes a student directly from intensive ground training to a height between 9,000 and 12,000 feet, where he is launched from the aircraft firmly held between two suitably qualified instructors. Comforted and controlled as necessary by their physical presence, he is guided through a sequence of basic skills as they fall together. His instructors stay with him until he has opened his 'chute. If necessary they do it for him, and there is an automatic opening device as the ultimate back-up. The concept is not new. It is a refinement of Jim Hall's 'Buddy System' developed by Para Ventures in the early 1960s, and adopted in a no-contact form to train Britain's military free fallers since 1972. It makes sense. Those early and solo free falls of traditional progression teach little but an exit technique and the confidence to advance further. Time in the air, and particulary in terminal velocity air, is the key to rapid progression in free fall skill: time to relax, and to feel, and to learn. Yet paradoxically the 'traditional' unaccompanied trainee cannot spend that time in the air until he has advanced to altitude through those slow but necessary categories.

At more than £1,200 for an eight-jump course, and further limited by the availability of qualified instructors, AFF is unlikely to replace the traditional training system. It remains a means of introduction to skydiving for the more affluent and for the one-jump sensation-seeker. Richard Branson tried it in his preparations for his epic balloon flight across the Atlantic, and demonstrated before the mid-air cameras that the system is not entirely fool-proof.

An alternative method of rapid introduction to free fall is 'Tandem Jumping'. It involves a pupil being buckled to the harness of an instructor and so carried through free fall and under the canopy. It has been made possible by the introduction of a ram-air parachute capable of supporting a double load during opening and descent; by the addition of a small drogue to assist free fall stability and slightly reduce terminal velocity; and by the training of instructors capable of operating the system. Developed by Ted Strong and Bill Morrissey in the USA, Tandem is now accepted as a safe and exciting introduction to skydiving. One of its most

The RAF 'Falcons' fly a diamond formation during practice over Texas. (Photo: Sergeant Alistair Wright)

valuable contributions is that it can extend the delights of free fall parachuting to those who would never otherwise experience them — the disabled and the blind.

Molly Sedgwick was in no way disabled when she made her first parachute jump buckled to the harness of Dave Morris of Action Enterprise at Peterborough, but she *was* sixty-six-years-old. Of course, she had tradition to help her, for Molly is the daughter of that great Edwardian lady parachutist, Dolly Shepherd. In fact Molly was a third-generation jumper, for while Dolly was recovering from that broken back after her mid-air rescue of Louie May, her own mother had made an exhibition jump in her place. Now it was Molly's turn.

'Tuesday, 22 September 1987 dawned fine and warm, with sun and blue skies, and sufficient cloud to produce interesting photographic effects. After a morning of press interviews and innumerable TV 'shots' (it was to be shown on the *Blue Peter* programme) the magic moment approached.

'I wriggled into a canary-coloured jump-suit over my navy track-suit and was zipped up, then helped into a sturdy harness. Thus girded, my training began: lying on my tummy on a high 'stool' with canvas top, I was instructed how to use my arms and legs for exit from the plane in free fall. I was anxious to experience as much as possible in the short space of time between the exit and the landing, so I was shown the method of movement across the sky. It all sounded so easy and magical — I was in a dreamworld!

'I donned the tightly-hugging red and grey striped cap, goggles were attached, and my hands automatically slipped into the red leather gloves with black palms. I really *was* making my way to the plane! We entered and I made a practice exit, then the crew arrived; pilot, 'spotter', three cameramen and the *Blue Peter* presenter, Mark Curry. The tiny plane revved up, taxied and left the ground. My eyes became moist and I blinked hard to prevent emotion overtaking me, as I realized that my dream world had become a reality! I peered out of the open doorway and saw the landscape gradually diminish — to be replaced by a Lilliputian scene — just as my mother had told me.

'The plane circled and by 10,000 feet the air was cold. I spoke into the microphone periodically pushed in front of me, and hoped I had given sensible answers to questions I could not hear! The 'spotter' made signs that indicated we were nearing 12,000 feet when we would be parting company. I moved on to the instructor's lap as I had been told, and I felt the pull backwards and heard the clinks as the large clasps snapped tight, holding me fast to my parachuting partner. Together we shuffled towards the exit. He held the handles on the sides whilst I, more out than in, obediently tucked my legs under the plane and folded my arms in readiness for the most exciting moment of my life — but as calmly as if it were an everyday occurrence! I looked around me and was stunned by the magnificence of the view, the countryside, in miniature, stretching for miles to a distant horizon. I laughed as I saw Garry, hanging onto a handle outside the plane, his camera fixed firmly to his forehead!

'Three — two — one . . . ! I swallowed a mouthful of deliciously pure air as we fell out. I looked all about me. "Where is Garry?" I called out, "I can't find him . . . Oh fantastic . . . it's fan-tas-tic . . . !" Suddenly Garry was in front of me! I laughed at him. A touch on the shoulder by my companion indicated I was in control! I moved my arms as instructed — and there I was, swimming about in the heavens, revelling in this new-found freedom, and unable to find sufficient words to express the exhilaration and sheer delight that filled my whole being!

'There was a sudden tug and I felt the top half of my body being pulled upwards. There was a quick whooooosh! The 'chute had opened, and we were floating down, turning this way and that by pulling on different toggles. All too soon, as we gently descended — with intermittent super-lative exclamations from me — the miniature pocket handkerchiefs and toy figures regained their rightful size and became fields, the dropping zone, and a cluster of animated men and women peering up at us.

'My instructor-companion pulled on the toggles and I waved my little Union Jack, as my mother used to do. A "brake" having been applied, we landed spot on, as gently as if hurrying down a couple of steps, to be greeted by the waiting group of camera- and press-men. Oh! It was all too wonderful, too unbelievable — and over far too soon!'

Not everyone would be as fearless as Molly undoubt-edly was, but then not everyone would have a famous parachuting mother holding their hand.

Like many other first-time parachutists today, Molly was jumping for charity — in her case the Guide Dogs for the Blind Association. Some have criticized 'charity jumping' as the wrong motive for something as potentially dangerous as leaping from an aircraft in flight. It may not be the best of reasons, but it is unlikely that it is ever the only one. There must still be, lurking somewhere, that sense of adventure, that willingness to accept a challenge to the mind and a risk to the body.

Where next, skydiving?

How much further can the skydiver progress in body flight? No doubt we shall see larger formations in the sky than that flown by 136 jumpers over Belgium in 1987, but that is a product of logistics and excellent organization as well as individual skill. So, will we see *faster* formations and *faster* sequences? Faster in terms of smoothness and the elimination of error rather than in brute speed? And if skilled body flying is a product of time in the air — preferably recorded on video for instant analysis — can we not expect a revolution in those skills if anticipated wind-tunnel technology allows skydivers to practise for hours each day, instead of minutes?

Might the advancing standards and specialized nature of top class RW competition take it beyond the reach of the part-time weekend jumper? Might he then return to more individual forms of competition? Will style and accuracy survive on this basis? Will they survive in their present form, as truly 'classical' events, just as throwing the discus has survived in athletics? Might we see a freestyle event added — a form of aerial ballet, not easy to judge, but not impossible either, if ice-dance is seen as an analogy?

The increasing internationalization of skydiving; the visual appeal that it makes through the air-to-air camera and the TV screen; sponsorship; the demon-strations at the Seoul Olympic Games — might these combine to bring full Olympic recognition to the sport?

Might the adoption of new training techniques for immediate introduction to 'square' canopies eventually lead to the disappearance of the 'round' in sport parachuting? And will those 'squares', with further design advances and more effective means of achieving rigidity, approach even more closely the performance of the hang-glider, and thus add the potential for soaring flight to parachuting?

The answer to all these queries must be 'Most likely,' for whatever else changes, one thing remains constant: the nature of the skydiver himself. He is an adventurer. A visionary. A constant seeker after fresh challenge. With the future of skydiving in such hands, who would place limits on its potential?

André Jacques Garnerin! Do you see what you started?

References

The Pioneers

1. Milton's *History of Britain*, 1670.
2. 'Medieval Uses Of Air', Lynn White, *Scientific American* Vol. 223, No. 2.
3. From Leonardo Da Vinci's *Codex Atlanticus*.
4. Simon De La Loubère's *A New Historical Relation of the Kingdom of Siam*, Vol. 2.
5. Garnerin's account, in *The Annual Visitor*, 1803.
6. Charles Green in the London *Penny Mechanic*, 29 July 1837.
7. *Through The Air* by John Wise, 1873.
8. *My Life and Balloon Experiences* by Henry Coxwell, 1887.
9. Thomas Baldwin to the *Edinburgh Evening Dispatch*, 1 October 1888.
10. *When The Chute Went Up* by Dolly Shepherd, Robert Hale, 1984.
11. Bud Morriss to Lloyd Graham for manuscript of *Ripcord*, 1933.

The Show-jumpers

1. *When The Chute Went Up* by Dolly Shepherd, Robert Hale, 1984.
2. Leslie Irvin testimony at Irving v. Russell Hearing, 1933.
3. *Spirit of St Louis* by Charles Lindbergh, Charles Scribner's Sons, New York, 1953.
4. Floyd Smith to Lloyd Graham for manuscript of *Ripcord*, 1933.
5. Harry Ward to *The Daily Mirror,* 5 February 1952.
6. See 5.
7. 'Secrets of the Silken Angels' by Floyd Smith, *Popular Mechanics*, February 1934.
8. *Nine Lives* by John Tranum, MacMillan, 1933.
9. See 8.
10. Jump Reports by Johnny Rallings and Ollie Owen to Apex Group members, 1949, 1950.
11. *See* 10.
12. *See* 10.
13. *Panic Takes Time* by Dumbo Willans, Max Parish, 1956.
14. *Bird Man* by Leo Valentin, Hutchinson, 1955.
15. *See* 14.
16. *See* 14.
17. *See* 14.
18. Reported by Howard Gregory in his *Parachuting's Unforgettable Jumps*, Pageant, 1968.

The Caterpillars

1. Milton St Clair to Don Glassman as related in *Jump*, Simon and Schuster, 1930.
2. Leo M. Brown letter to Irving Air Chute Company, 7 August 1940.
3. Guy Ball to Lloyd Graham for manuscript of *Ripcord*, 1933.
4. Floyd Smith to Lloyd Graham for manuscript of *Ripcord*, 1933.
5. Air Corps Technical Report No. 2916 of 24 November 1928, *Determination of the Rates of Descent of a Falling Man and of a Parachute Test Weight*.
6. Lord Malcolm Douglas Hamilton letter to Irving Air Chute Company, 1930.
7. Tony Wood-Scawen's letter to Irving Air Chute Company, June 1940.
8. *Doolittle's Tokyo Raiders* by Lt. Colonel Glines, Van Nostrand.
9. Frank Hulbert letter to Secretary Caterpillar Club, 1987.
10. *The Long Lonely Leap* by Joseph Kittinger, E. P. Dutton & Co. Inc., 1961.
11. *See* 10.
12. Wing Commander Bob Iveson letter to secretary Caterpillar Club, 28 July 1982.

The Paratroopers

1. *Memoirs of World War One* by William Mitchell, Random House, 1960.
2. *On the Sidelines* by Wedgewood Benn, Hodder & Stoughton, 1924.
3. *By Air to Battle*, the official account of the British Airborne Divisions, HMSO, 1945.
4. *Daedelus Returned* by Von Der Heydte, Hutchinson, 1956.
5. *Prelude to Glory* by Maurice Newnham, Sampson Low, 1947.
6. 'The Parachute Test Platoon' by William T. Ryder in *Gung Ho Airborne Special* magazine, 1984.
7. Letter from PFC James Martin to his parents, 15 July 1944, recored in *D-Day With the Screaming Eagles* by George Koskimaki, Vantage Press Inc.
8. *Currahee!* by Donald Burgett, Houghton Mifflin Co., 1967.
9. *Inside SOE* by E. H. Cookridge, Arthur Barker Ltd., 1966.
10. *The Los Banos Raid* by Lt. Gen. E. M. Flanagan Jr., Presidio Press, 1986.
11. *Airborne to Suez* by Sandy Cavanagh, William Kimber, 1965.
12. *A Drop Too Many* by John Frost, Cassell, 1986.

The Skydivers

1. Sue Burges to Ministry of Transport & Civil Aviation, February 1959.
2. Sue Burges to author, March 1988.
3. *United We Fall* by Pat and Jan Works, RWunderground Pub. Co., 1978.
4. Jackie (Smith) Young to *The Sport Parachutist*, April 1987.
5. Jackie (Smith) Young to author, March 1988.
6. Article, *The Sport Parachutist*, April 1987.
7. *United We Fall* by Pat and Jan Works, WRunderground Pub. Co., 1978.
8. *The Wisdom of the Sands* by Antoine De Saint Exupery, Hollis & Carter, 1952.
9. Molly Sedgwick to author, 1988.

Bibliography

This is a selective bibliography. Where there is some overlap in subject matter, books are listed in the most appropriate category. Not all the accounts of early parachuting are accurate: there is some repetition of errors made by the earliest writers on the subject. That apart, the following are recommended:

General History and The Pioneers

Parachutes by Charles J. V. Murphy, Putnam's, 1930.
Parachuting by Charles Dixon, Sampson Low, 1930.
Parachutes In Peace and War by A. M. Low, The Scientific Book Club, 1942.
Panic Takes Time by Dumbo Willans, Max Parrish, 1956.
Parachuting and Skydiving by Dumbo Willans, Faber & Faber, 1964.
The Parachute from Balloons to Skydiving by James R. Greenwood, E. P. Dutton & Co., 1964.
The Silken Angels by Martin Caidin, Duell, Sloane & Pearce, 1965.
The Aeronauts by L. T. C. Rolt, Walker & Co., 1966.
Parachuting's Unforgettable Jumps by Howard Gregory, Pageant, 1968.
Bailout by Don Dwiggins, The MacMillan Co., 1969.
Parachutes and Parachuting by Bud Sellick, Prentice Hall Inc., 1971.
The Big Umbrella by John Lucas, Elm Tree Books Ltd., 1973.
Parachutist by Peter Hearn, Robert Hale, 1976.
Parachuting Folklore by Michael Horan, Parachuting Resources, 1980.

The Show-jumpers

Nine Lives by John Tranum, John Hamilton Ltd., 1933.
Aerial Maniac by Art Starnes, Hammond, 1938.
Bird Man by Leo Valentin, Hutchinson & Co., 1955.
Barnstorming by Martin Caidin, Duell, Sloane & Pearce, 1965.
Flying Daredevils of the Roaring Twenties by Don Dwiggins, Arthur Barker Ltd., 1969.
When the 'Chute Went Up by Dolly Shepherd and Peter Hearn, Robert Hale, 1984.
The Yorkshire Birdman by Harry Ward and Peter Hearn, Robert Hale, 1990.
Falcons by Peter Hearn, Grub Street, 1995.

The Caterpillars

Jump! by Don Glassman, Simon & Schuster, 1930.
Delayed Opening Parachute Jumps by Arthur H. Starnes, Parachute Science Service, 1942.
Jump for It by Gerald Bowman, Evans Bros. Ltd., 1955.
Into the Silk by Ian Mackersey, Robert Hale, 1956.
Long Lonely Leap by J. W. Kittinger, E. P. Dutton & Co., 1961.
The Man in the Hot Seat by Doddy Hay, Collins, 1969.
Sky High Irvin by Peter Hearn, Robert Hale, 1983.
Eject! Eject! by Bryan Philpott, Ian Allen, 1989.

The Paratroopers

By Air to Battle, HMSO, 1945.
Prelude to Glory by Maurice Newnham, Sampson Low, 1947.
Airborne Warfare by Lt. Gen. James M. Gavin, Infantry Journal Press, 1947.
Daedelus Returned by Von Der Heydte, Hutchinson, 1958.
Airborne to Suez by Sandy Kavanagh, William Kimber, 1965.
Currahee! by Donald Burgett, Hutchinson, 1967.
Airborne to Battle by Maurice Tugwell, William Kimber, 1971.
German Paratroopers in World War Two by Volkmar Kuhn, Ian Allen Ltd., 1978.
Assault From the Sky by John Weekes, Westbridge Books, 1978.
Paratrooper by Gerald M. Devlin, Robson Books, 1979.
Out of the Sky by Michael Hickey, Mills & Boon Ltd., 1979.
The Paras by Frank Hilton, BBC Publication, 1983.
The Red Devils by G. C. Norton, Secker & Warburg, 1984.
A Drop Too Many by John Frost, Cassell, 1986.
The Making of a Para by Rory Bridson, Sidgwick and Jackson, 1989.
Red On . . . Go! by Jon Davison, Inspired Images, 1990.
Men of the Red Beret by Max Arthur, Hutchinson, 1990.

(This is but a selection of the many books written about The Paratrooper. A comprehensive range is available at the Airborne Forces Museum, Aldershot).

The Skydivers

Alone in the Sky by Mike Reilly, Robert Hale, 1963.
The Space Age Sport by Ray Darby, Julian Messner, 1964.
Sport Parachuting by Russ Gunby, Herald Printers, 1969.
Skies Call (3 volumes) by Andy Keech, 1974-1981.
The Art of Free Fall Relative Work by Pat Works, RWunderground Publishing Company, 1975.
Parachuting — The Skydivers Handbook by Dan Poynter, Parachuting Publications, 1978.
United We Fall by Pat and Jan Works, RWunderground Publishing Company, 1978.
The Best of Sport Parachuting by John Meacock and Charles Shea-Simonds, British Parachute Association, 1979.
A Complete Guide to Sport Parachuting by Charles Shea-Simonds, A & C Black, 1986.
Body Flying by David Howerski, Mike Truffer diving' 1988.
Skydiving Basics — A Parachute Training Manual by Doug Peacock and Andy Allman, Parachute Training Services, 1996.

Index